R00970 07792

LP

GARLAND STUDIES IN HIGHER
EDUCATION
VOL. 1

THE FUNDING OF HIGHER EDUCATION

GARLAND REFERENCE LIBRARY
OF SOCIAL SCIENCE
(VOL. 919)

GARLAND STUDIES IN HIGHER EDUCATION
Philip G. Altbach, Series Editor

1. **THE FUNDING OF HIGHER EDUCATION**
   International Perspectives
   by Philip G. Altbach and D. Bruce Johnstone

THE FUNDING OF HIGHER EDUCATION

International Perspectives

Edited by

Philip G. Altbach
D. Bruce Johnstone

GARLAND PUBLISHING, INC.
New York & London / 1993

Copyright © 1993 Philip G. Altbach
and D. Bruce Johnstone
All Rights Reserved

Library of Congress Cataloging-in-Publication Data

The Funding of higher education : international perspectives /
edited by Philip G. Altbach and D. Bruce Johnstone.
    p.   cm. — (Garland reference library of social science ; vol.
919. Garland studies in higher education ; vol. 1)
    Main results of the 6th International Conference on Higher
Education (ICHE), held in Washington, D.C., August 21–23, 1992—
CIP pref.
    ISBN 0-8153-1335-7
    1. Education, Higher—Finance—Case studies—Congresses.
I. Altbach, Philip G. II. Johnstone, D. Bruce (Donald Bruce),
1941– . III. International Conference on Higher Education (6th :
1992 : Washington, D.C.) IV. Series: Garland reference library of
social science ; vol. 919. V. Series: Garland reference library of
social science. Garland studies in higher education ; vol. 1.
LB2341.98.F85   1993
378'.02—dc20   93-7388
                                                                           CIP

Printed on acid-free, 250-year-life paper
Manufactured in the United States of America

CONTENTS

Series Editor's Preface	vii
Acknowledgments	ix
Preface	
Ignaz Bender	xi
Introduction	
Ernest L. Boyer	xv

Part 1: Comparative Perspectives

The Costs of Higher Education: Worldwide Issues and Trends for the 1990s	
D. Bruce Johnstone	3
Optimizing Allocation Strategy	
William F. Massy and Michael C. Hulfactor	25
University Strategies for the Third Stream of Income	
John Fürstenbach	45
The Future of Higher Education Financing	
George Psacharopoulos	61
Sources of Revenue	
Ihsan Dogramaci	71
Are University Funding Systems in Need of an Overhaul?	
Karel Tavernier	83
Industry-University Research Collaboration: An Option for Generating Revenue	
Linda Parker	101

Part 2: Case Studies

Higher Education Funding in Open Door China
    Richard A. Hartnett   127

Toward Understanding the Economics of African Higher Education
    Teshome G. Wagaw   151

Allocating Budgets Using Performance Criteria
    Michael A. Brown and David M. Wolf   173

Changing Patterns in the Funding of University Education and Research: The Case of the Netherlands
    Cornelius A. Hazeu and Peter A. Lourens   189

Issues in Funding Higher Education in Eastern Europe: The Cases of the Czech Republic and Slovakia
    James E. Mauch and Daniel S. Fogel   207

Problems of Funding the Transformation of Higher Education in East Germany
    Helmut de Rudder   237

Higher Education Funding in Australia
    Brian G. Wilson   253

Canadian Universities and the Politics of Funding
    Howard Buchbinder and P. Rajagopal   271

Constructing the "Post-Industrial University": Institutional Budgeting and University-Corporate Linkages
    Janice A. Newson   285

Contributors   305
Index   309

SERIES EDITOR'S PREFACE

Higher education is a multifaceted phenomenon in modern society, combining a variety of institutions and an increasing diversity of students, a range of purposes and functions, and different orientations. The Series combines research-based monographs, analyses, and discussions of broader issues and reference books related to all aspects of higher education. It is concerned with policy as well as practice from a global perspective. The Series is dedicated to illuminating the reality of higher and postsecondary education in contemporary society.

Philip G. Altbach
State University of New York at Buffalo

ACKNOWLEDGMENTS

Any edited volume requires a great deal of collaboration. We appreciate the prompt responses of our contributors to our requests for revisions and changes in their chapters. We have depended on the editorial assistance of Hyaeweol Choi and Penka Skachkova of the Comparative Education Center and Patricia Glinski of the Center for Educational Resources and Technology, both at the State University of New York at Buffalo. Penka Skachkova prepared the index. The Carnegie Foundation for the Advancement of Teaching has provided support. This volume is co-sponsored by the International Conference on Higher Education (ICHE) and is a research activity of the Comparative Education Center, State University of New York at Buffalo.

Philip G. Altbach
Buffalo, New York

D. Bruce Johnstone
Albany, New York
January, 1993

PREFACE

Ignaz Bender

Higher education needs rational forms of funding. Rationality is absent if there is no correspondence between the number of students entering universities and the costs involved in educating them. In order to obtain a wider perspective, it is wise to look from time to time comparatively and learn how other countries fund universities or successfully raise money for their higher education institutions.

These are, in short, the main results of the sixth International Conference on Higher Education (ICHE), held in Washington, D.C., August 21–23, 1992. The conference, jointly organized by the ICHE Steering Committee and the Carnegie Foundation for the Advancement of Teaching, assembled experts in higher education from thirty-six nations, among them heads and administrators of higher education institutions, scholars, researchers, and representatives of interested organizations and foundations. Earlier conferences held in Ankara (Turkey), Trier (Germany), Maastricht (Netherlands), and Edinburgh (United Kingdom), dealt with topics like university governance, public versus private universities, university leadership, specialized versus multidisciplinary universities, the role of "buffer" institutions in higher education, etc.

Higher education needs significant funds. Although money is not everything in higher education, without money nothing is possible. During the Washington conference, it was therefore widely agreed that under current circumstances, it is important for academic institutions to search for diversified sources of funds. Sources of income are mainly governmental subsidies, research grants from public or private enterprises, revenues from business, student tuition for instruction, income from endowments, real estates, capital, and money earned by the institution itself. Which form of funding dominates depends on certain conditions like the status of the university as a public or private institution, tax regulations regarding charitable donations to universities, the financial involvement of university founders or trustees, property owned by the university, the success of fund-raising campaigns, the engagement of alumni organizations, historical traditions of student tuition, the socio-cultural readiness to invest into universities, and others.

A simple but often forgotten truth: universities tend to be poor if their income is based on only a limited number of financial sources. They tend to be wealthy if their income comes from a broad variety of sources. Centuries ago university founders were aware of this fact. It is impressive how in the Middle Ages even the Pope was interested in funding higher education institutions. In many of their university founding bulls, various Popes enumerated the institutions (cloisters, abbeys, parishes), which had to contribute to the budget of the university.

It was George Washington who, 200 years ago, favored a federal university in the capital of the United States and provided it with land. Today, the George Washington University (G.W.U.) in Washington, D.C., is, after the federal government, the largest landowner in the District of Columbia. Many of the buildings along Pennsylvania Avenue belong to G.W.U. and are rented by United States government departments, the World Bank, and commercial firms. Renting buildings provides the university with an annual income of $300 million. This excellent financial base does not hinder this institution in applying for federal or foundation grants, organizing fund-raising campaigns, or charging tuition fees to students. Similarly, Harvard University, considered the wealthiest university in the world with a fortune of billions of dollars, obtains funds from a variety of sources.

Owning capital stock or real estate may be a characteristic of private universities, whereas public universities primarily depend on governmental subsidies. Nevertheless, there exist many examples in the world in which public universities own land, buildings, or endowment funds and can benefit from these. Both public and private universities in the United States charge tuition fees. Many state universities have always financed part of their budgets through student tuition. The difference is that in private institutions, the percentage of the budget financed by student tuition is generally twice or three times as high as in public institutions.

It is unusual in the current period for students to pay no tuition fees. In the last ten years, many countries, particularly in Europe, introduced student tuitions. There is, as Chancellor D. Bruce Johnstone

Preface xiii

of the State University of New York summed up the Washington conference in his keynote speech, a "definite worldwide trend ... toward shifting a larger share of costs, both for instruction and student living, onto parents and students mediated by means-tests grants and governmentally sponsored and subsidized loans."

It seems that students and their instruction will receive special attention in the coming years. This follows the six-decades-old recommendation of Ortega y Gasset, the Spanish philosopher, who in his 1930 "Mission of the University" speech recommended that students should be the center of the university's attention. Why, therefore, shouldn't students be the center of teaching-cost-calculation for universities?

Sometimes states responsible for higher education institutions subsidize public universities irrespective of enrollments. If the state budget for a university increases three percent while the student number increases ten percent (because of an open door policy of the same state), the financial situation of the university will over the years become precarious.

Belgium provides at least one answer. The new Flemish Higher Education Funding System demonstrates how a state parliament, by fixing costs per student, contributes to a rational form of university funding. The new system is extremely simple. The budget consists, on the one hand, of a fixed lump sum (mainly for research activities) and, on the other hand, of a sum based strictly on the number of students. A student of the humanities counts "one student unit," a student of natural sciences two units, a student of medicine or engineering three units. More detailed information is given in the contribution of Karel Tavernier, general manager of Leuven University, one of the keynote speakers at the Washington ICHE conference.

As chairperson of the ICHE Steering Committee, it is a great pleasure for me to thank all those who contributed to the outstanding success of the sixth International Conference on Higher Education. These colleagues include Professor Henry H. Wasser, director of the Center for European Studies at the City University of New York, Dr. Ernest L. Boyer, Dr. Mary Huber, and Ms. Jeanine J. Natriello from the Carnegie Foundation for the Advancement of Teaching. I thank all keynote speakers and contributors of papers. I thank in particular Professor Philip G. Altbach, director of the Comparative Education Center at the State University of New York at Buffalo, and Chancellor

D. Bruce Johnstone of the State University of New York for their competent and energetic editing of this volume.

INTRODUCTION
Ernest L. Boyer

The essays collected in this book stem from the 1992 International Conference on Higher Education, hosted in Washington, D.C., by the Carnegie Foundation for the Advancement of Teaching, with assistance from the American Council on Education. The theme for the 1992 conference was "Funding in Higher Education," a topic which is at the heart of a worldwide crisis for colleges and universities today. In many nations, academic institutions are faced with insufficient funds. The recession has placed constraints on government funding for higher education throughout the world, and has strengthened resistance to increasing tax burdens. Almost everywhere, it seems, colleges and universities are being asked to do more with less.

At the same time that budgets are being trimmed, academic institutions must continue to provide access, and in many countries there are pressures to further expand enrollments. Academic institutions are still central to the hopes of many nations for social equity, civic values, and economic productivity, and expectations for colleges and universities remain high. Yet in the midst of current fiscal problems, institutions of higher education are facing a crisis of confidence in their ability to meet these hopes and expectations. Colleges and universities in many countries are being held to stricter standards of accountability, not only for their budgets, but also for their productivity in instruction and research. Teachers and administrators find these pressures new and perplexing, and students face deteriorating conditions of study and increasing costs.

Since World War II, colleges and universities have been seen as central to the development of a modern technologically based society and as necessary to create a skilled labor force, and thus worthy of significant public financial support. Today, however, academic degrees are increasingly looked on as being for private benefit rather than serving the public good. The implications for funding and for academic life are very significant, indeed. Influential voices in many countries have proposed that higher education be privatized, either by creating or expanding private institutions, or by asking students (and parents) to directly pay a larger share of the cost of instruction in public universities.

Several common international trends are documented in this volume; for example, the effort to diversify the financial base of universities, privatization, and the operation of the "free market" in higher education, and directing research to meet national needs. It is important to note, however, that common funding issues, like privatization, can take different forms in different countries. Higher education in some nations, including the United States, Japan, Korea, and the Philippines, has long depended significantly on private institutions, while other countries, such as those in Central and Eastern Europe and even China, are just now exploring the establishment of private institutions to relieve the fiscal burden on public universities. Access also differs across countries. In much of Western Europe, the expansion that was evident in the 1960s and 1970s has slowed or stopped, and access has not grown significantly. The rapidly expanding countries of the Pacific Rim, however, have continued to expand the size and scope of their academic systems, while in Africa, dramatic economic and political crisis has devastated the universities. In short, while concern with financing issues exists almost everywhere, fiscal problems and policy responses differ widely throughout the world.

What can be learned from such varieties of fiscal experience in higher education? While it is seldom possible to directly apply policies or practices from one country to another, important lessons can be learned from abroad. For example, a number of countries are finding the British experience in measuring academic quality and productivity through national assessments of disciplines and departments useful in thinking about accountability and the measurement of outcomes. A comparative study of the "management of decline" could yield interesting results. Efforts in countries such as Brazil, the Philippines, and Japan to utilize private higher education should provide useful insights into the role of private higher education internationally.

An international perspective offers a unique view of issues relating to higher education finance, and it is critical that we attend to its lessons. The world has become increasingly interdependent, and the next century will be a time when national boundaries will be further blurred, despite the divisive struggles going on today. Future survival surely will depend on our capacity to examine the issues that bring us together in common cause—ecological, medical, and educational. In response to this global challenge, it is imperative that scholars and policy makers extend their agenda beyond national horizons. In today's interconnected world, an international perspective is essential in understanding how education can be strengthened at home, as well as abroad.

PART 1
Comparative Perspectives

THE COSTS OF HIGHER EDUCATION: WORLDWIDE ISSUES AND TRENDS FOR THE 1990s

D. Bruce Johnstone

Higher education is considered throughout the world to be the key to both individual and societal aspirations. For individuals, education beyond the secondary level is assumed to be the way to social esteem, better paying jobs, expanded life options, intellectual stimulation—and frequently a good time in the pursuit of any or all of the above. For societies, higher education is assumed to be the key to technology, productivity, and the other ingredients of international competitiveness and economic growth. Higher education also shapes and preserves the values that define a culture. And it is believed to be a major engine of social justice, equal opportunity, and democracy.

For all of its importance, higher education throughout the world is increasingly troubled by costs that are high and rapidly rising and that seem to be outrunning available revenues. Governments are cutting outlays to universities and other institutions with consequent loss of staff, deterioration of plant and equipment, erosion of salaries, and loss of capacity to expand to meet student demand. Where costs are passed on to students and parents, debt levels are increasing and access is being threatened, if not outright curtailed. Exacerbating the political tensions of the cost-revenue squeeze are charges of higher education's inefficiency and lack of cost-benefit accountability. In a recent review, Jean-Claude Eicher and Thierry Chevaillier of the University of Dijon's Institute for Research on the Economics of Education write: "The conclusion is clear. There is a financial crisis in education in most countries. That crisis is much deeper than macrostatistics reveal; and it is not going to disappear soon, especially in developing countries, if new solutions are not found."[1] This paper examines the nature and the dynamics of higher educational costs and summarizes some trends and patterns that are observable worldwide as institutions and governments deal with rising costs and faltering revenues.

The Categories of Cost

It may be useful to view four broad categories of higher educational costs. First are the basic costs of instruction, categorized by American accounting standards as "education and general." These are the costs of faculty and staff salaries, equipment, libraries, administrative and basic academic computing, and certain capital or locational costs such as rent. In effect, this is what it costs the institution to do its mission of teaching and whatever basic research or scholarship its faculty is expected to do without special grants or contracts.

Second are the costs associated with sponsored research or special activities covered by their own funds or appropriations and that would presumably not be incurred without such specially-designated revenues. Although the costs incurred at a particular university by the conduct of sponsored research and other special activities may be high, these costs to the institution's basic missions of teaching and scholarship ought, in principle, to be low or zero because of the nontransferability of the revenues. Expressed another way, a sponsored research activity should have no cost *to the institution* because all costs, direct and indirect, should be picked up by the sponsor. Similarly, cessation of the sponsored activity should not benefit the institution in the sense of permitting the expansion of an alternative activity because the revenues would be lost along with the expenditures.

A third category of costs associated with higher education are the costs of student living: room, board, clothing, laundry, entertainment, and other expenses that would be incurred whether or not an individual was a student. In this sense, these costs are not strictly attributable to higher education. To students and their families, however, they are every bit as real as the costs of tuition or books, and must be met from the same combination of sources (students, parents, taxpayers, or institutional resources) that meets the costs of instruction.

The Costs of Higher Education 5

The costs of student living will vary according to whether a student lives at home with parents, with a spouse, or in a student flat or dormitory. The costs will similarly vary according to the prevailing standard of student living, which may range from traditional student penury to a standard of living commensurate with non-student age peers. Finally, these costs may be evident and easily measurable, as when they are paid directly by students or their parents, or quite obscure and sometimes virtually immeasurable, as when the expenditures are in the form of subsidies to canteens and residence halls or tax benefits to parents.

The fourth category of cost is the cost of foregone earnings (actually, foregone real production) of students while disengaged from the productive work force. While this is a perfectly valid cost in theory, it presumes productive labor force alternatives for persons of university age, foregone by the decisions of some who choose to be students. It is a very real cost in a society with labor shortages and where the loss of students from the work force causes real lost production. It is less relevant where the marginal productivity and employment options of young unskilled labor are minimal.

Cost Issues

The costs of higher education present three mega-issues in virtually any nation.[2] First, how much of a nation's total resources ought to be, or can be, devoted to higher education? Essentially, this issue translates to questions: how large a proportion of any age cohort should go on to higher education (as opposed, presumably, to labor market alternatives), and how long should they remain there, or to what average degree levels should they aspire?

Second, what ought higher education to cost—per-student or per-degree granted, or per-unit of learning, or per-any other reasonable unit of higher education's output? This issue deals with efficiency and productivity of institutions, in contrast to the preceding issue that dealt more with the total resources that a nation devotes to its higher educational enterprise. The unit costs of higher education are elusive because of the multiple and hard to measure outputs. At the most simplistic level, per-student costs (ignoring real learning outputs or any outputs of faculty scholarship) are a function of:

- faculty workloads (class size, course loads, etc.);
- ratios of support staff to faculty and students;
- average faculty and staff salaries; and
- the richness or leanness of libraries, laboratories, and other resources of plant and equipment.

The issue of efficiency or productivity, then, is whether the outputs or products of higher education can be produced with fewer or cheaper inputs, or whether a given monetary value of inputs can yield a greater volume or value of outputs. The search for greater efficiency leads to considerations of, e.g., better management, more effective incentives, consolidations and economies of scale, and more application of technology.

The third mega-issue is how the costs of higher education ought to be shared among the general citizens/taxpayers, parents, students, businesses, and philanthropists or donors? Whatever the costs, and in whatever country, they must be borne by some combination of the following:

- *all citizens*—through taxes or through the debasement of purchasing power brought on by the inflationary printing of currency;
- *parents*—through direct payments for tuition or through the direct or indirect support of the costs of student living;
- *students*—through payment of tuition or living expenses either through term or summer work, depletion of savings, or the assumption of future loan repayments or graduate tax obligations;
- *businesses*—through the assumption of some or all of the student loan repayment obligations of employees, or through special tax assessments in proportion to, e.g., total payroll or number of graduates hired; or
- *philanthropists*—through current gifts or the investment return on past gifts.

In fact, the three issues interact. Higher education as a strictly private expenditure, supported mainly by tuition, may be thought by some to be overly expensive, but that is no more a public issue than the high cost of any luxury good freely purchased by persons affluent enough to pay. The concern with unit costs or even with total spending arises mainly from public expenditures—that is, to the degree to which the costs of higher education are borne by the general citizen/taxpayer.

The Costs of Higher Education

Furthermore, it is when the costs of higher education are both large in the aggregate and borne mainly by the general citizen/taxpayer that the equity of the distribution of benefits becomes a public issue. As Gareth Williams puts it in his summary of OECD country financing patterns: "The larger the number of people who obtain the benefits of higher education, the greater the relative deprivation of those who do not have it. Other claimants on public funds begin to see higher education as a voracious competitor of public resources and not merely as an insignificant fringe activity."[3]

"Who pays" may also have a bearing on unit costs as well as on the social goals of expanded opportunity and equity. Efficiency and equity alone, for example, would suggest that users or beneficiaries—in this case, students and, to a degree, their parents—should bear most of the costs of higher education, as they do in the private sectors of, e.g., the United States, Japan, the Philippines, Korea, and much of South America, or as they do in those public sectors that have begun covering a substantial portion (say, 20–40 percent) of unit costs by tuition as in, e.g., the United States, Canada, or Australia. The reasons are obvious and conventional. The requirement to cover more nearly the full costs with tuition fees should discourage waste and encourage a reallocation of resources to the most productive uses. The reliance on tuition as a significant revenue source also places a substantial share of the burden on those who benefit (and who are more likely to be affluent anyway) rather than on those general taxpayers who do not so directly benefit and who are also likely to be from less-advantaged backgrounds.

At the same time, the goals of expanded opportunity for the disadvantaged and of expanded participation for the social and economic benefits enjoyed by all citizens suggests the appropriateness and even the necessity of some taxpayer subsidy for higher education generally, as well as the need for means-tested subsidies for those families otherwise unable to pay. Thus, the goals of access, efficiency, and equity interact with the issues of aggregate expenditures, unit costs, and the apportioning of the burden.

Unit Costs and Quality: Efficiency Versus Mere Parsimony

Efficiency must be measured by the relationship between costs (as a measure of inputs) and outputs. Although cost per student (usually refined to "full-time equivalent student") is the conventional measure of efficiency in higher education, it is clear that "student," meaning a single student enrolled full time for a year or its equivalent in part-time students or in total course units taught, is not higher education's *output*, at all, but only an easily-calculated proxy.

Real efficiency comes about as we find ways to increase the amount of additional student learning or newly discovered knowledge per dollar spent. Sometimes, we would become more efficient by investing *more* dollars—as with better instructional equipment, for example, or with better paid and more dedicated professors, or with more instructional support staff, all of which might be presumed to increase the real outputs of added learning and research. However, in the absence of reliable real output measures, the quest for efficiency can be reduced to mere parsimony: cutting costs without regard to the effect on real benefits or outputs. Equipment and library budgets may be cut. Full-time faculty may be replaced by part-time faculty or, as is the case in many developing countries, by faculty paid so little that their attention to teaching and scholarship becomes effectively part time, with a virtually inevitable diminution of quality teaching and of the real learning that could otherwise be taking place.

The Rate of Increase of Costs Over Time: Higher Education's Inflationary Engine

The costs of higher education may present problems less for the aggregate expenditure, or even for the unit costs at a point in time, than for the seemingly pervasive rate of increase of those costs over time. Unit costs, for example, tend to rise at rates generally mirroring the rates of increase of wages and salaries of the faculty and staff, reflecting the general absence in higher education (as in most of the service sector of the economy) of the kind of sustained productivity increases characteristic of the goods-producing sectors of most national economies. Non-labor costs peculiar to the enterprise of higher education, such as library acquisitions and scientific equipment, tend also to rise at rates that are above the average of cost increases generally.

But this means that the unit costs of higher education—assuming only a "steady state" of teaching loads, student/staff ratios, and accessibility of academic equipment—will tend always to rise at rates in excess of the average increase in costs: *that is, faster than the rate of inflation.* If the sheer volume of students or degree programs, or research expectations is also increasing, the rate of increase of total expenditures, or at least the pressure for increased expenditures, will rise inexorably and pervasively. Obviously, this means that the revenue sources, mainly from taxes and/or tuition fees, must rise at the same high rate as the costs—or else higher education must suffer cutbacks either in total number of staff or in relative wage and salary increases or, in capital and equipment.

The Politics of Higher Educational Costs

Because higher education in most countries is either governmentally-owned and operated, or at least publicly funded, or both, its cost structure is usually subjected to the pressures and distortions of politics and public sector management practices. While all nations are not alike, of course, nor are all institutions alike in many countries, four common practices, or political phenomena, form a context in which higher educational efficiency and productivity in most countries are severely tested:

- civil service employment practices;
- public sector budgeting and control practices;
- public subsidies and the politics of tuition; and
- universities as regional political prizes.

Civil service employment practices. In most countries, faculty and staff are employees of the state, like other governmental employees, rather than of the institution itself. Governmental or civil service employment tends to feature job protection and level, or generally equivalent (if sometimes very low), salaries. One result is that universities are frequently unable to match private sector salaries in high demand fields such as engineering or computer science and are forced instead to employ very large classes or part-time faculty, or in any event to a less-than-optimal match of salary costs with benefits. Another consequence is that universities typically have great trouble retrenching or laying off faculty or staff whose contributions have become minimal and thus have difficulty reallocating resources from low-need to high-need departments.

Public sector budgeting and control. Most governments seek to maximize financial control of their key agencies, including colleges and universities, and to minimize the outlays of what the finance ministry or budget office bureaucrats tend often to consider "their money." The discretion of universities or agencies to reallocate resources to meet the highest priority needs may thus be limited. It may be difficult, or at least very risky, to effect economies or savings in one function or in one fiscal year in order to increase spending on, or in, another function or year without losing the saved funds altogether. Increased nongovernmental revenues—e.g., from tuition fees or private giving—may be met with a commensurate withdrawal of taxpayer-originated funds. In short, traditional practices of public sector budgeting tend, to greater or lesser degrees, to discourage savings, resource reallocation, the augmentation of public resources with private funds, and decentralized decision making, all of which are thought by most observers to be important ingredients of productivity and efficiency.

Public subsidies and the politics of tuition. Where goods or services have been traditionally free or heavily subsidized by the taxpayer or general citizenry (whether those goods be bread, housing, higher education, or public transportation), the lessening of the subsidy, or sometimes even the mere passing on of real underlying cost increases while maintaining a constant relative subsidy, can elicit a political firestorm. Thus, attempts to impose tuition where costs have hitherto been borne only by the general taxpayer can mobilize what in many countries are politically powerful student unions, joined by other parties of the political left that generally support high subsidies and entitlements, price controls, and high taxes. (The most vivid recent example has been the attempt of the National Autonomous University of Mexico in early 1992 to raise a tuition rate that had been frozen since 1948 when it was 25 percent of instructional costs, and which had subsequently fallen in real terms to a United States dollar equivalent of some six cents. Student leaders opposed the increase and threatened to shut down the university.)

Universities as regional political prizes: the consequences of geographic dispersal and small size. Since the end of World War II and the explosive growth, worldwide, of higher education, one of the real prizes for a regional political leader has been to induce the government to build an institution of higher education (preferably a university) in his or her home town or region. A new university meant jobs during its construction and other (albeit different) jobs during its subsequent operation. It meant opportunities for the local electorate. It meant regional prestige. What was less important was the critical mass of enrollments, faculty, disciplinary coverage, and operating budgets that were required, over time, to achieve both quality and some reasonable economies of scale. Furthermore, an institution once built has enormous political staying power—even if it no longer has the students or programs or resources needed to maintain itself.

New Factors Influencing Higher Educational Costs and the Willingness or Ability of Governments to Meet Them

Almost every country has experienced in recent years some manifestation of "financial crisis" in its institutions of higher education: loss of faculty and staff, erosion of salaries, deterioration of equipment and plant, tuitions rising beyond the reach of traditional consumers, and the like. Underlying all of these difficulties is the phenomenon of costs that press upward beyond the ready ability of revenues to support them. Contributing to this financial squeeze affecting public higher education in most nations as of the early 1990s are the following trends and events:

- the upward cost pressures of technology and the competitive meritocracy of higher education;
- economic stagnation in most of North America, Europe, Latin America, and Africa;
- the collapse of governments, institutions, and the economies of Central and Eastern Europe; and
- new social priorities.

The upward cost pressures of technology and the competitive meritocracy of higher education. Contrary to some popular wisdom, universities are not complacent or conservative or resistant to change. Rather, they are constantly attempting to incorporate new technology, new scholarship, and new missions (albeit, we must add, finding it difficult to shed the old). Computers *can* save on costs, but only if outputs and quality and capacity are held constant. But they are not, of course, so the computer usually allows us to manage *more* effectively, write *more* voluminously, and calculate and analyze with vastly *greater* speed and sophistication—and, in the end, at greater cost. The same phenomenon is found with advances in scientific equipment, pedagogy, assessment, and attention to the student's life outside of the classroom. Higher education is an aggressively competitive and meritocratic institution. The faculty, the governing leadership, the students, and generally the controlling boards or ministries all want to do ever better: to keep up with other scholars and other universities, to master the available technologies and methodologies, and to earn higher degrees or more peer recognition. And "better," however appropriate and even efficient, generally means "more costly," contributing to the inflationary engine of higher education.

Economic stagnation in much of the developing world (outside of Asia's Pacific Rim) and a slowdown, in the early 1990s, of economic growth in much of Western Europe and North America. The effects of slower economic growth are fewer tax revenues, heightened cost pressures on the various socioeconomic "safety nets" such as unemployment insurance and public assistance, and a diminished ability of students and families to afford whatever shares of the cost of student living and the cost of instruction are to be borne by them. Unfortunately, the very economic hard times that argue for more investment in higher education, by both individuals and societies, also make ministries and universities cut back and forego the needed new investments in human capital.

The Costs of Higher Education

The collapse of the governments, economies, and higher educational systems of the former Soviet Union and the nations of Central and Eastern Europe. This extraordinary event has brought about new cost pressures on salaries and all other goods and services traditionally purchased by the universities of these regions, plus the enormous added costs of bringing their faculty and curricula up to date. The challenge of meeting these new costs is made especially daunting by the major (it is to be hoped only temporary) breakdown of the economies and the near absence of taxing capacities, along with continuing political instability and uncertainty of what the future may bring.

New social priorities. For two decades or more after World War II, higher education was a high priority of nearly all countries, reflecting national aspirations for social, political, and economic progress. The last decade, though, has seen (in some countries at least) some relative slippage of higher education's once-vaunted priority—and perhaps even of its esteem. The developing world has turned more toward elementary and secondary education and to vocational, short-cycle, and other non-university forms of tertiary schooling. The industrialized nations are seeing a relative enhancement of such public needs as environmental conservation, health, and public infrastructure. Ironically, the undiminished private value placed on higher education by those willing to pay dearly for it may be one of the reasons why some governments seem less inclined to spend scarce taxpayer money on it.

Trends in Containing Costs and Enhancing Productivity in Higher Education

Several trends are discernable worldwide in response to the forces just described. This section summarizes four trends in containing costs and enhancing productivity. The following and final section will describe trends in diversifying revenues and expanding private, or non-taxpayer borne, sources.

Adjusting sector balance: expanding non-university sectors of higher education. "Non-university" higher education, although an unfortunately negative term, refers to institutions that deliver shorter and more vocationally-oriented curricula, taught by faculty for whom research is a secondary, and hence less time-consuming and thus less expensive, obligation. Such institutions include polytechnics in the United Kingdom, fachhochschulen in Germany, community colleges, and, to a degree, comprehensive colleges in the United States, Institutes Universitaires de Technologie in France, higher vocational schools (HBO Institutes) in the Netherlands, technical institutes in Mexico, special training schools (Senshu Gakko) in Japan, and so forth. A variation on this theme are those institutions delivering "distance learning" by telecommunications and correspondence: the British Open University, Thailand's Sokothai Thammathirat Open University, or the State University of New York's Empire State College.

Such institutions generally have lower per-student costs for some combination of the following reasons:

- higher student/faculty ratios, made possible by faculty who spend more time teaching and less on scholarship;
- (sometimes) less extensive and less expensive academic support in, e.g., equipment, library, or computing;
- in general, lower salaries than typically enjoyed by research-oriented university professors;
- frequently, more use of part-time, nontenured, and less expensive adjunct teaching staff; and
- degree programs of shorter duration (than the typical university degree), thus further lowering the cost per degree.

It is likely that more and more countries will turn increasingly toward non-university institutions, especially to absorb new demand for student places and to respond rapidly to the training and retraining needs of business and industry. Countries like Spain and Italy, where the non-university sector is negligible, or the countries of the former Central and East European Socialist Bloc, where it is relatively undeveloped, as well as the developing nations of Latin America, Africa, and Asia can be expected to place increasing emphasis on the expansion of their non-university institutions.

At the same time, the per-student costs in the university sectors of some countries—Spain, Greece, Italy, Portugal, come to mind[4]— are so low (due to enormous class sizes and student/faculty ratios) that a shift to a reasonably-funded non-university sector might well increase

The Costs of Higher Education 15

the cost per-student, even though it could lower the costs per-degree granted.

Shedding non-essential activities. Many universities and other postsecondary institutions, especially in developing nations and in nations long dominated by central planning and Marxist ideology, are extensively engaged in activities unrelated to the core functions of a university. Such activities may relate to student life or to the maintenance of employees—such as university-run dormitories, restaurants, bookstores, apartments, and social camps—or they may be remnants of a political ideology that attempted to immerse universities, faculty, and students in the politically noble work of farms and factories. Some university-owned enterprises, such as medical clinics, may be useful or even essential to teaching and research, although it may not be necessary to own, manage, or subsidize them. Still other activities (all with costs) may have emerged from faculty entrepreneurial activity and may be viewed simply as eventual net revenue sources—"moneymakers." Cost pressures and modern managerial thinking, however, are likely to "spin off" more of these activities to private or quasi-private forms and to force those that remain to stand financially "on their own bottom." Even if such activities warrant continuing subsidization, the process of setting them up as separate and supposedly self-sufficient entities can inject them with discipline, motivation, and entrepreneurship and can make clear exactly how much they cost in revenues that have alternative uses.

Reforming practices of public sector budgeting and management. The United Kingdom in the late 1980s and early 1990s radically altered the governance and financing of both the universities and the polytechnics. These changes greatly lowered per-student, taxpayer-borne costs, with considerable pain and probably some real losses. But they also engendered more effective planning, some reallocation of resources, a devolution of control from the ministry and the local authorities to the polytechnics, and a great expansion of entrepreneurial activity.[5] Planning and "outcomes assessments," or "quality indicators" are being introduced throughout Europe and North America. It is likely that such reforms will continue not just because they are reasonable and desirable (which may have little correlation with the likelihood of their adoption), but because intrusive and inefficient management is becoming a political liability. The tougher the decisions to be made, the wiser it will be for ministry officials and elected politicians to let the campuses make their own decisions—both for the greater likelihood of a good decision and also for the opportunity to let someone else make those decisions that are most likely to cause unhappiness.

Applying technology to research, to more effective and efficient management, to the more effective assessment and guidance of students, and to the learning process itself, through distance learning and self-paced instruction. Technology has already transformed financial controls and student registration. During the 1990s, digitized information storage and retrieval will actually begin to see returns in library efficiency, inventory management, and energy control. Even more important, new learning technologies should allow the more productive use of the time of the students: less redundancy, less attrition, more genuine "mastery learning," and less time to the degree. In a few countries—e.g., China, Thailand, Indonesia—a significant amount of the new student demand is being met by distance learning, albeit as yet of relatively low technology.

To date, with the exception of the aforementioned national open universities, technology has arguably added as much cost (with greatly added benefits) as it has cut. In time, however, technology can still be expected to lower unit costs significantly through:

- greatly increasing the teaching power of a single faculty member—i.e., expanding effective student/faculty ratios through electronic storage and the widespread dissemination through telecommunications of lectures and demonstrations;
- greatly lowering the per-student costs of libraries and both the storage and retrieval of information;
- lowering per-student capital costs as well as the costs of student living by reaching students in their homes and places of work; and
- lowering the opportunity costs of foregone earnings by facilitating simultaneous work and study and shortening the total real time to the final degree.

Trends in Enhancing Revenue

Trends in cutting costs, or the enhancement of productivity, are being complemented by trends in the enhancement of revenue. Because revenue from the government, or taxpayers, may be assumed to be maximized at a point in time, given the prevailing fiscal and political realities, the "enhancement of revenue" generally means shifting a greater proportion of costs onto non-taxpayer sources: principally parents and students, but to some degree businesses, philanthropists, and institutional entrepreneurial activities. This final section summarizes seven trends, or techniques, of enhancing non-governmental revenue.

Reducing taxpayer-borne subsidies for the costs of student living—e.g., for residence halls, meals, transportation, and the like. Direct government (taxpayer) contributions to the costs of student living were estimated in 1980 to constitute about 14 percent of government recurring expenditures on higher education in the OECD countries, but as much as 47 percent (1988 figures) in the lowest income countries.[6] Clearly, substantial public funds can be saved, or shifted, to support of instructional costs if these subsidies can be reduced, and parents and students, to the limit of their financial capabilities, be required to pay more of the costs of student living. In fact, such a shift will probably precede the imposition of, or significant increases in, tuition fees for reasons both of politics and economics. There are clear users and non-users of subsidized student canteens and housing, and while free or highly-subsidized tuition has at least an intellectual defense and substantial precedent (including most of Europe), there is very little defense for the practice of highly-subsidized room and board other than affordability for the poor—which can arguably be handled more efficiently and equitably through means-tested loans and grants for the costs of student living. Beyond the sheer relief to government budgets (or the shift of public revenues to more generous support of instructional costs), placing enterprises such as restaurants and student residence halls on a "break-even" basis introduces all of the signals and incentives of the market into enterprises that can easily have become both inefficient and unresponsive under the cover of government subsidies.

Establishing at least modest tuition fees and requiring them to increase annually as underlying costs increase. Tuitions have long covered a significant portion of instructional costs in the public institutions of the United States, Japan, and Canada, and have recently been introduced, via a graduate tax obligation, in Australia.[7] Eicher reports that tuition levels in Europe, traditionally zero or insignificant, have recently been increased to levels that are "not nominal" (i.e., from $200–800) in Belgium, Spain, Netherlands, and Switzerland.[8] In the developing world, tuitions are significant in the public colleges and universities of Korea, Indonesia, the Philippines, and in some of the anglophone nations of Africa; they have been minimal in Bangladesh, China, India, Malaysia, and Thailand, but have been introduced or seriously considered for a more significant role in most of those countries.[9]

On the negative or at least precautionary side, however, the ability of students and parents to bear substantially greater shares of the institutional instructional costs via tuition is limited by three significant factors. First, student living costs alone are very high in all countries and, as suggested earlier, these costs are likely to make the first claim on possible additional revenues from parents and students; the proportion of families (even accepting the upper-middle class enrollment bias in virtually all countries) who can now afford to meet all student living costs and also cover a more significant portion of instructional costs via newly-increased tuitions may be minimal in many countries. Second, any significant cost borne by students and parents requires the complex and not inexpensive administrative machinery of means testing and of grant and loan programs. Third, tuition remains politically unpopular, perhaps especially in Europe and other countries that have lacked either a tradition of public sector tuition or a genuinely private higher educational sector to demonstrate its viability. Nevertheless, the need for expanded and diversified (i.e., nongovernmental) revenues for higher education is so pervasive that the trend toward some greater reliance on tuitions, and thus toward parent and student revenues, will undoubtedly continue.

Encouraging the development of private higher education, with substantial reliance on tuition. Another way that nations are drawing more revenue from parents and students is the encouragement of a private sector with a substantial reliance on tuitions. It is possible, of course, for there to be private sectors that are nearly entirely publicly financed, as in the United Kingdom, the Netherlands, Finland, or India, and have thus become virtually absorbed into the public system.[10] But

The Costs of Higher Education

private sectors can also be largely self-supporting, as in the United States, Korea, Japan, the Philippines, Indonesia, Brazil, Colombia, Argentina, and Mexico;[11] such private sectors take a substantial burden of support off of the state, and they generate revenues from parents and students that would otherwise have to come from taxpayers. Arguably, private institutions can also provide higher educational benefits at lower costs than state-owned and state-run institutions through their greater managerial flexibility and their independence from state civil service rules and work habits. Private higher education, mainly outside Europe, is encouraged by government through capital and operating grants, access of their students to means-tested grants for the costs of student living, tax advantages to donors, and liberal policies of licensure and control.

Maintaining access, while increasing parent and student contributions toward the costs of higher education, through means-tested grants and government-sponsored student loans. If revenue is to be increased through greater dependence on parents, provision must be made for "means testing," or the determination of what in the United States is termed a fair "expected parental contribution," so that families unable to contribute can receive state (i.e., taxpayer-borne) support through means-tested grants or subsidies. In nations like the United States, the United Kingdom, Germany, and Japan, such means testing draws on an extensive, reasonably well-accepted, and reasonably well-policed system of taxation on income and assets. Nations without such systems, however, find means testing difficult to implement with confidence.[12] Some East European countries continue to leave the distribution of means-tested grants up to the students themselves, through student governments, apparently on the theory that the students know best who is and is not truly needy and also have a strong self-interest, in the face of scarce grant funds, in maintaining a fair system.

Students can bear a significant portion of costs only through borrowing, and the use of student loans is spreading throughout the world.[13] Student loans have been major features of higher educational finance in Scandinavia, the United States, Canada, the Netherlands, and Japan. Germany's student support scheme requires a partial repayment, as an interest-free loan. After decades of fierce opposition to student loans from the National Union of Students and their Labor Party allies, who saw student loans as essential to any significant burden sharing by students and thus to be resisted, England and Wales have adopted a "top-up" loan program, supposedly to shift a portion of student living costs, over time, from parents and taxpayers to students. Australia's Higher Education Contribution Scheme is more of a graduate tax than a loan, *per se,* but most students are nonetheless emerging from their higher educational studies with a repayment obligation, even if it is discharged as a progressive income surtax. Turkey has a student loan agency, YURT-KUR. Colombia's student loan program dates back to 1953, and loans in Latin America have become significant in Argentina, Brazil, and Jamaica. In Asia, student loans are well-established in Japan, Hong Kong, and Singapore, and are under serious study for initiation or revival in China, Korea, Malaysia, and the Philippines. In Africa, student loans are employed in Ghana, Kenya, Lesotho, Malawi, Nigeria, and Zimbabwe. In short, there is a definite worldwide trend, albeit uneven and fraught with both administrative and political pitfalls, toward shifting a larger share of costs, both for instruction and student living, onto parents and students mediated by means-tested grants and government-sponsored and subsidized loans.

Increasing revenues from business. Because of the obvious links and dependencies between business and higher education, and because of the increasing need for non-tax revenues, universities and other higher educational institutions are trying several approaches to more directly tap business revenue:

- Universities and polytechnics in the United Kingdom have been given both the incentive and the latitude aggressively to seek funds from business, both as donations and for sponsored research.
- The French Tax d'Apprentisage is a 5 percent payroll tax deferred for those firms contributing a like amount to worker training, much of it through higher educational institutions.[14] Universities worldwide have sought similar policies, but business opposition is understandably powerful.
- The Soviet Union in 1988, just prior to its breakup, was reportedly planning a surtax on businesses and other enterprises in proportion to the graduate specialists they employ.
- In Korea, which has one of the highest proportions in the world of students in private institutions, paid for largely by parents and the students themselves, the giant Pohang Iron and Steel Company has established and funded an entire private research university, the Pohang Institute of Science and Technology.[15]

While the number of business enterprises worldwide able to sponsor an entire university may be small, the emergence of large and highly

The Costs of Higher Education

profitable firms in the nations of the Pacific Rim, and potentially in other developing nations, makes this a model that may see replication. As yet, however, contributions from businesses, aside from their contributions to the general tax coffers (the incidence of which is almost certainly passed directly to consumers, not unlike a general sales tax) are uneven and in most countries not yet significant.

Increasing revenue from alumni and other philanthropic sources. The United States has long led the rest of the world in obtaining revenues for higher education from alumni, foundations, friends, and corporations. Other nations are now turning to fund raising as a continuous and significant revenue source. Success in fund raising, however, requires a tradition of philanthropic activity generally, plus good alumni records and fund-raising techniques, a cadre of alumni or friends with large fortunes capable of major gifts (say, $500,000 and up), and income, capital gains, and estate tax laws deliberately designed to encourage eleemosynary giving. Without such conditions—not easily or quickly put in place in countries where they do not now exist—"fund raising" as we know it in the United States, at least for most institutions, will remain costly and of increasing, but nonetheless marginal, importance.

Universities themselves engaging in entrepreneurial, profitable activities. Institutions of higher education perform many functions that have potential value on the market and that can, with good management and favorable regulatory treatment, become sources of revenue for certain programs or for the institutions generally. Sponsored research for private enterprises, for example, can potentially turn a real profit, at least through aggressive marketing of patents, copyrights, and licensing possibilities. Medical and other health profession schools operate clinics, the income from which, at least in the United States, has become a significant source of salaries and departmental operating revenue. Certain schools catering to "executive training seminars" and various short-course "refresher" and certificate programs can earn revenue in excess of their costs to support other programs of the institution. Big-time athletics, for a few American universities, is a money-maker. Universities in China, the former Soviet Union, and other formerly socialist nations frequently own factories and farms, which might, with good management, someday turn profits for the benefit of the institution.

Two significant cautions should be observed in considering more aggressive entrepreneurial activities as revenue producers. First, such activities can compete, and sometimes even conflict, with the academic mission and principles of the university. Second, such activities can appear to be profitable when, with more complete and forthright accounting of all costs and revenues, they might in fact prove to be financial drags on their institutions. A general guideline is to account carefully and to pursue activities, such as short course certificates and applied research, that are intimately connected to the university's basic activities.

Conclusion: Trends in Cost Control and Revenue Enhancement

Higher education's formidable appetite for revenue, coupled with the slowdown of many economies and thus of tax revenues, plus in some countries a reassessment of priorities, not necessarily to the advantage of higher education, will place universities and other higher educational institutions and the governments that support them in an increasing financial squeeze. Part of the response to this pressure will be an increasingly aggressive quest for non-tax revenue from parents, students, businesses, and donors. At the same time, there are important limitations to the capacities of most of these non-tax sources in most countries, and it may be well to sound a note of warning that higher education will continue to need stable and generous support from the general citizen/taxpayer, and that higher educational institutions are going to have to earn more of that support by their own aggressive actions of controlling costs and assessing outcomes.

The solution to the diverging trajectories of cost and revenue is going to have to come at least as much on the cost side. Higher education must become more productive through sector differentiation, more attention to the economies of scale, and rigorous cost control that constrains the natural inclination of higher education always to do more and better, at more cost.

NOTES

1. Jean-Claude Eicher and Thierry Chevaillier. "Rethinking the Financing of Post-Compulsory Education." *Higher Education in Europe*, 17, no. 1 (1992): 6–32.
2. D. Bruce Johnstone. "The Costs of Higher Education," *International Higher Education*. Edited by Philip G. Altbach. (New York: Garland Publishing, 1991), pp. 59–90.
3. Gareth Williams. *Financing Higher Education: Current Patterns.* (Paris: OECD, 1990).
4. Frans Kaiser, Jos. B.J. Koelman, Raymond J.G.M. Florax, and Frans A. van Vught. "Public Expenditures on Higher Education: A Comparative Study in the EC-Member States, 1975–1990." *Higher Education in Europe*, 17, no. 1 (1992): 33–64.
5. Gareth Williams. *Changing Patterns of Finance in Higher Education.* (Buckingham, England: Open University Press, 1992).
6. Douglas Albrecht and Adrian Ziderman. "Deferred Cost Recovery for Higher Education." (Washington, D.C.: World Bank. 1991), p. 11.
7. D. Bruce Johnstone. "Tuition Fees." *The Encyclopedia of Higher Education.* Edited by Burton R. Clark and Guy Neave. (Oxford: Pergamon Press, 1992).
8. *Ibid.*
9. D. Bruce Johnstone. "Public and Private Financing Strategies for Higher Education in Asia." (Washington, D.C.: Economic Development Institute, The World Bank, 1992); and Jee-Peng Tan and Alain Mingat. "Educational Development in Asia: A Comparative Study Focusing on Cost and Financing Issues." (Washington, D.C.: World Bank, 1989).
10. Gareth Williams. *Op. cit.*, p. 21.
11. R. L. Geiger. *Privatization of Higher Education: International Trends and Issues.* (Princeton: International Council for Educational Development, 1988); and D. C. Levy. *Higher Education and the State in Latin America.* (Chicago: University of Chicago Press, 1986).
12. Douglas Albrecht and Adrian Ziderman. *Op. cit.*
13. Douglas Albrecht and Adrian Ziderman. *Op. cit.*; D. Bruce Johnstone. *Sharing The Costs of Higher Education: Student Financial Assistance in the United Kingdom, the Federal Republic of Germany, France, Sweden, and the United States.* (New York: College Entrance

Examination Board, 1986); David A. A. Stager. *Focus on Fees; Alternative Policies for University Tuition Fees.* (Toronto: Council of Ontario Universities, 1989); and Maureen Woodhall. "Designing a Student Loan Programme for a Developing Country: The Relevance of International Experience." *Economics of Education Review,* 7, no. 1 (1988): 153–161; Maureen Woodhall. *Financial Support for Students: Grants, Loans, or Graduate Tax?* (London: Kogan Page, 1989); Maureen Woodhall. "Changing Sources and Patterns of Finance for Higher Education: A Review of International Trends." *Higher Education in Europe,* 17, no. 1 (1992): 141–149.

14. Jean-Claude Eicher and Thierry Chevaillier. *Op. cit.*

15. Kim Hogil. "The Contribution of Public and Private Education to the Development of Asian Higher Education." (Washington, D.C.: Economic Development Institute, World Bank, 1992).

OPTIMIZING ALLOCATION STRATEGY*

William F. Massy and Michael C. Hulfactor

Introduction

The decade of the 1980s was a period of affluence for many of America's colleges and universities. Private institutions experienced high returns on investments and were able to raise tuition with apparent impunity. Public institutions enjoyed the benefits of healthy state budgets supported by robust economies. The glow of prosperity was tempered only by the rumblings of a few critics, such as former Secretary of Education William Bennett, who decried the escalating costs of an undergraduate education.[1]

But the rumblings were soon to grow to a roar. Not only were costs increasing, but mounting evidence indicated that educational quality was declining. Several national reports criticized American higher education's lack of commitment to its mission of teaching undergraduates. For example, studies commissioned by the National Endowment for the Humanities,[2] the Association of American Colleges,[3] and the Western Interstate Commission for Higher Education[4] found that many undergraduate programs were neglected and in serious disarray.

Government officials, the media, and families sending their children to college began to question the efficiency and effectiveness of American higher education. Higher education had been regarded unquestionably as a public good. Lay people took the value of an education for granted, even if they could not understand how that education was formulated or delivered. Although faculty and academic administrators tended to be aloof and sometimes arrogant, they carried forth the image of lofty subject matter. However, as both cost and quality issues arose, people began to question whether higher education had become more of a private good than a public good. They voiced concerns that institutions and their faculty had become self-serving. In effect, the U.S. system of higher education experienced a loss of public trust.

The loss of public trust has hit colleges and universities hard in the recessionary years of the 1990s. This has been especially evident in state governments where, when faced with fiscal crunches and competing demands for entitlement programs and other social services, legislatures are forcing public institutions to accept large funding cuts. They seem to believe there is so much fat in the system that a 10, 15, or even 20 percent cut can be sustained without significant harm to quality. Private institutions also are experiencing similar problems in the form of tuition resistance and, in some cases, cutbacks by public funding agencies.

American colleges and universities certainly are no strangers to recessionary times and retrenchment. The sharp recession of 1974 caused a collapse of investment returns while stagflation triggered by the Arab oil embargo prompted many institutions to retrench financially. Overarching these events was the loss of institutional consensus and confidence caused by campus conflicts over the Vietnam War and faculty reaction to new funding limits and regulations. In the 1970s, the predominant reaction to retrenchment was to treat it as a "one-time" phenomenon, to be gotten past as quickly as possible with little long-term disruption.[5] The 1990s are different. To regain the public's trust in higher education's quality and efficiency, institutions will have to restructure themselves.

By restructuring, an institution reorganizes fundamental elements of its work processes and management systems. Restructuring can help colleges and universities realign themselves with their fundamental educational missions, and, at the same time, hold down costs during hard financial times. The need for restructuring is not delimited by international boundaries. Western European colleges and universities, for example, are experiencing increased student demand as well as shifts in government views of research and research policies, and these pressures are stretching the resources of many campuses. Political and economic events are changing higher education at a dizzying pace in the emerging eastern European democracies. Though some of the oldest institutions of higher learning are in eastern Europe, many suffered greatly in the post-World War II years. They are struggling to redefine their educational missions and their programs, and to secure stable funding.

Elements of Restructuring

Four elements are necessary for restructuring in higher education. They are (1) aligning academic objectives with institutional mission and vision, (2) reengineering administrative and support services, (3) redeploying the faculty resource, and (4) reforming resource allocation systems.

Aligning Academic Objectives to Mission

Many colleges and universities have drifted away from their fundamental missions. It is easy for divergent goals and objectives to be added incrementally to an institution's perceived mission over time. When goal diffusion is allowed to proceed unchecked, the result is numerous constituencies promoting many narrow objectives but no constituency supporting the overall institutional purpose. Yet, a mission which includes something for everybody may be so broad and bland that it lacks focus and coherence. A mission is only meaningful when some things are left out or downgraded in importance relative to others.

Reengineering Administrative and Support Services

The second restructuring task entails reengineering administrative and support services to gain more efficiency and effectiveness. Administrative and support service bureaucracies, which make up the so-called "administrative lattice," have proliferated in many colleges and universities over the past two decades.[6] One estimate places staff increases at 60 percent nationwide between 1975 and 1985, while faculty grew by only 8 percent in the same period.[7] Familiar causes of such additions include responses to increasingly complex regulatory and institutional environments. Less familiar causes are the "growth force," where administration and its products become goals in and of themselves; the practice of consensus management, which effectively diffuses risk and responsibility for decisions; and the off-loading of tasks formerly the province of the faculty, such as student advising and counseling.

Redeploying the Faculty Resource

The third restructuring task calls for colleges and universities to reacquire the capacity for redeploying the faculty resource in support of the overall instructional mission. Over the past three decades or so, faculty have gradually shifted their allegiance away from the goals of their institutions and toward those of their academic specialties—a process we call the "academic ratchet."[8] This process has led to an increased emphasis on research, publishing, and teaching in specialties at the expense of more general undergraduate courses. Faculty have, in effect, become more independent and entrepreneurial. They are more accountable to the agencies providing their research funding than to their own institution. They also are more accountable to their profession, through which they achieve professional standing and the peer endorsements needed for tenure. Less faculty discretionary time and attention are made available for instruction, which reduces curricular coherence and increases institutional cost.

Reforming Resource Allocation

The fourth task requires institutions to reform their resource allocation systems. Institutions that fail to do this risk forfeiting gains from other restructuring efforts, whereas systems that are aligned to restructuring goals reinforce new procedures and provide incentives for operating units to change their behavior. Thus, how resources are allocated can make or break efforts to contain costs and improve productivity. Budgeting systems can empower operating unit leaders to do things which improve productivity, or they can stifle such efforts. Budgeting responsibilities can be delegated in ways that either promote overall institutional goals, or they can allow operating units and individuals to pursue their own goals at the expense of the institution's.

Resource Allocation Systems

Before considering reform strategies, we will discuss the main types of resource allocation systems used by governments, higher education systems, and individual campuses. Resource allocation systems distribute funds for (1) the cost of education, (2) the primary cost of research, and (3) research overhead. Although there are inevitable overlaps and tradeoffs among them, each type is quite distinct.

Methods for Distributing the Cost of Education

Every college and university distributes funds in one way or another to pay for the cost of educating students. Three alternative allocation methods are in use: (1) traditional line-item budgeting (also known as specific responsibility budgeting), (2) block allocation budgeting, and (3) responsibility center budgeting.

Line-Item Budgeting

Centralizing resource allocation through line-item budgeting is a common response to concerns about accountability. According to conventional wisdom, one way to insure that funds are spent properly is for the central administration (or state authority) to allocate them, line item by line item. While this method may be appropriate for small institutions, it quickly becomes unwieldy for large or complex ones. Line-item allocation presents a formidable decision-making challenge for the central administration, as the number of proposed items can run into the hundreds. Furthermore, it is difficult to compare the value of, say, a teaching assistant with the value of disposing of a package of hazardous waste. The difficulty of seeing what is gained from a heterogeneous collection of incremental budget items represents one strategic problem with line-item budgeting. The fact that it disempowers local unit leaders represents another. Controlling overall budgetary growth also presents difficulties, even though such control represents the process's main rationale. It is difficult to persuade operating heads that fund reallocations among units are equitable, and the resulting pressures produce add-on budgeting and institutional expenditures that spiral out of control.

Block Allocation Budgeting

Block allocation budgeting presents an alternative to line-item budgeting. There are many variations in practice, but what happens is essentially this: a central funding authority engages in negotiations with each operating unit about its operations and funding, a mutually acceptable plan is agreed upon, and a block allocation is made. The money goes to the unit as a block with few or no strings attached, so the unit can spend money for whatever it deems necessary. However, the unit is responsible for delivering what was promised. Funding next time around depends upon how well the operating unit performed in achieving the agreed-on objectives.

Block allocation budgeting places responsibility for local decisions in the hands of the operating unit, yet those decisions have consequences for the unit's overall performance as judged by the central funding authority. The method is relatively easy to integrate with other elements of an institution's strategy. However, block allocation budgeting does not delegate revenue responsibility to operating units, so demand and market forces are not likely to be very important in unit level planning. Furthermore, the central authorities are apt to allocate similar budget increments to all units, regardless of how well each is meeting institutional goals. This can reduce efficiency and blur incentives, since unit heads will come to expect a "fair" block allocation regardless of performance.

Responsibility Center Budgeting

In responsibility center budgeting, the central administration delegates budgetary authority to "responsibility centers," such as schools or major academic programs. Centers receive credit for the income they generate, so they must pay attention to demand for their services. They also are responsible for the full costs of their operations, which may include indirect costs as well as direct costs. The central administration retains responsibility for centrally-provided support services, paying for them with overhead charges. It also may tax

income and develop pools of "non-attributable" income to augment capital budgets and to help financially-strapped units.
    Responsibility center budgeting has much to recommend it, but it also has several disadvantages. Attributing tuition income to schools and programs can be difficult, and this may not be compatible with overarching institutional objectives. Responsibility centers may be induced to maximize their income at the expense of institution-wide efficiency. Additionally, some responsibility centers may not be able to survive on their own, even though they may be critical to the overall institutional mission. For example, an undergraduate program in mathematics may be important to the general education of undergraduates, although there are few mathematics majors. Taxing other programs to pay for such a program may mitigate the problem, but this also creates dissension among units that are heavily taxed. Finally, the methods used to allocate overhead can become lightning rods for controversy within the institution.

Methods for Distributing the Primary Cost of Research

We define "primary research cost" as consisting of expenditure items whose benefits flow directly to a particular project; for example, the salaries of workers, laboratory supplies, and equipment. Primary research costs may be allocated in a variety of ways. These include (1) project funding, (2) program funding, (3) departmental (or non-sponsored) research funding, and (4) institutional funding.

Project Funding

Project funding is the prevalent form of research funding in the United States. Some agencies distribute funds in a block allocation for a given project, with restrictions only on the purchase of capital equipment, foreign travel, and overhead allocations. Others place very tight restrictions on individual line items, such as types of salaries, fringe benefits, and different kinds of supplies.
    Evaluations of quality and relevance to sponsor goals are performed on a project-by-project basis, with the probability of repeat funding depending significantly on past performance. Hence, this

allocation form maximizes market forces. On the other hand, the transaction costs of such a system can be high and it is difficult for an institution or academic department to develop a coherent research strategy. Nevertheless, this seems to be the most efficient system, and it is being adopted in country after country.

Program Funding

Project coherence tends to be improved when funding is allocated on a program basis. Such funding was popular in the United States in the 1950s and 1960s, but its popularity declined as research became more expensive relative to the available funds. While a good many national centers do exist at present, project monitors from the funding agencies often carefully control the individual projects even within centers. Currently, most program funding goes to interdisciplinary undertakings of national scope, so they do not contribute much to the development of coherent institutional research strategies.

Departmental Research Funding

"Departmental research funding" is common in the United States and Europe. Such research usually is considered a by-product of the educational function, and funding is not allocated or accounted for separately. In such cases, allocations take the form of enhanced faculty-student ratios and additional support services, which lead to reduced educational workloads. This is a fine way to get research resources into faculty hands, but it begs the question of whether the money is spent effectively. In fact, reduced teaching loads become entitlements—to be enjoyed by faculty whether or not they currently are productive in research. Lack of clarity about the degree to which departmental funding levels are intended to support research as opposed to education can represent an additional problem. For example, those who fund undergraduate education may not understand the purposes of their expenditures, and significant ill will can result when the truth becomes apparent.

Institutional Funding

Finally, research funding can be provided on an institutional basis. This permits a school to decide on its research priorities—probably in consultation with funding agencies—and then take the steps needed to carry it forward. This method is used to fund specialized research institutions, but the sums going to universities are minor. Its principal drawback is as that noted earlier for block budgeting: once a given level of funding is established, it is difficult to reduce it unless there are truly significant priority shifts or performance problems.

Methods for Distributing Research Overhead

Research "indirects" represent costs which are not "primary" according to the previous definition, but which nevertheless support research projects in meaningful ways. Allocation methods which may be used to distribute research overhead include: (1) incremental attributable costs, (2) average attributable costs, (3) average overhead costs, and (4) incremental overhead costs. Of course, the option of making no provision for indirect costs exists as well.

Incremental Attributable Cost

Research overhead payments may be limited to those costs which are "caused" by a particular project, and which usually are paid by the project sponsor under the "direct expense" category. Clerical and project administration expense provide good examples of incremental attributable costs. There are no formulas for determining the appropriate level for incremental clerical or administrative cost, so the dividing lines are hazy. In the United States, the practice typically has been to include whatever seems reasonable under the circumstances. The difficulty with this approach is that it may produce contention between institutions and funding agencies, with projects receiving quite different funding in relation to activity levels.

Average Attributable Cost

Sometimes indirect costs can be pooled and then allocated on the basis of usage. Service center costs, which are charged on a rate-times-volume basis, represent the most familiar instance of this genre. However, the creation of formal service centers is not necessary. Take the case of facilities, for example. Facilities utilization might include depreciation, energy consumption, operations and maintenance, and hazardous materials disposal. Each service operation would calculate its average cost per square foot for a particular category of space, such as laboratories or offices, and then allocate the cost to projects according to the square footage utilized. Since it is virtually impossible to precisely identify the specific costs of particular spaces or to attribute such costs to a particular accounting period, one averages the costs on the basis of multiperiod data for generic space types. It is not too difficult to track the amounts of space assigned to individual projects and programs, so the average costs can be assigned with reasonable precision. As a further benefit, the methodology discourages projects from hoarding space—which is in short supply on many campuses.

Average Overhead Cost

In the average overhead cost allocation method, a computed overhead rate is applied to all projects at an institution and typically paid as a single line item by the project sponsor. The rate is derived from averaging the costs for services like central administration and libraries, which are difficult to attribute to individual projects. The U.S. government's OMB Circular A-21 provides detailed guidelines for computing average research overhead rates. Theoretically, these rates allow institutions to fully recover all overhead attributable to research. In practice, however, negotiations with sponsoring agencies result in much lower rates—in effect, rates that come closer to representing incremental cost than full average cost.

Incremental Overhead Cost

An incremental overhead cost allocation system would require institutions to compute an overhead rate based on the incremental cost of the overhead services used by research projects. However, it would not go so far as to allocate costs based on the actual use of particular services by particular projects (that would be an "incremental attributable cost" allocation). In an incremental overhead cost allocation system, the rate calculation would exclude the fixed cost of administrative and support services. For example, since the institution would need a president even if it had no research projects, the president's salary would be excluded. Clearly, the analytical and accounting requirements of such a system are formidable. Moreover, it might well fail to capture the less-well documentable indirect research cost, which under average-cost oriented systems are compensated by contributions to the fixed cost of overhead operations.

Centralized Versus Decentralized Resource Allocation Systems

As in many enterprise types, the trend in higher education resource allocation is toward decentralization. Centralized systems, which are characterized by line-item control and stringent restrictions on how unit operations can spend funds, impose a limited number of objectives and a consistent set of operational procedures. However, centralized systems carry high transaction costs; for example, the central funding authority must monitor program details and give permission to spend relatively small amounts of money. The system also can stifle innovation in operating units, since the units are expected to perform in lockstep fashion. Finally, a high degree of "gaming" behavior occurs in operational units. Units attempt to get around the rules, and often manage or fabricate information in order to satisfy the central funding authority.

Allocation system decentralization has been prompted by the realization that attention to increasingly complex environments requires more decision-making authority at local levels. Decentralization allocates resources in blocks, which reduces transaction costs for the central administration. It also empowers those who are at the local level and close to the action. In the case of higher education, faculty members, department chairs, and others who are close enough to know about quality firsthand are the ones who can make the most effective decisions. Decentralizing resource allocation can increase morale, while reducing the amount of time spent gaming the central authority. Institutions that have recently decentralized their resource allocation systems sometimes confront department chairs who say, "Look, you decentralized, so why are you now telling me that I didn't do what you wanted?" However, decentralizing does not mean abdication: operating units still must be held accountable for their performance. The money was provided for a purpose, and departments should be judged on how well they deliver on that purpose.

Despite its good qualities, decentralization can increase an institution's vulnerability to what we shall call value incongruity. The value incongruity problem has two parts: goal differentiation and value externalities. Operating units may have different goals than those of the central authority, and these goals can substitute for those of the larger institution. Goal differentiation produces the so-called "agency problem," in which principals cannot fully control the actions of their agents. Mitigating the agency problem requires either detailed regulation—the antithesis of decentralization—or the development of incentives that cancel out the value differences. The development of new incentives represents a major new area for study and innovation in higher education.

Value externalities arise when one decentralized entity reaps the benefits of an action while another pays the price. The classic example is polluting the atmosphere; the pollution blows downwind and affects not the polluter, but its neighbor. In academia, the analogy is a department thinking, "I don't have to do an especially good job teaching beginning calculus because the students are going somewhere else." (Such thinking is unlikely to be stated out loud, but it still has an impact.) Conversely, if education is funded on a formula basis using enrollment numbers, a department may want to teach its own calculus in order to get the average cost funding that comes with those enrollments. Externalities may be mitigated though countervailing incentives or by limiting their scope, as we will describe later.

The Tension Between Teaching and Research

The tension between teaching and research on many campuses illustrates value incongruity and some of the other difficulties

Optimizing Allocation Strategy 37

associated with decentralizing resource allocations. Higher education's critics argue that institutions and faculty over-value research relative to teaching. However, institutional initiatives to improve the quality of teaching often make little headway with professors. Let us examine this problem in more detail. The conventional wisdom, of course, is that research enhances educational quality, but the real situation is more complex. Figure 1 depicts what economists call a "production possibility curve": in this case the alternative combinations of educational quality and research that are feasible given that enrollment and resource levels are held constant.

[Figure: Trade-off diagram showing Educational quality (vertical axis) vs. Research (horizontal axis) with a curve. Point 1 is near the top-left where the curve slopes upward (labeled "complements"); point 2 is on the right portion where the curve slopes downward (labeled "substitutes"). A triangular shaded region indicates "Alternative production possibilities with fixed resources". Source: see note 9.]

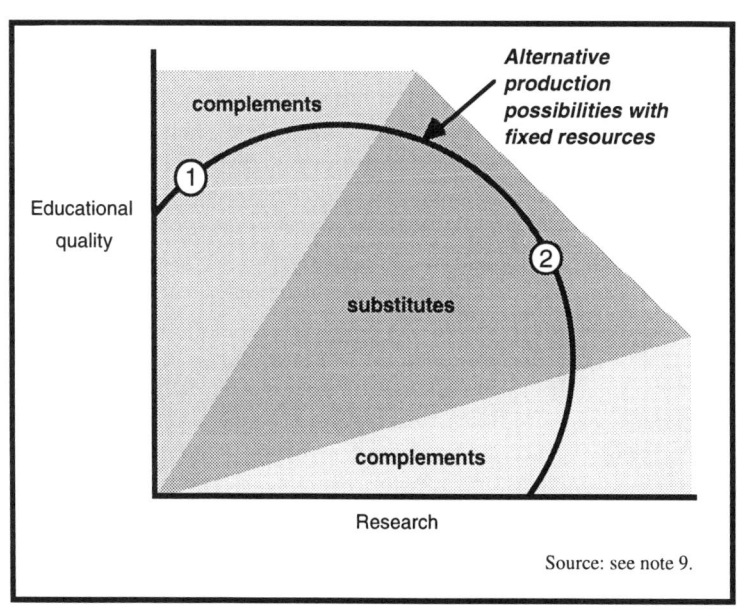

Figure 1. The Trade-Off Between Educational Quality and Research

Imagine an institution that does little research. Its production is near the left-hand axis at point 1. For this institution, when research is increased, educational quality increases as well. Faculty members become more stimulated by their subjects and become better informed, thus benefiting their classroom teaching. Educational quality and research are complementary goods in production in the region where the curve slopes upward. When there is more of one, there is more of the other, too.

Unfortunately, the curve eventually begins to slope downward, so that more research results in lower educational quality. Powerful forces drive institutions toward point 2 on the curve, where research substitutes strongly for education. To illustrate this process, suppose that a faculty member acquires some new research sponsors. A deadline approaches, and she slips up on preparing for a class. The world does not end, so the next time around it is a little easier to shortchange the class. Another faculty member knows he should have five office hours this week, but needs to board an airplane and go to Washington to give a talk, so he reduces his office hours to four. Next time it might be three office hours. It happens gradually—norms that shape faculty professional behavior change very slowly over time. The process has been going on in the country's best institutions for more than thirty years now; in the next echelon of institutions for twenty years, and so on down the line. Many institutions are sliding further down that curve as new faculty are being hired with research degrees and expectations for research.

Critics think that American higher education is at point 2, whereas the conventional wisdom holds that we are further up the curve. Obviously, these are gross generalizations. Different institutions are at different points along the curve, though it seems that research universities have, in fact, gone over the hump and are well down the slope. In some research universities, goal differentiation has allowed the production of research to substitute for educational quality. Yet, while research confers prestige and can produce larger faculties, it leads to greater costs and reductions in overall educational quality at the institution. Educational clients thus end up paying more and getting less.

Lessons from Hospitals

Higher education is not the only sector where rising costs and concerns about quality have triggered public concern. Issues facing hospitals over the past fifteen to twenty years have analogies in higher education. By analyzing policy solutions in hospitals, insight can be gained about their applicability to colleges and universities. Hospitals also have had to change their management processes and relations with physicians in order to cope with cost containment measures imposed by the payers of services. There is an analog here, too, since colleges and universities also rely on highly independent and mobile professionals (faculty) for their primary production work.

The basic problem for hospitals is that doctors have shifted their value system from "do no harm" to "do all you can." The value shift coincides with the tremendous advances in biotechnology since World War II, and it has been stimulated by malpractice lawyers. Entitlement programs, such as Medicare, have added fuel to the cost-rise fire by decoupling the receipt of services from the economic tradeoffs required to pay for them. The result is that hospitals have been caught in a ratchet of ever-escalating costs.

Several schemes have been devised to grapple with excessive cost-rise in health care. These schemes try to contain costs by regulating medical decision making, building price resistance, or changing cost reimbursement procedures. The schemes include utilization reviews, capitation, copayments, preferred provider programs, and prospective payment systems such as diagnostic-related groups. The returns from applying these remedies are not all in, but they appear to have slowed the rate of medical cost increases.[10] At the same time, ethical considerations and the threat of malpractice lawsuits have worked to maintain quality in the face of cost-reducing efforts.

The left-hand side of Figure 2 depicts the situation graphically. The downward-pointing arrow represents the pressure induced by the new cost-reducing programs. The left- and right-pointing arrows represent pressures for quality—pressures which we regard as symmetric to contrast them with the asymmetric quality pressures in higher education. Symmetry tends to prevent cross-subsidies between different medical services; heart transplant patients, for example, are not systematically shortchanged to aid cancer patients. The result is a decentralized system in which doctors make the best possible decisions about what is appropriate for patients, consistent with funding limits.

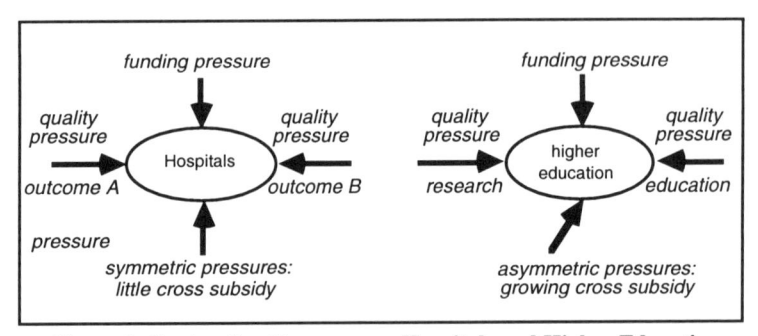

Figure 2. Contrasting Pressures on Hospitals and Higher Education

Higher education, represented by the right-hand diagram in Figure 2, operates differently. Increased funding pressure is placed on the system, but the quality control pressures for education and research are asymmetric—originating disproportionately from the research side. To illustrate, faculty promotion and tenure typically depend on research, which can tap peer-group review for publications and other scholarly work. However, there are no peer reviews of students who graduate from college. Thus, organized judgments on the research side are matched up with fuzzy impressions on the education side, creating an asymmetric net quality-control vector. Therefore, as fiscal pressures mount, colleges and universities do less for undergraduates because of the pressure to maintain the quality of research and scholarship.

The central lesson for higher education from the hospital experience is that expenditure discipline is absolutely necessary. Without funding pressure, college and university costs will expand without limit. However, expenditure discipline is not sufficient. Effective quality control measures are required for all the important dimensions of higher education performance. Such measures already are in place for research and scholarship, but they are woefully inadequate for education. Managing educational quality does not come naturally to the academy, but higher education must find a way to do it.

Strategies for Reforming Resource Allocation

Colleges and universities must reverse the academic ratchet and roll back the administrative lattice if they are to keep costs in line. This will require fundamental restructuring on many campuses. Such restructuring will not succeed unless resource allocation systems are reformed to reinforce institutional choices about academic objectives, administrative and support services, and faculty deployment. We offer the following principles as general guides for the reformation process.

1. Decentralize whenever possible.
2. Enforce expenditure discipline in all areas.
3. Clearly define responsibilities and performance criteria.
4. Transmit appropriate "market signals" to operating units.
5. Expose operating units to the consequences of value incongruity and inefficiency.
6. Reward units that meet institutional goals.

Allocation systems should decentralize and transmit market signals, but they also should structure information flows and focus issues so that negotiation is a central feature of the process. Participants should agree on their respective responsibilities and the measures that will be used to track outcomes, despite differences in their values and goals. Failure to reach agreement should persuade the central authority to withhold funds, lest it lose the ability to discharge its accountability to external constituencies. Conversely, the central authority should remain mindful of the risks to faculty morale and retention associated with imposing its will on academic units, and avoid pushing top-down goals beyond the point needed to achieve the institutional mission.

Resource allocation systems are varied, and no single template will apply to every institution. Indeed, institutions will probably want to select the best features of several allocation methods. Once installed, it is likely that a given system will evolve over time as new needs are discovered and old ones are dropped. For example, an institution may align itself with the decentralization principle by abandoning line-item budgeting in favor of block allocations. Later, as part of its restructuring efforts, the institution may elect to add a market-signaling component by adopting some features of responsibility center budgeting.

We have come to believe that an optimal resource allocation system will include elements of both block budgeting and responsibility center budgeting. Such a plan would begin by identifying the flows of incremental revenues and costs that are attributable to each operating unit. The next step would devolve selected revenue flows to the operating units in order to transmit market signals; however, flows that generate incentives counter to institution-wide goals would be withheld. For example, tuition from undergraduate general education might not be allocated in order to avoid course duplication and retain the capacity for teamwork. The plan also would allocate only incremental overhead costs to units, not the average overhead cost associated with responsibility center budgeting. Fixed indirect costs would be covered by the central administration from centrally-retained income.

The plan would allocate some revenues according to formulas (e.g., tuition for undergraduate majors might be allocated on the basis of enrollment), but only for those revenue flows for which market signals need to be reinforced and where there are no major value externalities. The remaining revenues would be allocated in blocks based on specific operating unit plans, which would be thrashed out in negotiations between department heads and the central administration. In typical block-budgeting fashion, the allocations would reinforce those operating unit goals and plans which are congruent with the institution's overall mission. Such a plan also could borrow features from educational and research-overhead budgeting methods as circumstances warrant.

The resource allocation system should provide a powerful set of tools for improving efficiency and effectiveness, and for enhancing public accountability. It should provide equality of opportunity and access to process, but there must be no doubt that resources flow for a purpose and that there are no implied property rights. In other words, academic units should be exposed to the negative consequences of value incongruity and inefficiency, and rewarded when they produce institutionally-desired outcomes.

Resource allocation reform should be considered as part of an overall institutional restructuring program, one that aligns academic incentives to the institutional mission and markets, reverses the academic ratchet, and breaks down the administrative lattice. It should grow out of deep discussions within the academic community about the institution's mission, and its strengths and weaknesses. This is the only way that colleges and universities can regain the public trust, and thus maintain their resource base and autonomy into the twenty-first century.

NOTES

*Preparation of this manuscript was supported by the Finance Center of the Consortium for Policy Research in Education (CPRE), under a contract from the U.S. Department of Education's Office of Education Research and Improvement.

1. Jean Evangelauf. "Bennett Castigates Colleges Over Skyrocketing Tuition, Proposes Changes in U.S. Student Aid to Control Costs." *Chronicle of Higher Education,* vol. 33, no. 13 (Nov. 26, 1986): 1–21.

2. William J. Bennett. *To Reclaim a Legacy: A Report on the Humanities in Higher Education.* (Washington, D.C.: National Endowment for the Humanities, 1984).

3. Joseph S. Johnston, Susan Shaman, and Robert Zemsky. *Unfinished Design: The Humanities and Social Sciences in Undergraduate Engineering Education.* (Washington, D.C.: Association of American Colleges, 1988).

4. Charles S. Lenth, Robin E. Zuniga, and John J. Halcon. *Setting the Agenda: Reform and Renewal in Undergraduate Education.* (Boulder, Colo.: Western Interstate Commission for Higher Education, 1989).

5. William F. Massy. "A Paradigm for Research in Higher Education." Stanford University, 1986.

6. William F. Massy and Robert Zemsky. "Faculty Discretionary Time: Departments and the Academic Ratchet." *Policy Perspectives Papers* (1992), Pew Higher Education Research Program, Philadelphia.

7. William F. Massy and Timothy R. Warner. "Causes and Cures of Cost Escalation in College and University Administrative and Support Services." Stanford Institute for Higher Education Research, Stanford University, 1991.

8. Robert Zemsky and William F. Massy. "Cost Containment," *Change* (November/December 1990): 16–22.

9. Adapted from Marc Nerlove. "On Tuition and the Costs of Higher Education: Prolegomena to a Conceptual Framework." *Journal of Political Economy,* Part II, 3: (1972), S178–S218.

10. William F. Massy. *Productivity in Higher Education.* (Stanford Institute for Higher Education Research, Stanford University, 1990.)

UNIVERSITY STRATEGIES FOR THE THIRD STREAM OF INCOME

John Fürstenbach

The Definition

"The third stream" was chosen as a term to describe the money earned by institutions of higher education in return for services such as research, education, and consulting to contractors outside the higher education sphere. In this context, "the first stream" naturally refers to government appropriations for education and basic research and "the second stream" to the flow of public money channeled through research councils and similar agencies designated for this task.

More precisely, the third stream of income is earned through contracts. The contractors are enterprises, organizations, and in some cases government agencies outside the higher education system. The tasks performed by the universities range from basic research to applied research and development tasks to routine analyses in university laboratories. In addition, standard academic or custom-made courses are sold as parts of industry's staff development programs.

The boundary between the second and the third stream is not crystal clear. The organizational status of the contractor alone is not enough to discriminate between the two; the interest of the contractor is also important. If the contractor has any interest other than to promote the development of research, the sponsored project obviously falls within the third stream, even if the contractor is a government agency.

National Situation and Trends

In this section the amount of third stream funding and the percentage this constitutes of the total turnover are given for participating universities nation by nation. The figures have been reported by each university for the fiscal years 1989–90 or 1990. The present European recession may have affected reported trends as well as the amount of third stream funding today. It has proved to be difficult to establish internationally unambiguous definitions, and comparisons should be made with a certain amount of caution. However, these examples illustrate the problems and raise questions for further research.

Belgium

Third stream income has been increasing for a long time. This has to some extent offset the effects of a decrease in public funding. University support to exceptionally good projects has enhanced the chances of contract income. It is not uncommon that the contracts taken are for routine processes. Such work, which is of low academic interest, is often subcontracted outside the universities. The university authorities are trying to improve their control over these activities for outside contracts. Full cost recovery is not yet possible.

At some universities (e.g., Université Louvain-la-Neuve), policies stressing that scientific results must be published have been adopted. Science parks and spin-off enterprises are favoured as a means to widen the academic community. Cooperation with non-profit organizations, such as the Vlerick School of Management in Gent, is pursued with the same objective. The University of Gent reports the amount of third stream funding to be 16.9 million ECUs, which is 12 percent of the turnover. The Universities of Leuven and Louvain-la-Neuve report 19.3 million ECUs (9 percent) and 29.8 million ECUs (16 percent) respectively.[1] (ECU, the European Currency Unit, is worth approximately US$1.30.)

France

At French universities, the volume of third stream funding is increasing rapidly. Outside contracts are most often initiated and managed by individual departments or professors. Contracts have to be formally approved by the university board, research contracts must also be approved by the scientific board. Contracts that have financial implications must also be signed by the financial director. Depending on university policies, externally financed activities are more or less closely monitored at central levels of the university. The control exerted may typically include legal issues, cost recovery, the distribution of benefits and the evaluation of projects. A university may adopt a policy to leave much freedom to entrepreneurial faculty members to increase the volume of third stream funding.

The president's power regarding third stream activities is reduced, as much of the personnel management such as recruitment, promotions, and salaries are heavily influenced from the national level, while at the same time professors are allowed to earn supplementary income as long as this does not more than double their income. In principle, the professors must inform the university of all external commitments, but how tightly this is implemented varies between universities. Universities are allowed to establish subsidiary enterprises. The four participating French universities have reported third stream funding as follows: Paris Dauphine 2.2 million ECUs (6 percent); Paris Sorbonne 2.8 million ECUs (4 percent); Bordeaux 5.6 million ECUs (6 percent); and Grenoble I 5.6 million ECUs (7 percent).

The Netherlands

The University of Nijmegen reports a 33.7 million ECUs turnover from third stream financing, which constitutes 20 percent of the operating budget. The general impression from the Netherlands is that the increase of third stream income has been strong and has resulted in administrative, personnel, and space problems. Dutch university leaders are trying to identify what contracts fall within university policies and missions. The objective is to accept only contracts which contribute to institutional development and quality. This would also lead to a welcome stabilization of levels of third stream funding.

Spain

The universities of Oviedo and Autonoma Barcelona report 3.6 million ECUs (4 percent) and 8.5 million ECUs (8 percent), respectively. Spanish universities are in fierce competition for industry contracts and other sources of third stream money. The third stream, which is seen as an important additional financial source, has been available for only the last six years. The growth has been fast: at some universities third stream money accounts for 10 percent of the budget. The law allows professors to take on contracts on their own, and university managers try to establish structural and financial control; the latter also includes charging contracts for university overhead.

Sweden

The importance of third stream funding has increased in Sweden, too. On the average, research institutions rely on contracts for about 20 percent of their budgets. Stockholm University, which only comprises the faculties of humanities, law, social sciences, and natural sciences, received 6.4 million ECUs through third stream funding.

Externally financed research and education are usually conducted within one and the same organization and with the same division of responsibility as the government financed activities at the institutions. Recurrent education is available on a broad basis, financed by the same grants as conventional undergraduate education. Nevertheless, the money earned for education within the third stream is significant. In fact, Swedish universities have taken a 10 percent share of the Swedish market for personnel development activities.

Externally financed projects must cover all direct and indirect costs incurred by the institutions. Academic staff have patent rights to their inventions. This gives the researcher a strong position in a well-regulated system like the Swedish one. Institutions have experienced severe problems of obtaining full cost recovery on their contracts as researchers and funders have found a common interest in reducing the amount of money that is not directly transferred to projects. Since 1991, universities have followed a recommendation from the Swedish Rectors Conference to charge 12 percent for university overhead. In addition, rent for the use of university premises must be levied and delivered to the state.

The Issue

In all participating nations, third stream financing is increasing and the significance of the state monopsony in higher education appears to be declining. If the saying is true that "he who pays the piper calls the tune," this will have a considerable impact on several levels of institutional strategy. Four important strategic fields are indicated as follows:

Influence on Institutional Autonomy

Institutional autonomy means that the institution can make decisions in its own interest which can not be overruled by government or its buffer organizations. However, universities are sensitive to financial restrictions. Consequently, it is clear that the balance between the different streams of income is of importance to the true autonomy of the institution, quite irrespectively of the legal status of the university. Too much third stream money will most probably shift the influence on the priorities for institutional development from the institution to the contractors. Too little third stream financing might make it difficult to finance activities which fall outside the established policies of governments and research councils.

Governance of Universities

Within the institution, power patterns change as the balance between the different streams of income changes. The shift from mono- or oli*gopsony* to a free-market like situation requires new leadership and new control systems. The growing interest of industry in university research also increases the conflict between institutional assignments and the private consulting opportunities opening up to a large segment of the faculty.

Within European universities, this could mean the end of strong centralized leadership based on control of the inputs and the processes of research and education. Instead, the devolved organizations, in which operational decisions to a larger extent are made at the departmental level, will become more competitive. Thus, the role of the vice-chancellor and the central administration becomes less that of making decisions on resource allocation and operational issues and more that of monitoring the environment and disseminating information and formulating policies for the institution as a whole.

National and Regional Development Policies

It is often felt that higher education and research are levers for national and regional economic development. From that point of view, the time between invention and application in industry should be reduced. Governments have therefore tended to encourage cooperation between universities and industry. Third stream financed projects are part of such a cooperation.

However, it is not only a matter of political interest whether cooperation will emerge or not. From the contractors' point of view, other infrastructural elements, first of all communications, must be available. A large international supplier of computers indicated to the working group that the company chooses sites for its development centres where there is a good international airport and an excellent university in the vicinity.

Academic Freedom

It is true that many contracts are won because of the academic excellence available at an institution. But it is also true that in many cases the new buyers of research and education do not understand that academic quality is a product of academic values. They may therefore be expected to honor academic values to a much lower extent than do governments and their buffer agencies. The freedom to choose the nature of a project is, of course, restricted by the contract, but the freedom to choose the method and to publish the results may be adverse to the interests of the contractor. If a contract is given to a department because of its skill in applying a known method, the contractor will expect the department to use that method. If publication of the results implies that the contractor risks losing competitive edge, the contractor will require that the results be kept secret. Contracts for routine work may be accepted, but universities have to maintain the position that scientific results must be published.

Impact on Institutions

In a number of areas, third stream financing has a clear impact on institutions.

Autonomy

Even though it may well be argued that government funding makes universities extremely dependent on government policies and that a fair share of third stream income provides an opportunity to balance that, most concerns are about the dependency of each single university or department on one or a few companies. Not only may this influence the development of an institution's research profile towards more applied science, but it may also influence quality or quality control through restrictions on publication or methods and values to be adhered to in the pursuit of research. It is clearly a responsibility of university leaders to keep professors aware of the long-term effects of their involvement with industry.

In democratic states, the need to balance government influence is not as urgent as it may be in states where governments have a narrower base of power. Generally, European governments accept and respect academic values. The major controversies are normally on the level of public funding, and in some cases on priorities within higher education politics. In most cases, industry contracts do not provide such surpluses that a balancing effect on government funding is achieved. The effect of independent donors, such as research foundations, is more important for academic freedom, even when their funding is marginal.

However, contracts with industry may also serve as a link between an institution and the community. Large companies and relevant social organizations have a considerable political impact. If relations are good, this may support the institutional image and the institution itself in negotiations with the government and public agencies.

Quality

Quality is associated with the expectations and values of those assessing quality. Within institutions of higher education, there is generally a consensus on what quality really is. Even if we cannot describe it, we know quality when we see it. Contractors outside the higher education sector often have other values. To them, quality means prompt delivery, relevance to the problem they have defined, and at worst, compliance with company or society policies and goals. Consequently, the quality faculty members value and protect differs from what they are paid for by the contractor. And, as indicated earlier, in the end, it is what was paid for that is likely to matter.

Cost Accounting

Universities were traditionally organizations consuming resources according to availability. That is, all the money was used during the fiscal year by the professors to whom it was allocated. If there were sufficient funds, a new chair, often in a new field, would be established by the university. The only financial control lay in professors not exceeding their budgets. The problems of allocation and cost accounting are late arrivals in twentieth-century European university management. Remarkable though it may seem, this is quite naturally related to the development of the role of universities. Before the 1960s, when mass education was introduced, education was not financially planned, professors delivered lectures, and the only change in resource input due to increased class sizes was larger auditoriums and more time used for examinations.

The increased level of government financing following the larger student numbers also brought a higher level of accountability. The advent of research councils, to which researchers were made responsible for individual projects, added to the increased ambitions in accounting. As long as the second and third streams of income were marginal, accounting standards could be maintained at a low level. With the third stream gaining in importance, greater emphasis has to be put on cost accounting to give researchers and managers information for decisions on project plans and resource inputs. However, from an academic viewpoint, these demands are often considered to be irrelevant.

Cost Recovery

One way or another, all costs incurred by a university must be covered. If all costs of a project cannot be financed within that project, someone else will have to cover the deficit. As long as the second stream was marginal and the third stream insignificant, subsidies from the first stream in the form of covered indirect costs were normal. In some countries (e.g., Sweden until 1990), governments and research councils maintain the idea of marginal cost recovery for projects sponsored by them within the second stream of funding. The view taken is that the appropriations made in the first stream for basic research are also to cover the costs of the base organization for second stream projects. This has led researchers to believe that they do not have to recover the full costs of third stream projects, either. In some states, that is actually the case. There, first stream or other financing includes the basic costs of resources used in third stream financed activities. Then, full cost recovery could imply only that all marginal costs are covered by the contractor.

Non-profit organizations (foundations) are often willing to pay direct costs only. They have two convincing arguments for this. First, foundations have to show their donors that they get a good effect from their contributions, and second, their research interests are often in line with the academic interests of the researchers. This is a dilemma for institutions. They may require full cost recovery from all financiers for all projects, or they may allow recovery of direct costs only for projects of significant value to the research activities, providing subsidies from other funds. In the first case, there will be a considerable risk of controversy over a university's costing principles. In the second case, the institution will face an ever-growing number of projects where the contractor and the researcher claim to qualify for recovery of only the direct costs. Now and then, this leads to problems with covering indirect costs. The special relation between an institution and affiliated foundations, e.g., science park operators, may also initiate divergencies from a full costing principle. These foundations often operate mainly for the benefit of the university. It also happens that they turn out to be even more non-profit than was originally intended—they make losses. One way to help is to make university assets available at direct cost. Thus, the university gets contracts which could not have been won without the foundation, and the foundation gets a more than normal business margin to subsidize its other operations. But eventually, it will be the university's regular education and research that pay to cover the total deficit.

Spin-Off Enterprises

One of the aims of science parks is to provide opportunities to establish spin-off enterprises. The business strategy of these companies is often based on the competence of individual researchers who feel that their results can be used more profitably outside the university organization. In many respects the establishment of such enterprises offers the same or better opportunities to the university than contracts. The number of researchers in a field can be increased without further strains on the university budget, new projects can be launched in cooperation with the enterprise, and there may even be profits that contribute to the development of the institution.

On the other hand, the problems that may arise if the institution is too deeply involved in the enterprise can be far worse than those generated by a failing third stream project. In the beginning, most spin-off enterprises require managerial and financial support, which in the short run can easily be supplied by the institution with a payback expected as soon as the enterprise makes a profit. But managerial resources are often scarce in universities, and in the long run, further financial support conflicts with the primary interests of the institution. Eventually, the institution may have to reassess its involvement with the company. If the institution has taken responsibility as a partner, a situation may develop in which losses have to be covered for legal, ethical, or just public image reasons.

Tension Between the Researcher and the Institution

Projects financed by external contracts are often perceived to be quite independent of the university. This is obvious in the French case, where institutes report directly to the university and the Centre National de la Recherche Scientifique (CNRS). In all countries, researchers often refer to contracts as "my contract," and see university interference with their projects or their flow of money as infringements. Seldom do they understand that if it had not been for their association with a recognized institution, they would not have received a contract in the first place. The notion of "my contract" contains the notion of "my money." Sometimes, this is extended to "my department's" or "my faculty's" money. To a varying extent, these ideas are reflected in the allocation principles of universities. In the history of university administration, there has always been a conflict between this principle, "each tub has its own tap," and the principle of funding "on the basis of need, not on income earning capacity." The strategies chosen have most often been compromises between these two principles.

Clearly, the institution has to deliver what the government expects when it makes its appropriations and what a company expects from a contract. This requires that the resources agreed on be available to the researchers and teachers who are responsible for the fulfilment of these tasks, without interference from university managers. However, the more freely the massed funds of an institution can be used, the fewer the restrictions on decisions made by university leaders, and the more likely that the strategic goals of the institution can be pursued.

Cash Management

The third stream of income creates considerable cash flow at the institutions. In many countries, government cash management regulations are more liberal regarding this income than for grants in the first and second streams of income. Even when the money must eventually be used in a project, massed university cash management may minimize the institution's capital service costs. With correctly assessed internal interest rates, these gains may be distributed within the institution.

Prestige

It appears that the problems we are discussing at least in some countries are linked to the prestige, or the lack of prestige, of the academic professions. University teachers lost in prestige and consequently also in salaries relative to other professions two or three decades ago. It was quite natural that those faculty members who were in a marketable position tried other means to achieve recognition and wealth. Depending on how permissive the universities have been—variations in national legislation account for the largest differences—professors have found different combinations of academic and contract work. It must be well understood that this is not only a matter of private income. It is also a matter of prestige outside the academic society. For a long time now, it has been far more prestigious to be a successful lawyer than a professor. There are, however, tendencies reported from some countries that professors who left the universities ten to fifteen years ago are returning in recognition of the advantages of academic life now that society's appreciation of academia has improved.

Institutional Strategies and Recommendations for Institutional Action

In this situation, institutions have to adapt strategies to maintain autonomy and academic values and find ways to manage in a changing environment. Here, six strategies are suggested. With each is included a number of recommendations on institutional action to pursue the strategies.

Strategy 1: Institutional Mission Consistency

Third stream activities must fall within or directly support the institution's mission.
Recommendations:
1a. Accept only contracts that directly contribute to research or educational programs. Nonspecific contributions (e.g., basic research in a field of priority) are to be considered the most valuable. If these contributions are negligible, financial surpluses that support primary activities are required.
1b. Formulate policies on how contracts for routine activities (e.g., chemical analysis using known technologies) have to contribute to institution and/or department finances.

1c. Institutional management must itself adhere to and communicate the institutional mission. Regarding third stream activities, the institutional mission may be defined broadly, indicating areas of activity and quality requirements.

Strategy 2: Full Academic Quality Required

The same quality must be required in third stream activities as in other research and education activities within the institution.
Recommendations:

2a. Use the same recruitment criteria and procedures for third stream financed staff as for ordinary academic and support staff.
2b. Third stream financed research should, with as few exceptions as possible, be free for publication. Secrecy must not be accepted in a project, or part thereof, that includes the work of postgraduate students or may otherwise be included in a doctoral thesis.
2c. Assess third stream activities in the same way as other education and research activities. For example, include student evaluation of education and seminars on project reports within departments.

Strategy 3: Responsiveness to Market Demands

Increase and/or maintain the institution's responsiveness to market demands. Success factors may include better market understanding, shorter response times, and clear points of external contact.
Recommendations:

3a. Decentralize contacts with international, national, and private third stream financiers.
3b. Establish central offices which support researchers in external contacts, make it easier for third stream financiers to approach relevant researchers, and advise researchers on legal and financial issues.

Strategy 4: Institutional Right to Inventions

Under the restrictions of national legislation and depending on the terms of third stream contracts, inventions by university staff are to be the property of the institution.
Recommendations:
   4a. Develop a policy on patent rights and formulate procedures on how inventions are to be protected and patents eventually applied for.
   4b. Distribute income from inventions to create incentives for departments and researchers to exploit inventions.
   4c. Share risks and costs by seeking to exploit inventions in cooperation with industry.

Strategy 5: Full Cost Recovery

All costs incurred by the university for a third stream project are to be covered by the financier.
Recommendations:

   5a. Introduce this strategy with due consideration to other institutional interests.
   5b. Increase academic awareness of direct and indirect costs at the institution.
   5c. All contracts accepted must provide for full cost recovery. However, look for ways to achieve full cost recovery through counter-balancing inputs (e.g., teaching in first stream financed programmes) from personnel financed under the contract.
   5d. Establish similar costing principles for all activities. Then, full cost recovery can be more easily maintained also in third stream financed activities.
   5e. Enforce accounting practices that recognize the cost of space and equipment to each project or (at least) department.
   5f. As far as possible, match the terms of employment in third stream projects with the contract period.
   5g. As far as feasible, the responsibility to cover deficits in third stream projects should stay with the lowest organizational level in the institution.

Strategy 6: Make Allocation Decisions Independent of the Sources

When allocating resources within an institution, the decision should, to the extent that various constraints permit, be independent of the source of income.
Recommendations:
- 6a. Adopt a policy that all income is primarily institutional income.
- 6b. Within that policy, recognize the need of incentives for departments and researchers to attract third stream money.
- 6c Surpluses from third stream contracts are to be allocated according to institutional priorities by the relevant authority (researcher, department head or chair, dean, rector), without taking the source of income into account.

THE FUTURE OF HIGHER EDUCATION FINANCING

George Psacharopoulos*

The financing situation of universities in developing countries has drastically changed during the last decades. Up to the early 1960s, only a small proportion of the eighteen to twenty-four age group attended university, hence the state could afford to provide such education free of charge to the students. This is no longer the case. The demand for higher education and enrollments have grown by such proportions that governments can no longer foot the university bill, admit to the university all those who want to enroll, or provide education of the same quality as they did before. This paper argues that the way of the future is some form of cost recovery or privatization in higher education, where the beneficiary and/or his/her family will have to bear at least part of the social cost of higher education. Such cost recovery, although politically unpalatable, will be a more efficient and (paradoxically) equitable way of financing higher education.

There are many complex and common issues facing most university systems in today's developing world. Higher education systems have multiple and various tasks, including nation building, training of high level manpower, satisfying the social demand for education, conducting research and being centers of excellence. As shown by experience, this above batch of laudable objectives is seldom, if ever, achieved. Why?

In what follows I attempt to briefly explain why the dynamics underpinning the development of university systems in low income countries might have changed drastically relative to, say, thirty years ago, and offer a vision of inevitable directions higher education might be heading.

The Changed Scenario

Until the middle of this century, only a small fraction of the eligible population attended university. Higher education systems were able to accommodate the demand for education at the tertiary level based mainly on public funding. As shown in Table 1 and Figure 1, higher education enrollments increased dramatically during the second half of this century to a multiple of what they were in the 1950s. In Latin America, for example, the higher education enrollment ratio increased more than ten times since 1950.

Table 1. Higher Education Enrollment Ratio (percent of age group)

Region	1950	1960	1970	1980	1990
Africa	0.8	0.7	1.5	3.5	7.0
Asia	1.5	2.6	3.5	5.6	8.2
Latin America	1.6	3.0	6.3	13.5	18.7
Europe	2.2	10.3	17.3	22.1	27.3
Northern America	7.2	28.9	45.4	54.3	70.4
Developing Countries	*	2.1	3.0	5.7	8.3
Developed Countries	*	13.5	23.4	30.3	36.8
World	2.8	5.3	8.5	11.5	13.5

Source: UNESCO, Statistical Yearbook, 1980–1991.
* Data not available

Figure 1. Higher Education Enrollment Ratio by Region

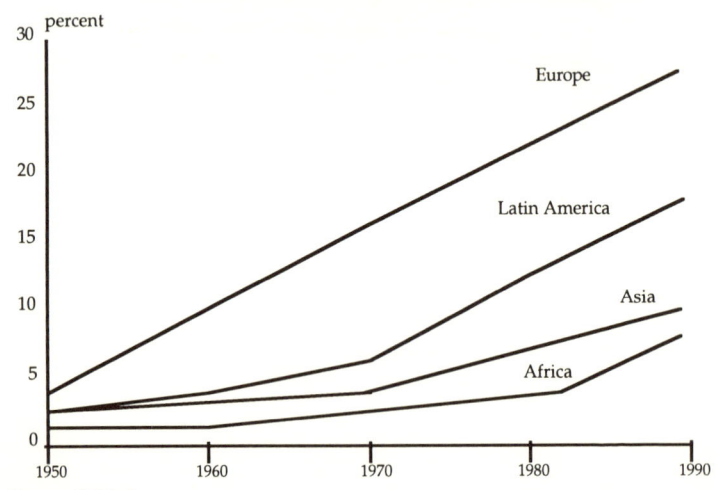

Source: Table 1.

However, as shown in Tables 2, 3, and 4, the public resources for education in general, and higher education in particular, have not increased *pari passu* with enrollments. For example, the share of the public budget devoted to education has remained constant, if not declined, throughout the period under consideration in all parts of the world. There are explanations for both of these trends.

Enrollment growth. Industrialized countries first took the lead in increasing enrollments in the early 1960s. The main reason for the sharp rise in enrollment in the developed world, I believe, was the Sputnik effect. The United States first, followed by European countries, felt that they were lagging behind in technology relative to the Soviet Union. Hence, universities (along with the accompanied R & D) were given a great boost. Developing countries followed as a demonstration effect (or to catch up with the metropolis), and because of the rise of the indigenous civil service in these countries. As the expatriates went home, the country had to produce its own high-level manpower. The thinking was that civil servants should preferably be educated locally, rather than be exposed to a "foreign model."

A secondary effect boosting higher education enrollments in both developed and developing countries was the rise in real incomes. As per capita income increased, so did the demand for luxury goods that could not previously be afforded. The demand for university attendance, regardless of career plans after graduation, increased, along with the demand for cars and refrigerators. Also, the rise in the public sector in general fueled the demand for higher education—a university degree became the sine qua non qualification for entering the public sector.

Table 2. Public Expenditure on Education as a Percentage of the GNP

Region	1975	1980	1989
Africa	4.5	5.0	6.4
Asia	4.3	4.5	4.2
Latin America	3.4	3.8	3.9
Europe	5.7	5.5	5.5
Northern America	6.4	6.7	6.8
Developing Countries	3.5	3.8	3.8
Developed Countries	6.0	6.0	5.8
World	5.5	5.5	5.5

Source: UNESCO, Statistical Yearbook, 1991.

Table 3. Public Spending on Education as a Share of Public Budget, Major World Regions, 1965–80 (percent)

Region	1965	1970	1975	1980
Africa	16.0	16.4	15.7	16.4
Asia	14.2	13.1	12.1	12.7
Latin America and Caribbean	18.7	18.9	16.5	15.3
Europe, Middle East, and North Africa	12.4	12.5	11.5	12.2
Developing Countries	16.1	15.8	14.5	14.7
Developed Countries	16.0	15.5	14.1	13.7

Source: *Financing Education in Developing Countries: An Exploration of Policy Options*, World Bank, 1986.

Table 4. The Share of Higher Education in Public Recurrent Expenditure, 1965–80 (percent)

Region	1965	1970	1975	1980
Africa	10.8	11.7	21.2	22.1
Asia	16.0	17.0	17.8	20.2
Latin America and Caribbean	14.3	15.9	23.4	23.5
Europe, Middle East, and North Africa	10.4	18.3	21.8	21.7
Developed Countries	13.9	18.6	19.4	19.1

Source: Based on World Bank, 1986, p.54.

A third reason for university expansion, especially in developing countries, lies in the development model used in the post-World War II period known as manpower forecasting: For a country to grow economically, it should have a given number of engineers, architects, and other high-level manpower that only a university could produce.[1] Much of the university expansion in Africa, for example, was based on this rationale.

It should be noted at the outset that the numbers in Figure 1 refer to actual enrollments and not to the demand for higher education. Demand for university studies vastly exceeds enrollment because many systems cannot offer as many university places as demanded by students and their families.

Finance trends. The main reason why public funds for higher education, and education in general, have not increased *pari passu* with enrollments is that there are many other sectors competing for scarce resources. Food and shelter might be more important than education. Often, education ministries are in a weak position relative to other

The Future of Higher Education Financing 65

ministries in persuading finance ministries to allocate more resources to education. Another reason is that there are limits to the generation of public funds through taxation.

In fact, regarding the split of public funds allocated to education, there has been a shift toward higher education (see Table 4). The reason is that the incidence of university attendance is higher among the wealthier parts of the population whose families are more articulate than those of the farmer. Hence, richer groups appropriate more public funds for the education of their offspring.

The Present Response

Different higher education systems have responded in different ways to increased demand for university entry in the presence of financing constraints. Some have accommodated more students at a reduced unit cost, flagging "mass education," but tacitly sacrificing quality. Others have reduced the number of years required for graduation or changed the mix of subjects offered toward the less expensive social sciences. Of course, other systems have shifted toward more reliance on private, rather than public, funds for university financing.

Among the various responses, perhaps the one that relies on greater private sector participation is the most sustainable one, leading to higher efficiency and equity in a given society. In order to understand why this is so, let us briefly analyze the current state of affairs in a typical developing country university system.

Fact No. 1: There is more demand to enter public universities than the state budget can respond to—what economists call "excess demand."

Fact No. 2: The demand for university entry is fueled by the following factors:

- the low cost of entry (no fees, or token fees being charged);
- the high benefit of being a university graduate (higher lifetime earnings, better working conditions); and
- the requirement of a university degree for entering the civil service.

Fact No. 3: The incidence of university attendance is higher among wealthier groups in the population. There are not as many students per 100,000 population whose fathers are farmers relative to those whose fathers are white collar workers.

The combination of the above facts leads to a series of economic inefficiencies and social inequities.

Inefficiencies. In the first place, anything that is free of charge can be abused. If I have to pay for the electricity I use, I am more likely to turn off the lights before I leave home. If I do not have to pay, the lights may stay on. The university analog is that many may wish to enroll as "students" and stay in the university nearly forever in order to appropriate secondary benefits associated with university attendance (e.g., reduced bus fares, subsidized lunches). If someone has to somehow contribute to the cost of his/her study, it is more likely that this person will think twice before enrolling. And it is less likely that he/she will become an eternal student.

The pressure for university entry by the most articulate, often wealthiest, groups in the population may result in the country misallocating resources devoted to education. If (a) the education budget is more or less fixed, as is the case in most countries, (b) the country has a high incidence of illiteracy, and (c) the most articulate classes divert resources to higher rather than primary education, the country might be underinvesting in what it needs most: primary education to create a literate population and labor force.

Inequities. Who is most likely to be excluded from the present higher education financing system? The offspring of high income families certainly will not be excluded. They will either enroll free of charge at the public university (perhaps because of better coaching, or because attendance at a private secondary school gave them more chances to compete successfully at the national university entrance examinations). Or, if they fail to enter the domestic public higher education system, they will enroll in a private university or go abroad for their studies.

Of course, it is those who come from the lower income classes that are most likely to be excluded from "free higher education" because, although they will also pay no enrollment fees, the income foregone while studying deters them from even applying for entrance. Or, if they compete at the national university entrance examinations,

The Future of Higher Education Financing

they might be at a disadvantage relative to those from wealthier families because they did not receive equivalent coaching.

Also, if (a) universities are supposed to select the most able among the pool of candidates, (b) the distribution of abilities is the same among the two socioeconomic groups described above, and (c) selection is made principally by social class rather than ability, this adds a further inefficiency to the system. [2]

The Alternatives

Now compare the situation just cited to one in which the financing of higher education relies to a greater extent on private resources and contributions from users. What would be the efficiency and equity implications of this change?

First, excess demand for university education would be reduced. This reduced pressure for university entry may translate into more public resources being used for primary education, which is still investment priority number one in developing countries.

Second, tapping private finance sources means more resources for universities as a whole. Whether it is by means of the establishment of private universities, or the paying of fees at public universities, the great unsatisfied demand for university places will translate into more money coming to the sector. Of course, more money would translate, although not automatically, to better education.

But perhaps the ultimate efficiency effect of the introduction of a system of even partial cost recovery in higher education lies in the accountability it brings with it. If universities charge fees, consumers must see a value to what they are getting in return. If not, such universities will not survive and will give way to better ones. At the individual student level, the charging of fees means greater accountability to themselves, in the sense of being motivated to study hard and complete courses on time.

The charging of fees also provides a more efficient student selection mechanism, as only those who are likely to succeed would be willing to pay the fees. Note that cost recovery does not automatically mean privatization. Fees could be charged at public universities so that accountability is introduced at both the university and student level.

It may sound paradoxical that the introduction of student fees is equitable. Yet if one compares a cost recovery scenario to the present one (where neither rich nor poor pay any fees at all, and where the poor might be deterred from entering university because of the foregone earnings involved), things become clearer. Selective cost recovery (directly related to some measure of parental wealth), can redress inequities in the financing of higher education. In addition, students from low income families cannot only continue to study free of charge, but also receive a scholarship in order to compensate for their foregone earnings.

When combined with the availability of student loans, cost recovery in higher education is associated with further equity gains. Anybody, poor or rich, could then borrow to finance university studies. The equity effect comes from the fact that those who later in life will have higher earnings (due to their university education) relative to the rest of the population (who are not university graduates), will finance their studies themselves—not the general taxpayer.

Political Feasibility

These propositions might be considered theoretical, given the tremendous political cost of introducing cost recovery in education. Yet several countries have done it. It is my prediction that selective cost recovery cum student loans will be the higher education financing scenario of the future. Given the political costs, this will not happen overnight. However, higher education systems around the world are inevitably heading in that direction. The simple contrast of the private demand for higher education and the available public resources do not permit any other sustainable financing system in the long run.

NOTES

*George Psacharopoulos is associated with the World Bank, Washington, D.C. 20433. The views expressed here are those of the author and should not be attributed to the World Bank. This paper draws from George Psacharopoulos. "Higher Education in Developing Countries: The Scenario of the Future." *Higher Education*, 21, no. 3 (1991): 3–9.

1. G. Psacharopoulos. "Assessing Training Priorities in Developing Countries: Current Practice and Possible Alternatives." *International Labor Review*, 123, no. 5 (1984): 569–583.
2. S. Pinera and M. Selowsky. "The Optimal Ability-Education Mix and the Misallocation of Resources within Education Magnitude for Developing Countries." *Journal of Development Economics*, 8 (1981): 111–131.

SOURCES OF REVENUE

Ihsan Dogramaci

Different sources of revenue for the funding of tertiary education are being sought in developed as well as developing countries. Governments around the world are reexamining the question of how to finance and fund higher education as they attempt to find new solutions to the perennial problem of sharing this financial burden efficiently and equitably. A university may have such diverse sources of revenue as student tuition and fees; government appropriations; contracts and grants from governments, private institutions, or various national/international agencies; student aid grants; services of teaching hospitals; auxiliary enterprises (including dormitories, food services, etc.); sports activities; gifts; income from existing endowments; debt financing (such as revenue bonds); real estate development options, and other sources. Since it takes effort to generate revenue from any source, which one(s) should the university management pursue? How much effort should be put into tapping additional funds from each potential source? Should revenue sources be prioritized based on which generate maximum revenues with the least effort? These topics, as well as other considerations, need to be taken into account.

Each source of university revenue may be characterized by different attributes. Some of these attributes include the magnitude of the cash flow and its variation over time, the degree of uncertainty in terms of the timing and magnitude of the cash flow, the set of current and future obligations to which the university is subjected due to each specific revenue decision or revenue source, and finally, the social, behavioral, and ethical implications.

When evaluating the attractiveness of a potential source of revenue, one thing which needs to be taken into account is the size of the cash flow and how it varies over time. For example, a university owning a piece of real estate (residential buildings, for example) may have to choose among options such as immediately selling the assets, renting them out, or using them as faculty housing. Each option has different cash flow implications. Comparison of the options based on the present values of their individual cash flow streams may not be enough. The needs of the university are not necessarily spread uniformly over time. Timing the revenues flow with the cash needs of the university can help to reduce the risk of future cash bottlenecks. Obligations may also accompany revenues and must be taken into consideration. Money to cover the capital cost of a laboratory is welcome, but not quite so welcome if in future years the university is to be saddled with the operating costs. Such obligations may come in explicit as well as implicit forms. For example, in receiving large funds for an astrophysics facility and its necessary researchers, a university's original physics department faculty may be outnumbered by the newly arrived astrophysicists and lost its decision-making power in what used to be internal departmental affairs in basic physics. Similar tensions could arise in departments or faculties and impact, for example, applied versus basic research in engineering, or the choice of fields in applied research.

Relying almost exclusively on government funding, as in the case of the public universities of continental Europe, has "convenience," but it means that a great deal of autonomy has to be sacrificed. In those countries, the government is a powerful overarching force. The education ministry has broad formal authority regarding the distribution of subsidies and may attempt to exercise authority over access, curricula, and exam and degree requirements. A major goal of such tight control may be to guarantee the standardization of national degrees, which are often awarded by the state instead of by the different universities.

D. Bruce Johnstone, in his classic study, *Sharing the Costs of Higher Education*, argued that "Regardless of the system, society or country, the costs (of higher education) must be shared by some combination of the following four sources of revenue: Parents, students, taxpayers, and institutions (i.e., colleges or universities which derive extra revenues from philanthropists or donors to help students)."[1] He further argued that different countries "must balance very similar policy goals in apportioning these costs (e.g., equal higher educational opportunities, efficient use of public resources, and equitable distribution of costs and benefits), and each country can benefit in the refinement of its objectives and in the choice of its instruments (e.g., parental-need analyses, means-tested grants, student loan programs) by understanding what countries with similar higher educational systems and public policy objectives are doing."

Johnstone's comparative study of student financial assistance in the United Kingdom, Germany, France, Sweden, and the United States showed debate and controversy in all five countries during the 1980s about how higher education costs should be shared among taxpayers, students, and their parents. The study also revealed that during the 1970s and early 1980s, several countries attempted to shift part of the financial burden by changing their student financial aid system.

According to the 1989–90 *Fact Book on Higher Education*, in the United States:

- Tuition and fees made up nearly one-fourth of all current fund revenue for all universities. However, at independent institutions they accounted for a much larger share (39 percent) than at public colleges and universities (15 percent).
- State funds represented 45 percent of the public sector's current fund revenue, but only 2 percent of the independent sector's.
- Funds from federal appropriations, grants, and contracts provided 13 percent of overall college and university revenue. Here, however, contrary to the case of state funds, federal funds made up 17 percent of the independent institutions' income, but accounted for only 11 percent of the public sector's.
- Endowment income plus private gifts, grants, and contracts represented less than one-tenth (8 percent) of higher education revenues. In the public sector, they accounted for only 4 percent; in the private, 15 percent.[2]

The situation differs greatly from one institution to another. For example, the revenues in 1991 for the University of North Carolina at Chapel Hill, a distinguished public university, and Princeton University, a well-regarded university, were:

Table 1. Comparative Funding Patterns at the University of North Carolina and Princeton University

	University of North Carolina at Chapel Hill (dollars in thousands)		Princeton University (dollars in thousands)	
Tuition and Fees	$ 50,221	7.2%	$ 96,246	21.2%
State Appropriations	257,219	36.8%	–	–
Governmental Contracts and Grants	149,577	21.3%	147,274	32.4%
Private Gifts, Contracts, and Grants	53,685	7.7%	47,800	10.5%
Sales and Services	166,182	23.8%	37,191	8.2%
Investment Income	11,750	1.7%	3,727	1.0%
Endowment Income	6,851	1.0%	97,949	21.5%
Other Sources	3,923	0.5%	23,716	5.2%
Total Revenues	$699,408	100%	$453,903	100%

Source: Statistics provided by Princeton University and the University of North Carolina.

The Rise of Private Sectors

The role of private higher education in certain developing countries is also worth examining. Until the middle of this century, only a small fraction of the eligible population attended universities. Higher education systems were able to accommodate the demand for education at the tertiary level mainly through public funding. Higher education enrollments increased dramatically during the second half of this century to a multiple of what they were in the 1950s. In Latin America, for example, the higher education enrollment ratio increased ten times between 1950 and 1987 (Table 2).

Table 2. Higher Education Enrollment Ratio (percent of age group) in Developing Countries

Region	1950	1960	1970	1980	1987
Africa	0.8	0.7	1.5	3.5	4.3
Asia	1.5	2.6	3.5	5.6	7.3
Latin America	1.6	3.0	6.3	13.5	16.9

Source: UNESCO, *Statistical Yearbook,* 1980–1989.

Sources of Revenue

Well into the twentieth century, higher education in Latin America consisted almost exclusively of public institutions subsidized by the state and authorized to act in its name. Only two of twenty nations have private sectors predating this century, and only four have private sectors predating 1940. Higher education is now very much divided into two sectors, private and public, and the spectacular growth of private institutions has reshaped the regional panorama. The private sector has managed to gain on the public sector despite unprecedented public growth. By the mid-1970s, the private share had become 34 percent of Latin America's total enrollments.

The rise of Latin America's private sector is especially noteworthy when seen in comparative perspective. Most developing nations continue to conceive of higher education as a state responsibility properly handled through public institutions. And where, following World War II, changes have been made in the private-public balance, most have pointed decidedly toward the public pole. In both the United States and Latin America, the shifting private-public balance is a matter of great policy interest and debate, but the value orientations tend to be different. The U.S. private decline is widely viewed with concern, even dismay. One may speak of a fairly broad U.S. policy consensus favoring a dual sector structure, valuing the private sector, and crediting that sector with at least a proportional share of higher education's contribution to society. Latin American opinion is much more sharply divided. Many Latin Americans, unlike all but a few of their U.S. counterparts, still regard higher education as an exclusive responsibility of the state even though the growth of the private sector can be attributed in large part to a conscious abdication by the state to the private sector of the responsibility to absorb the region's exploding demand for higher education.[3] Even among those who would not bar the private sector altogether, many are concerned that the private sector has grown inappropriately powerful and that the state has abdicated too much responsibility.

In most developing countries, the government continues to dominate in financing and providing education. In many of them, in spite of the fact that public resources for education in general, and higher education in particular, have not increased at a pace equal to enrollments, the share of education in public spending has already become very large, reaching between one-tenth and one-third of the public budget, and it is increasingly difficult to compete for additional public resources. At the same time, poor macroeconomic conditions have constrained the growth of the public budget itself.

Primary, Secondary, and Higher Education Sector Balance

An important issue is distribution of the allocation to education among the higher, secondary, and primary sectors of education. In a number of developing countries, in absolute values, higher education has been drawing roughly the same level of public resources as secondary education, and at times almost approaching the level of primary education. In Table 3 we see that in Pakistan in the year 1989–1990, 23.31 percent of the budget allocated to education was used for tertiary education while 22.63 percent went to secondary, and 26.17 percent to primary education.

Table 3. Percentage Distribution of Budget Allocations for Education by Level in Pakistan

	Education levels		
	Primary	Secondary	College and University
1980–81	33.99	19.89	19.20
1981–82	32.49	17.62	19.71
1982–83	32.34	19.41	20.21
1983–84	33.73	21.20	20.47
1984–85	32.12	23.23	19.27
1985–86	30.97	21.91	18.18
1986–87	31.66	20.14	20.10
1987–88 (RE)	27.49	21.31	20.10
1988–89 (RE)	26.88	22.00	21.63
1989–90 (E)	26.17	22.63	23.31

Notes: RE=Revised estimates E=Estimates

Source: Calculated from *Economic Survey 1989–90*, Statistical Appendix (1990, p. 212).

An important consideration, especially in poorer countries, is the difference in social rates of return to public expenditures on different levels of education and how the pattern of public expenditure across different levels corresponds to these differential rates of returns. In this way, at least in theory, we may gauge whether the distribution of

Sources of Revenue

educational expenditures by sector is socially efficient. If the ranking by expenditure has no correspondence with the ranking of social rates of returns on education, one could infer that the allocation of resources among the educational sectors is not socially efficient. To equalize the social rates of return, allocational efficiency would require more expenditure on levels for which the rates of return are higher.[4]

Subsidies, Tuitions, and Social Justice

Some argue that education paid for by students contradicts social justice. This cannot be taken as absolutely true. The enormous subsidy drawn by students participating in higher education raises an important issue: Which income groups benefit more from this subsidy? Evidence suggests that the financing of higher education exclusively from the public budget is inequitable since in effect this is a transfer of income from the lower to the upper income groups.

It should also be borne in mind that anything free of charge can be abused. If one is obliged to pay for electricity, he is more likely to turn off the lights before leaving home. If not, the lights may stay on. The university analogy is that many may wish to enroll as "students" and stay in the university nearly forever in order to take advantage of secondary benefits associated with university attendance (e.g., reduced bus fares, subsidized lunches). If students have somehow to contribute to the cost of their study, it is more likely that they will think twice before enrolling. And it is less likely that they will become eternal students.

In Turkey, up until two years ago, the cost to students of higher education had been almost symbolic, ranging between 20 and 100 U.S. dollars per academic year. Two years ago, a law was passed whereby the student would be responsible for up to 50 percent of the current costs (i.e., excluding capital investment) per student. The exact portion (of up to 50 percent) would be decided annually by the government.

The student could be eligible for a loan, at practically no interest, from state-guaranteed sources (banks). Due to the reaction of the public and students, however, and to the objection of the left-wing political parties that "burdening students and their families by requiring that they pay tuition is against social justice," the portion of "up to 50 percent" fell to just over 1 percent. Therefore, in Turkey's case, contribution by students or their families continues to be insignificant.

Variations in Patterns of Higher Educational Finance

Financing higher education in industrialized countries shows no uniformity. For example, in Germany, higher education institutions are public. Germany has only a very small number of private institutions, which do not educate a significant share of the student population. In that country, it is the responsibility of the states (lander, as contrasted with the federal state, bund) to care for education in general and higher education specifically. Institutions are financed and governed by the state (land) in which they are located, usually a minister of science and arts, or of science and research being responsible for those institutions. Basically, German higher education consists of sixteen separate state higher education systems. While general frames of reference for laws and regulations do exist on the federal level, in details of finance as well as many other rules and regulations, Germany has sixteen *different* higher education systems. Institutions receive a basic subsidy from their state. Their budgets are part of the state budget and the state budget laws apply for higher education; therefore institutions cannot count on tuition fees as an additional source of income. Students, however, are eligible for financial aid to cover their living costs, depending on the income of their parents. The student aid program is a federal program financed by federal money. Half of the student aid is granted, the other half given as a loan.

Higher education in the Netherlands is mainly supplied by public institutions. The central government is the main source of subsidies. In addition to subsidies to institutions, student financial assistance is available. Every regular full-time student receives a non-repayable grant (about $4,000 per year for a student not living with his parents). For students from low- and middle-income families the grant is supplemented by a loan and, for the lowest incomes, also by a supplementary grant. The Dutch student assistance system is one of the

Sources of Revenue

most generous in the world, measured in terms of assistance levels and eligibility requirements.

Higher Educational Finance in Turkey

As mentioned earlier, the subject of financing of higher education has been looked at closely in recent years in Turkey. During the past five years there has been a steady growth in Turkish higher education.

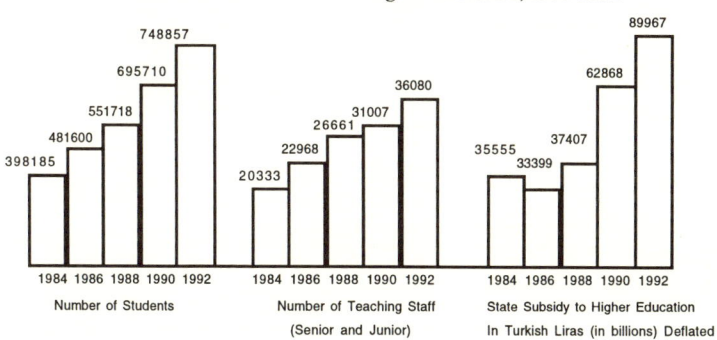

Table 4. Growth in Turkish Higher Education, 1984–1992

Year	Number of Students	Number of Teaching Staff (Senior and Junior)	State Subsidy to Higher Education In Turkish Liras (in billions) Deflated
1984	398185	20333	35555
1986	481600	22968	33399
1988	551718	26661	37407
1990	695710	31007	62868
1992	748857	36080	89967

Source: Ministry of Education, Turkey.

Total budget includes 20 percent from professional and academic activities and 12 percent from student tuition.

The number of students has doubled, including those in the open university, who also enter the national competitive exam and follow the same programs of study as full-time students in certain disciplines. Teaching is provided to open university students through television broadcasts as well as tutoring in their localities during evenings and on weekends. Even excluding them, the number of students has increased by 55 percent. Teaching staff has also increased in the same proportion, while state subsidies to higher education have more than doubled. In addition to this sum, universities are allowed to generate funds from contracts, research projects, and professional activities, including medical practice in university hospitals. This adds another 20 percent to the revenue of the university. Tuition, as mentioned earlier, accounts for about 1.2 percent of university revenues. The budgetary increase reflects the increase in the gross national product as well as government spending.

Table 5. Percentage of Enrollment in Higher Education of 18–24 Age Group

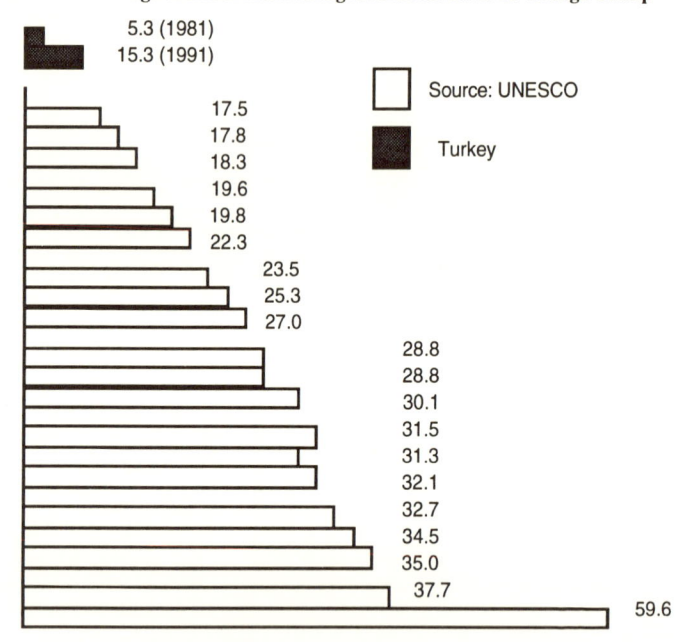

5.3 (1981)
15.3 (1991)

Source: UNESCO
Turkey

17.5
17.8
18.3
19.6
19.8
22.3
23.5
25.3
27.0
28.8
28.8
30.1
31.5
31.3
32.1
32.7
34.5
35.0
37.7
59.6

Table 6. Public Expenditure for Higher Education in Turkey

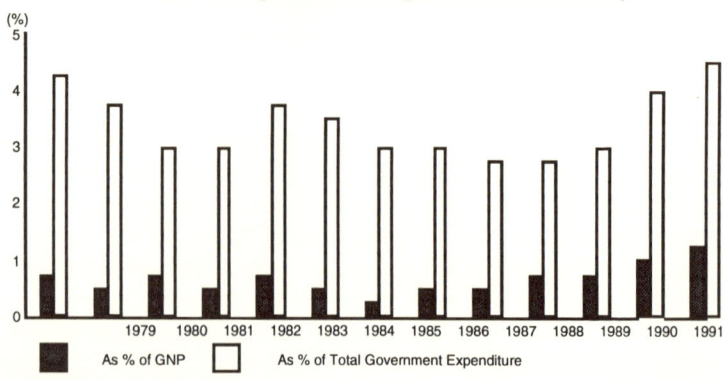

(%)

As % of GNP   As % of Total Government Expenditure

Source: Ministry of Education, Turkey.

Sources of Revenue

Turkish university faculty receive research projects, mainly from the Turkish Scientific and Technical Research Council. In addition, universities receive lump sum grants from the state for research, the use of which is decided on by the university. In other words, these funds are not earmarked. The university can, and usually does, add to these sums. For example, 63 percent of such unearmarked research money in 1991 came from the state and 37 percent from the universities' revolving funds.

Table 7. Research Funds (not earmarked) Allocated to Turkish Higher Education

	Total		State Subsidy		University Subsidy (from revolving fund)	
Year	TL (in Millions)	US Dollars	TL (in Millions)	US Dollars	TL (in Millions)	US Dollars
1991	119,807	28,130,200	75,066 (63%)	17,625,200 (63%)	44,741 (37%)	10,505,000 (37%)

Source: Ministry of Education, Turkey. TL = Turkey

If the Turkish law requiring students to pay up to 50 percent of current expenses were put into practice, instead of limiting their contribution to the present 1.2 percent, then our universities would have far more financial means. In that case, loans or even grants could be the answer for those in the lowest income groups.

Until recently, all twenty-eight universities in Turkey have been public.[5] This number will double in the next few years. Recently there has been interest in the establishment of non-profit private universities, also permitted by the University Law of 1981. So far, three private institutions have been licensed, but only one is currently in operation: Bilkent University in Ankara.

The financial resources of Bilkent University, which has just completed its sixth year of academic activity, come mainly from endowments, which consist of profitable business enterprises involved in such areas as tourism, construction, manufacture of construction materials, and a paper mill. Student tuition fees meet about 30–35 percent of operating expenses. During the past two years about one-third of its income has come from research contracts and government contributions.

About 20 percent of the students at Bilkent are on full scholarships, which include living accommodations and a small stipend to meet a part of other expenses such as meals. During the short period of its existence, Bilkent has set an example that has made it possible for this new university to attract some of the best scorers on the national competitive entrance exam. In national rankings of universities by academic staff publications as cited in the ISI *Citation Indexes*, Bilkent is first in number of papers per faculty member. By the end of its sixth year, Bilkent had attracted 7,000 students in seven faculties and five graduate schools, which are known as institutes. Foreign students from twenty-nine countries had enrolled. Each summer the university has a variety of scientific seminars and symposia as well as the Bilkent International Music School, which has attracted young musicians from fourteen countries on four continents. Bilkent's accomplishments in this short span of time provide an example of the viability of a private institution of higher learning at which the students pay tuition that covers about 35 percent of expenses. The university could be a model for Turkey and possibly some other countries with a tradition of a state monopoly on higher education.

NOTES

1. D. Bruce Johnstone. *Sharing the Costs of Higher Education.* (New York: College Entrance Examination Board, 1986).
2. American Council on Education. 1989–90 *Fact Book on Higher Education.* (New York: Macmillan, 1989).
3. Daniel C. Levy. *Higher Education and the State in Latin America: Private Challenges to Public Dominance.* (Chicago: The University of Chicago Press, 1986).
4. Shahrukh R. Khan. "Financing Higher Education in Pakistan." *Higher Education,* 21 (1991): 207–222.
5. Ihsan Dogramaci. *Ten Years of Turkish Higher Education: 1981–1991* (in Turkish). (Ankara: Council of Higher Education, 1991).

ARE UNIVERSITY FUNDING SYSTEMS IN NEED OF AN OVERHAUL?

Karel Tavernier*

Basic Statement

In recent decades, the university environment in most European countries has been changing so drastically that government steering systems and university funding methods have gone dangerously off course. More and more they are becoming unsuitable for ensuring an efficient and goal-oriented governance of modern universities. Therefore, opportunities remain unused and the contribution of traditional universities to society is suboptimal.

What holds true for national educational policies also holds true for the internal management and funding systems of many individual universities. If universities are unable to live up to the expectations of their customers, there is the danger of their tasks being taken over by others and by other methods of production. It is disconcerting to see just how difficult it is for European countries to rid themselves of the old fashioned conviction that universities are using tax money and therefore have to be treated as any other government agency. Even when policy statements tell the contrary, in practice, input-funding prevails over output-funding, detailed throughput-regulations over flexibility, equality in treatment over quality of results, and line-item budgeting and red tape over strategic management.

In this town-gown relationship, little progress is made for the simple reason that the fundamental changes which have recently taken place in society are insufficiently perceived and understood. If one just looks at the new environment, a set of criteria for renewal emerges. It is the intention of this chapter to discuss these criteria and use them to assess a new funding system for Flemish universities in Belgium.

Some consideration will also be given to the implications for the financial strategies of an individual university. It should be borne in mind that the underlying discussion is based on the situation in Europe, and more especially in Belgium and in Flanders. There is a wide variety of university systems, and what is self-evident in one country is a major problem in another.

Changes in the University Environment

University Tasks and Services Growing More Heterogeneous

The university product used to be rather unidimensional in the sense that it tended to focus selectively on educating a small elite of young people to be the leaders of tomorrow. The property of a university training resided in the confrontation with the inherently critical and relativising inquiry of scientific research. In this information age much has changed. Because of the premium put on knowledge, what were once selective universities now have become mass producers. Eighteen-year-olds regard a university degree as a much desired entry ticket to the labor market. For many of them, technical know-how and practical skills are better suited and better appreciated than the typical university component of abstract reasoning, critical questioning, and contextual thinking.

Undoubtedly the *content* of the university product has clearly been enlarged and the dividing line between a university education and non-university higher education has become blurred. Together with the enlargement of the product content, a *multiplication of the services* the universities can provide has occurred. There is a growing demand for graduate studies; what is new is an increased demand not so much for the traditional doctorate but for a second diploma which, once again, is hoped will win success in the labor market. Examples of these are the successful DESs and DEAs in France. In the emerging field of permanent education, heterogeneity is complete: it goes from corporate in-house training to sophisticated seminars at the front end of research, from language training to computer initiation, from basic accounting to history and cultural events. In scientific research the same extension is encountered. The available infrastructure and expertise leads to a

Are University Funding Systems in Need of an Overhaul?

potential extension from basic to applied research, to consultancy services and hiring out of computer capacity and other scientific facilities. Universities are also often expected to play a central role in the development of science parks, innovation centers, and in the economic exploitation of their findings.

The potential demand for university products is now so great and so varied that no single university can encompass this variety. Each university must choose what to do and what not to do. So-called full or comprehensive universities have become impossible. No two universities need to be the same.

In view of the wide range of ever-expanding opportunities facing universities, it may be concluded that a centralizing government will be hard put to define and circumscribe its omnivalent university type. Considering the heterogeneity of demand, a *heterogeneity of university types* should be allowed to develop. Governments cannot possibly possess the expertise to contain this process of ever-expanding opportunities. Any attempt to maintain a single system for organizing and funding universities will result in an overregulated paralyzing bureaucracy and an impoverishment of the university product mix.

The national university system should be based on heterogeneity and set up in such a way that universities have the *institutional autonomy* to make choices and to specialize.

Knowledge as a Factor of Production

The wide variety of university products and the inherent difficulty of governments to control it does not mean that universities should be of no concern to policy makers. On the contrary, in a modern society, the very product of the university, knowledge, has become an extremely important factor of production, not only for individuals and business, but also for society itself. More and more, the really important questions are becoming university questions insofar as they require a *long-term perspective* and a *multi-disciplinary* and even an *ethical approach*.

Where products become important, attention should shift from input and procedures to *quality and quantity of output*. Funding systems should be geared to performance and results. This also implies more emphasis on *competitive funding* and *centers of excellence*. Measuring a university's output is obviously no easy task. When it comes to teaching performance, one meets criteria such as "required time to graduate" (Holland and Germany), and the "number of doctorates actually conferred" (Belgium).

In research, measurement is even more delicate as the social and private benefits of university research tend to be of a long-term nature and are thus difficult to define. In the light of this it is by no means certain whether the recent practice of singling out particular disciplines for special *impulse funding* is wise. In many countries, these impulse topics suffer from partisan interference of politicians; they come too late and often fail to take enough account of the relative strengths and weaknesses of the institutions concerned.

Governments should limit themselves to broad mission statements and leave it to the universities to implement them. They have the expertise, not the governments. As to control, the Dutch approach of monitoring output performance through imposed *self-evaluation schemes* and through inter-university *visitation committees* deserves attention.

Universities Are Resource Intensive

The production process of multiproduct universities has become immensely resource intensive. When resources are scarce, *efficiency* and *effectiveness* should come to the fore. In this respect, management literature suggests that productivity increases when decisions are decentralized to where the expertise really exists. Again, this is an argument to free universities from *line-item budgeting, detailed control,* and *over-regulation.*

At a time when politics and public spending are getting a cool reception from the general public, this line of reasoning would seem to be self-evident. In reality, however, it is still very much absent in the small print of university regulations and especially in the interpretation of these regulations by government administrators. In their fight to retain control over complex institutions, these administrators often resort to absurdly literal interpretations of legal texts.

Increased Competition and Strategic Alliances

Technological and political developments as well as the process of European integration have all helped to open up the university market. In modern society, traditional universities have lost their monopoly position. They are facing increased competition from often unexpected angles. There is competition from foreign universities and open universities; from teleclassing and satellite education; from private and specialized institutions such as INSEAD[1] and IMED.[2] There are the big multinationals, which often have their own institutes for higher learning. These corporate colleges often have surprisingly broad fields of study. Universities also face increased competition in the field of permanent education, not to mention in fundamental research from industrial laboratories with their own share of Nobel prizes. In such a competitive climate the normal outcome is a stronger hierarchy of universities. For Europe, it might mean a European "Ivy League."

As the IBM-Apple case has shown, competitive business strategies often lead to the most unexpected alliances. What is true for multinationals should also be true for universities. Given the challenges, the stakes, and the size of the resources required, for many projects, international alliances with other schools, industries, and non-profit organisations will become a normal way of life. National legislation not only should not prevent this, but should actively encourage it. This encouragement is certainly present in many teaching and research programs and worthy examples can be found in recent pieces of EEC-legislation.

In Belgium, the funding programs which are intended to finance centers of excellence set the condition that at least two "satellite" research units in other universities should be associated with a program. Moreover, special funding conditions are granted for teaching programs when they are organized jointly by several universities.

The University Product: Less and Less a Public Good

It is increasingly clear that governments cannot and should not finance everything. In the broadened spectrum of university products there is an increasing number for which costs and benefits can easily be individualized. Those who clearly benefit from a university education or from research findings or other services should pay. Loans coupled with some form of insurance should ensure that the cost of education does not deter people from enrolling to study.

It is equally indefensible to impede valorization of university findings, participation in spin-offs, or charging for services. In Europe, it is not only a question of regulation but also of a mentality. With taxation rates rather high, universities are still too much considered as public goods in all that they are doing. The opposition to overhead charges is a striking illustration.

Increased EEC Funding

The development of the European Economic Community (EEC) has also been influential in changing the management and funding conditions for European universities. This new source of money cannot but further loosen the grip of national governments. More important, it drives universities into international cooperations with research centers and with industry. Many EEC programs, however, find their motivation in the objective of making Europe economically stronger; BRITE, EURAM, and EUREKA, therefore, have a predominantly technological orientation. It is no surprise that in many European universities the most successful groups are to be found in engineering schools.

These trends, however, have the disadvantage that participating laboratories are gradually moving to the application end of research, a development which, from a viewpoint of comparative advantages of university research, can be questioned. It is only recently that the "European Human Capital and Mobility Program" explicitly emphasizes fundamental basic research. But again, it is set up in terms typical of EEC funding. It aims at increasing human scientific resources for Europe through research networks made up of the best centers of excellence. These centers receive money for basic research and infrastructure, but are expected to receive foreign research fellows and to disseminate new knowledge by organizing highly specialized "Gordonlike" Euroconferences. Similarly, the Erasmus program, designed to promote international exchanges of students, has proved to be a great success and has increased the Europeanization of universities.

Resulting Guidelines for Funding

Vastly expanding opportunities, greater internationalization, decline in the dominant position of the traditional university, sharper competition, increasing privatization, and higher resource intensity are just a few of the recent trends which have affected modern universities. A first conclusion was that this situation makes the university sector too complex, too diversified, and too expensive for governments to maintain their traditional bureaucratic ways for steering and funding nationwide systems.

In the new environment, societal goals in higher education are realized more effectively by granting more institutional autonomy to the different schools. Governments and politicians should give up their distrust towards institutes of higher education. It is the only way to successfully survive in the new internationalizing environment, to maximally exploit the ever-expanding opportunities and to realize the potential value added for society.

For the funding system, institutional autonomy means first of all freeing universities from line-item budgeting and from the, still very common, purely formalistic but energy consuming practice of prior government approval for any major expenditure. It also involves replacing input and procedures control by *ex post* accountability. The funding system should accept that multi-source funding is unavailable, and that charging for university services, wherever benefits can be individualized, is perfectly justified.

Of course, more freedom means more responsibility. Therefore, it seems logical that legislation should be conceived so as to put pressure on universities to optimally pursue quality, efficiency, and effectiveness. This suggests—especially for research—a higher share of competitive money, for centers of excellence, and hence for inequality in treatment.

For the basic subsidy a block grant with a high degree of spending freedom would seem an appropriate solution. However, there is no reason why the basic grant for each university should not be determined by a *voucher-like system* or by other competitive arrangements.

Finally, the more distant steering formulae should financially encourage collaborations, cost sharing, and program rationalizations whenever possible.

The New Flemish Funding System: A Case Study

In this section, the new Flemish university law and its funding system will be explained and evaluated against the simple normative background developed in the previous section. With its six million people and seven university institutions, on a world scale Flanders is not central. Still, I believe that some of the basic features of the new concept deserve attention.

The new system is extremely simple and it seems to work. In Belgium, universities have always enjoyed more autonomy than in most of their European counterparts. The most likely reason for this is that the three largest universities have traditionally been private institutions: The Catholic University of Leuven (K.U. Leuven) now has 22 percent of all university students in Belgium. The French-speaking sister university, the University of Louvain at Louvain-la-Neuve has 16 percent, and the "Université Libre de Bruxelles" 15 percent. Since 1971, private universities and state universities have been funded on an equal basis.

Belgium hardly has any specialized non-university research institutes comparable to the French CNRS, the Dutch TNO, or the German Max Plank Institutes. For its basic research and technological know-how, Belgium largely has to rely on its universities. In Belgian higher education, a sharp distinction is made between research-based universities and other institutions of higher learning. A National

Science Foundation (NFWO) is the interface for research funding. In practice, it is the academic community and its rectors which determine its policy. NFWO-funds come to the universities on a fairly competitive basis. In addition to its own small endowment, the NFWO receives a yearly subsidy from government.

In moving toward more regional autonomy, a new university law was written in 1991. With it, the Flemish government seeks to increase the institutional autonomy of the universities and to switch to more distant steering formulae with a drastic reduction in the number of detailed regulations and procedures. As in the neighboring Netherlands, focus is on self-evaluation and on *ex post* accountability.

1. In Belgium, no *numerus clausus* exists. Every high school graduate is free to choose his or her university. This university is compelled to allow admittance. Only potential engineering students are required to take an entrance examination.
2. For each university a simple mission statement is written out. In practice, this boils down to listing the disciplines each institution is allowed to develop. Only K.U. Leuven, the University of Gent, and V.U. Brussels have a fully comprehensive curriculum.
3. Each university—private as well as state—owns its buildings, infrastructure, and other resources. The proceeds from any sale of university property is, however, channelled into the establishment's investment fund. This fund is entitled to a yearly investment subsidy.
4. For operating costs, each university receives yearly a basic budget. Once this is received, the university is free to allocate this budget according to its own priorities within its mission in research or teaching.
5. In the case of K.U. Leuven, this basic subsidy amounts to about 60 percent of the total operating budget. The remaining 40 percent is mainly for competitive research money, student fees, and a social envelope earmarked for cheap student housing, student meals, and the like.
6. The basic budget for each university consists of a predetermined and fixed lump sum and a variable component, the size of which depends strictly on the number of "student units" a university is able to attract. A "student unit" is a full-time student in humanities; a science student is counted as two units, and a student in medicine and engineering gets a weight of three.
7. The "lump sum" is historically determined and based on provisions laid down in older law. Roughly speaking, it is proportional to the

size of the university in 1990, but with an important adjustment for economies of scale: larger universities receive on average less per student, smaller universities more. Except for an automatic adjustment for inflation, the lump sum is fixed once and for all. In the starting year of the system, for the whole of Flanders, this shield against an expected demographic decline amounted to 50 percent. As each marginal student draws the same subsidy everywhere, the relative size of the lump sum in the subsidy of an individual university varies considerably. It goes from 70 percent in a small school to 46 percent at K.U. Leuven. In this way, the historical differences in average subsidy per student among universities might amount to 78 percent.

8. Within the context of their missions, universities are free to organize the study programs they wish. However, these programs are funded only when they maintain a minimum of about thirty students. For new programs the minimum level is doubled. A student can maximally be financed twice for the same year program. A series of additional features should be mentioned so as to give a clear picture of possibilities and constraints.

9. University staff paid for by the basic subsidy include the administrative and technical staff, the permanent academic or tenured staff, and the academic staff on temporary contracts.

10. Universities decide on the composition of their staff. However, they have to respect a few quantitative requirements: of the total academic staff, a minimum of 36 percent should be temporary assistants; a maximum of 25 percent of the total should be full professors (ordinarii), and the combined group of full and associate professors should not exceed 35 percent.

11. Out of the total subsidy, staff expenditures should be lower than 85 percent. This proportion is a warning light and requires official justification.

12. Unlike the situation in France, nearly all staff is hired and paid by the university itself according to its own selection procedures. The only requirement is a public call for candidates so as to foster competition.

13. Official salary scales are set by the government and are the same for all universities. Universities do, however, enjoy a certain freedom in fixing the entrance levels for new staff and in speeding up or slowing down promotion through the four academic categories.

14. Temporary staff are appointed three times for two year terms. They have facilities for achieving a doctorate. A maximum of four extra years may be granted after obtaining a Ph.D.

Evaluating the New System

An Extremely Simple Funding Formula

A main advantage of the system is that it is extremely simple. It allocates funds among universities through a very transparent formula. At the ministry of education only a small number of civil servants is required to steer the system. No yearly negotiations, nor discussions among universities are necessary. The only difficulty is effective control of the number of students attending subsidizable programs. A government commissioner within each university is responsible for this, in addition to his or her general task of watching over the financial equilibrium of the university. Of course, in this setup, the government automatically agrees to pay for any increase in student numbers over which the government has no control.

In fact, in the absence of the *numerus clausus,* it is very much the secondary school leavers who decide the size of the government subsidy for universities. If it should rise too fast in the future, the only defense for policymakers lies in tinkering with the yearly price indexation or in refusing to accept additional social security costs. Of course, a certain compensatory budget flexibility exists in the so-called "second stream" money flow for research funding. It is also true that with a declining birthrate, it is expected that enrollment will fall. In that case, it is the university that bears the burden of adapting to reduced funding. It is this fear which has pushed universities to accept a reduced dependence on student numbers.

An unexpected consequence of a European directive which prohibits cross-border discrimination has been an inflow of Dutch medical students. In the Netherlands the existence of a *numerus clausus* excludes a considerable number of possible candidates. For one Flemish university, half of its first-year students in medicine are from the Netherlands. For that university, which was facing a serious fallback in students, it has been a welcome relief.

A Competitive Voucher-Like System

A considerable part of research money is granted on a competitive basis. Even when to a certain extent university quotas are predetermined, competition still drains off much of the funds to better-performing groups. As this is the case in most countries, it is unnecessary to dwell on research. The basic subsidy is essentially a voucher system. Every high school graduate has the right to attend the university of his or her choice. The university cannot refuse, nor ask for additional qualifications. The only exception is an entrance examination for engineers. Once a student has made his or her choice, the university automatically receives the subsidy one year later.

As university finance depends on student numbers, universities have to compete for students and are compelled to remain attractive, especially for the better subsidized medicine and engineering students. More than in other countries, therefore, universities are obliged to make a serious marketing effort. The marketing campaigns mainly consist of offering honest and clear information about preliminary study requirements. They offer advice as to the most appropriate study choice, information on the organization of programs, and on opportunities in the labor market. All Belgian universities have considerable staffs of student advisers involved in this activity. Target groups are the students themselves, of course, but a great effort is made to reach secondary school teachers and professional study choice advisers. Annual open-house days at universities and visits to secondary schools by professors are standard techniques. Of course, in the past some universities, feeling the pinch of declining enrollment, have tried less orthodox methods including advertisements in public places or smiling ads in cinemas and newspapers. These methods, however, do not seem to have been very successful. A study choice is a serious matter. When a particular university is unable to fulfill its campaign promises, the word soon gets around in the student community.

Behind the marketing, there are the real reasons for the attractiveness of a university. According to a recent study carried out on behalf of K.U. Leuven, what seems to score highly is the establishment's reputation as a leading scientific university in Europe and the value of its diplomas on the labor market, for which evidently a large alumni association is also important. Also mentioned are student

Are University Funding Systems in Need of an Overhaul? 95

tutoring, well-designed programs, and teaching quality. For a university of 25,000 students in an old medieval town of 30,000 inhabitants, a lively student life is another major attraction. The ideology of a Catholic university seems less and less a determining factor. Indirectly it might still be important, as about 70 percent of all secondary schools are Catholic, a percentage much higher than actual church attendance or sociological stratification can explain. It is often said that pupils leaving these schools are better prepared for universities. State subsidies for low income students imply that the cost factor is not seen as important, whereas housing accommodations are.

From an educational policy point of view, several observations can be made:

- Undoubtedly, more students are attracted to try their luck at the highest level in the educational hierarchy. The highly valued societal goals of democratization and fully tapping the intellectual reserve of the population are frequently mentioned.
- As many students enroll without sufficient talent, working discipline, or preparation, there is a tremendous social cost: the dropout rate in the first year can be as high as 60 percent.
- Under this system, universities are permanently tempted to broaden their programs. With existing staff to a large extent on long-term contracts, every new student improves the financial situation. In this strategy it is often forgotten that, especially for undergraduates, the total number of students is limited. As participation rates rise and the birthrate declines, one program's gain is another program's loss.
- In looking for new students, universities often expand beyond the range of what can be considered real university tasks. Teaching capacity is spread too thin in many departments.

Multiplication of teaching hours is another undesirable consequence which is detrimental for research and hence for the quality of the institution. Because of the financial dependence on enrollment, most faculties are reluctant to skip underattended programs. The new law, having reduced the marginal revenue of new students and having added minimum enrollment conditions for subsidy, might bring a correction. However, looking at the behavior of academic authorities, especially at the postgraduate level, it is clear that new attitudes take time to take hold.

An Envelope Subsidy

In the new legislation, the funding formula (60 percent) is simply used to calculate the amount of the subsidy. Once received, it is the university which allocates it between departments and makes the distribution between research and teaching, between graduate and undergraduate programs, between academic staff and central services, and between present and future expenditures.

Of course, such legislation creates room for strategic choices, for centers of excellence, and for long-term policy. Greater autonomy, however, calls for more watchful and responsible policy. It is not yet clear whether the different universities are capable of this. Anyway, they will have to avoid a series of pitfalls which may seriously mortgage the future. One to particularly watch out for is excessive labor engagement. The pressure to use up immediately any financial leeway to increase the number of tenured staff can already be felt. Such a policy runs counter to fostering the vitally important intake of young assistants.

Another victim might well be maintenance of real estate, which again is trading the future for the present. As has been discussed before, policy makers have built in a system to protect against irresponsible behavior of university institutions. Especially strict is the rule that personnel expenses should not exceed 80–85 percent of the budget. Also, in order to retain a certain financial flexibility for future periods of distress, there is a minimum norm for temporary staff and hence a maximum for permanent staff. An often heard argument against this provision is that the basic subsidy should provide more for tenured staff and less for temporary staff because a fast-rising but volatile "second and third money flow" only allows hiring of temporary staff which requires seniors for their tutoring and guidance in research.

Universities in Flanders have yet to learn how to make full use of this new freedom. However, it should be mentioned that, in practice, the scope of action is much more narrow than could be expected. This is due to the long-term nature of labor contracts, the government imposed salary scales, and foremost to the narrow specialization of academic staff which limits interfaculty mobility. Traditionally, decision making is collegial and hence conservative. This too renders any redistribution of resources difficult and slow. It is felt that a structural reorganization might be necessary before strategic management gets on the right track. In the meantime it should not be forgotten that in several European universities, the growing competition for research money has probably done more to change the institutions and to focus them (almost unnoticed) on quality and centers of excellence.

Student Fees: A Controversial Issue

In 1992, a normal student would pay 17,000 Belgian francs, which is about $560 a year. This fee is hardly comparable with what is customary in the United States. But fees remain a controversial issue for students. They defend free access to universities with the argument of democratization of society through higher participation of lower social classes. In this same line of reasoning, as in many countries, a special subsidy exists for cheap housing, meals, medical and other student care, with students having a serious say in the allocation process. Universities can charge more if they agree that a program is not subsidized or when it concerns non-EEC students. Charging for a permanent education program is, of course, the normal rule.

A Funding Policy Within the University[3]

In trying to outline the basic elements of a funding strategy for an individual university, one should not only look at the drastically changed environment and at what national legislation allows. It is equally important to recognize what, from an organizational point of view, is specific in a modern university. Here the appropriate starting point is undoubtedly the labor intensive character of teaching and research. It is the quality of its staff which makes the quality of a university. We can even go one step further: what really makes the difference is the presence of a small group of top, internationally renowned scientists within the institution. This seems crucial for setting standards for younger scientists, for uplifting the whole staff, for inspiration, and for motivation. If this is true, a few basic principles for the organizational concept of the university and its financial organization come to the foreground: a high degree of autonomy for the academic staff, well-defined decentralization rules, a clear mission statement, and a competitive internal allocation of funds.

If academic staff is important, power should be with that staff. A university is typified by the fact that, for the realization of its purpose, expertise is to be found at the bottom, not at the top. It is in the centers and the laboratories, where this academic staff is operating, that the opportunities are. It is this academic staff that knows where and what to search for and what and how to teach, not the academic top. The rectorate or the presidency can at best create the proper environment and provide finance. Even this latter task is often more successfully done by the basic units themselves. More often, they know better where to compete for funds; they know how successful they can be. Strong decentralization, however, requires explicit decentralization rules and makes it necessary to define the boundaries for independent action.

As decentralized organizations, universities have a special need for a clear mission statement which is widely understood and accepted throughout the university, as well as mission statements for each of its units. Universities also require the setting of general recruitment standards and systematic performance evaluation. From an organizational point of view, we might add the need for overhead rules and perhaps a pricing system for utilized space.

If excellence is important, the allocation of staff and means should be flexible. These should flow to the units where the best performance in research or teaching can be expected; equal distribution over departments should be avoided. Procedures and rules should be set in such a way that quality and performance are rewarded. Also, within the institution, competition ought to be a way of life.

In this chapter it is argued that given the many challenges, universities will only successfully survive in an environment allowing a high degree of institutional autonomy and spending freedom. However, it is not only a question of government regulations. Much more important is the recognition by the university of the need to change its governance from administrating to strategic management, to make choices and to change procedures and allocation mechanisms so as to permanently favor quality and performance.

NOTES

*Thanks to Professors E. Meulepas and F. Bellefroid for their much appreciated suggestions.
1. INSEAD (European Institute of Business Administration).
2. IMED (International Institute for Management Development).
3. See also: K. Tavernier. *An Organizational Framework for Staffing Policies in Universities.* (Paris: OECD, 1992).

INDUSTRY-UNIVERSITY RESEARCH COLLABORATION: AN OPTION FOR GENERATING REVENUE

Linda Parker*

In many countries, obtaining desired levels of funding for colleges and universities is becoming increasingly difficult. Public institutions are often asked (or told) to do more with less. One option is to look to industry to fill the gap. The ramifications for institutions of pursuing this approach can be significant, especially with regard to institutional mission and priorities. There is no question but that in the process of turning to industry to solve financial problems, universities in Western Europe are starting to realize the possibilities of generating income from "commercialization of their specialist knowledge and facilities whether by means of publications, provision of continuing education, consultancy, contract research, licensing, new company formation, science park development, or other activities."[1] It is unclear whether colleges and universities going in this direction appreciate just how much more is involved than selecting a revenue raising scheme. This chapter will explore lessons learned in developed and developing countries about assembling successful industry-university collaborations. The underlying theme is that, unless collaborations are successful, colleges and universities are unlikely to generate significant revenue from them.

Obstacles to Getting Started

There are many obstacles to developing successful collaborations. Understanding institutional perceptions, norms, and values is necessary. Some clashes of institutional culture are predictable. For example, in academia, one common perception is that collaboration will threaten traditional academic values. Specifically, some faculty members and university administrators are afraid that industrial collaboration will endanger their institutions' basic research and graduate training missions.[2,3] Similarly, university researchers are sometimes concerned that engaging in industry-sponsored or applied research will be of no benefit, and could possibly hurt, their careers.[4] This constraint stems from the traditional academic reward structure not placing as much value on research with industrial or practical relevance as on basic research. Another perceived threat to academic values is that industrial influences will restrict academic freedom, especially when intellectual property rights conflict with the importance that academic researchers place on dissemination of knowledge.[5,6,7] Table 1 summarizes some of the differences between the academic and industrial research cultures:

Table 1. Academic and Industrial Research Cultures

TYPICAL ASPECTS	UNIVERSITY	INDUSTRY
Focus of R&D	Basic research; curiosity-oriented	Applied research; experimental development
Basic rationale	Advance knowledge	Increase efficiency
Aim	New ideas	Profits
Characteristics	Idea-centered	Practical; product-centered
Framework	Open	Closed, confidential
Evaluation	By peers	By the boss
Schedule	Open-ended	Tight, predetermined
Recognition	Scientific honors	Salary increases[8]

Barriers are not one-sided. As has been the case in Mexico, industries in developing countries often engage in little if any research. Reasons for this include:

- no immediate need;
- little or no incentive for firms to compete;
- sophisticated technology is imported as turnkey package deals;
- firms in international joint ventures rely on research and development (R&D) of parent firms; and
- small firms cannot afford to pay for R&D.[9]

If industries see little reason to invest in R&D and universities perform basic research with minimal relevance to the needs of the productive sector, the likelihood of collaboration is low.[10] Nonetheless, industry in developed countries cannot dismiss the increasing number of exceptionally successful collaborations. While industrial support for academic research is not, and has never been, high in any developed country, level of support is not an indicator of rate of collaboration or the value of a productive research relationship to companies.

The size of a firm affects the ease with which collaboration can develop. University researchers may not be interested in cooperating with small firms because they tend to be interested in problems that are not enough of a challenge to academic research. Additionally, small firms often lack adequate in-house research organizations or personnel to build a linkage, and funds to pay for university research. Small high-tech firms, however, are an exception.[11]

Finally, industry-university collaboration is not inherently natural for either party. One notable stumbling block is the "we haven't done this before" syndrome. A variation from industry's perspective is that, until collaboration with academia is tried, no one can see what good "outsiders" can be to the firm.[12] Nonetheless, resistance tends to lessen once both parties try working together and learn how to operate in each other's environment.[13]

Four Models of Collaboration

Developed and developing countries have been experimenting with a variety of ways to engage in industry-university research collaboration for years. These range in scale from programs that encourage one-to-one partnerships to vast technology parks. Some models have been copied, but new settings necessarily require making modifications to the original. The following four models provide a brief glimpse of the variation in existing approaches to collaboration.

Turkey—Revolving Funds

In 1981, Turkey's Higher Education Law established a mechanism that allowed universities to contract with industry to conduct research and perform consultancy work. Called *Revolving Funds* (RF), this source is one of four that support university R&D. A contract between a university and a client is simply a letter, but the university and faculty members involved sign a comprehensive contract in which the precise use of the funds is spelled out. Each university controls its own revolving fund, which is comprised of income earned from the industrial contracts.[14]

The university's income, which can be as high as several million U.S. dollars a year, is split between researchers' salary supplements (40 percent), the university research and equipment fund (35 percent), and university overhead (25 percent). According to the enabling legislation, the salary supplement may not exceed twice the total annual salary of the researcher. In reality, however, they amount to only about 80 percent of researchers' salaries; this is reached in engineering departments of universities with large RF income. Researchers in other fields and those in the less prestigious institutions receive little or no salary benefit from their contract work.[15]

The program could work more effectively. First, even though two of the universities receive several million U.S. dollars in RF income, universities do little to sell their research services. Second, the same institutions receive most of their RF income from large state enterprises, such as waterworks, highways, and the armed forces, not the private sector. Third, not all faculty members who bring in RF income receive a salary supplement. Fourth, there are enough implementation problems—most of which are due to the design of the program—that it would make sense to consider modifications of original restrictions, incentives, and optimal size of the activity. For instance, most of the contracts have been for applied research. However, with salary supplements as the basic incentive for faculty researchers to participate, it is possible that routine test work, rather than true research, will make up an increasing amount of the contracted activities. This amounts to underutilization of university researchers. Similarly, if RF growth continues at the present high rate, contract income may take the place of national investments to upgrade personnel capabilities and research facilities. The latter is needed to reverse brain drain.[16]

United Kingdom—Industrial Orientation in a University

The University of Salford hosts one of England's most diversified programs of industry-university linkages. As with many of the other programs, it is designed to reverse regional economic decline brought on by a decaying industrial base. The immediate stimulus for creation of the program was a reduction in the university's public appropriation in excess of 40 percent starting in 1981 and spread over three years. The university's new vice-chancellor responded by developing a strategy designed not only to generate income but also to establish a distinctive niche for the institution in the UK higher education system. The history of the university's development has been documented by Segal Quince Wicksteed.[17, 18]

The objective was to develop a different type of institution that would have a strong industrial orientation. To achieve this objective, the university set up a variety of mechanisms to link the institution with industry. In the first five years, the university set in motion a wide-ranging plan that included:

- obtaining industrial sponsorship for four endowed chairs as in the German model;
- appointing industrial leaders to sit on the university's research committee so that industry would play an active role in determining the overall research direction;
- developing a new mechanism to promote the capabilities of the university around the world;
- developing a collaborative project with large firms nearby to provide education and training in information technology; and
- establishing a technology park next to the university.

Unlike other examples of technology parks, the one at Salford is not considered the focal point of the institution's industry-university linkages. There are also applied research institutes with their own ties to industry, such as the Advanced Manufacturing Technology Centre, plus other mechanisms not mentioned. This multi-faceted approach to linkages has several interesting organizational consequences. First, university administrators have direct oversight activities. They direct and influence, if not control, as much as they can. Second, the administrators want to know as much as possible about what individual faculty members are doing. The latter must register their outside work with the university authorities. Third, academics do not always comply with what some perceive to be unnecessary and burdensome bureaucratic requirements; they conduct their industry work "underground." At some institutions, as much as 50 percent of the collaborative work is done covertly. The control that makes this approach necessary probably discourages those who do not want to bother with registering their outside work but who have no desire to resort to covert arrangements from collaborating altogether. In the long run, no one gains from this, except possibly those trying to control the academics.

Another result of the desire of university officials to control what they can is that faculty members are no longer allowed to form their own companies. However, university officials have allowed at least one faculty member to form a company as a division of the university's industrial liaison company.

It remains to be seen if the control aspect restricts the effectiveness of the overall program so that it never reaches its potential. Time will also tell if a university that shifts so sharply toward an industrial, short-term perspective makes a significant sacrifice in not continuing to create new knowledge that industry will need in the future. A university that performs little or no research cannot support the kind of graduate program that produces the kind of graduates that industry wants and needs.

It is far too early to determine if the university is successful in reshaping itself to an industrial orientation. Some of the services and programs may be more successful than others. Further, if the scheme succeeds, one consequence may be that the changes within the institution are so significant that the university ceases to be a university in the traditional sense.

Slovenia—International Center for Chemical Studies

Two decades ago, a group of enthusiastic young researchers at the University of Ljubljana, Slovenia (then Yugoslavia), sought ways to go beyond national and academic boundaries. Forming what became the International Center for Chemical Studies (ICCS), they pursued a variety of strategies for cooperation with international organizations and industry in both research and education. Through trial and error, not to mention years under Communist rule and a war in 1991, the center grew to become a model of what can be done with ingenuity and limited resources.[19]

From the beginning, center activities received only partial support from government funds, more of which were for basic research than for education or applied research. One of the founders explained, "This was the beginning of our cooperation with industry. At first, our group saw cooperation only as an opportunity to acquire funds for the improvement of the institute and for the support of international activities. At that time neither the faculty nor the industry thought that university-industry cooperation could improve teaching and research."[20] In the early days, companies requested a narrow range of assistance from the center.

The industry-university collaboration component, while always necessary for the survival of the center, was not a significant activity until the mid-1980s. Nonetheless, over the years, center researchers realized that successful collaborations involved working with clients from the very beginning of project development and selecting projects on the basis of product marketability. They developed a sophisticated system of information processing that allows them and their industrial clients to identify the most promising line of research before any bench work is done.

Along the way, center researchers learned rules of thumb that have led to many lucrative contracts with industry. Among the lessons that Kornhauser has documented are:

- Line up industry clients before commencing project selection;
- Reduce risk of failure and losing time and money in the proposal preparation process by selecting projects that "offer many approaches to possible products, or many applications of the selected technology"; and
- Recognize that being able to move an idea to the market in a short time is crucial. Academic researchers must focus their activity and work under time constraints.[21]

ICCS realized that academic researchers often oppose collaborative research because the time pressures stemming from industry's need to move from idea to market quickly make them work in a more concentrated fashion and discourage examination of all of the questions that appear while working on a project. The solution was to reserve approximately one-third of researchers' time for basic research beyond the scope of a collaborative project, but in the same field.[22]

Over the years, the center has had successful collaborations with a wide variety of companies around the world. Beyond this, one distinctive feature of the center is that not only do students gain experience working on collaborative projects, they also learn how to use the center's information processing techniques for project selection.

South Korea—Interdisciplinary Research Centers

South Korea established two types of university-based interdisciplinary research centers in 1989: the science research centers (SRCs) for advancement of new knowledge, and the engineering research centers (ERCs) for development of new technology relevant to industrial applications. Funded by the Korean Science and Engineering Foundation (KOSEF), the SRCs are similar to the U.S. science and technology centers. The ERCs resemble the U.S. engineering research centers. In both Korean programs, centers are awarded on a competitive basis, and funding for centers is obligated annually. As a result of the 1989 and 1990 competitions, fourteen SRCs and sixteen ERCs had been awarded to universities across South Korea. Each center receives approximately US$1 million per year.[23, 24]

The overall goal of the programs is that, collectively, the centers will be the future loci for innovation in Korea. During the development years, the centers are to increase in research quality and international visibility; disseminate information via seminars, workshops, intensive training, and publications; and provide continuing education for and collaborate with staff in industry and government research institutes (KOSEF, 1991). The main difference between the programs is that SRCs focus on pure research, while ERC research must have industrial application.[25]

While research is the primary focus in both programs, education is a close second. The centers are intended to provide excellent preparation for students who, in ten years, will lead South Korea's development. Graduate students and postdoctoral fellows are already involved, and undergraduates will be included in the future. In order to improve the quality of research and professors at the centers, KOSEF intends to entice more and more of the South Korean students who

Industry-University Research Collaboration

previously would have studied abroad to study at universities with SRCs and ERCs instead. Program designers also intend for the centers to play a significant role in reversing South Korea's earlier brain drain problem by conducting research that is sufficiently interesting to convince researchers who stayed abroad after schooling to return home.[26]

Perhaps the most notable feature of the programs is that they were designed to do a number of things simultaneously. While raising revenue from industry was not a goal, industry-university collaboration certainly was. KOSEF expected the ERCs to begin building collaborations almost immediately, while the SRCs were given several years to do so. Since government funding was allocated annually, there was great incentive to move ahead with the collaborations. Each participating company paid membership fees to the center, so the more collaborating companies, the more additional research support a center had.

These programs are noteworthy. While in their design they are similar to programs supported by the U.S. equivalent of KOSEF, they are tailored to meet the needs of South Korea. In many ways, they are quite different from the U.S. models. The SRCs and ERCs are clearly elements of a national strategy for strengthening research, education, and technology development capabilities. Goals are clear and incentives for participation are built into the designs of the programs.

Necessary Conditions for Collaboration

In 1989, Decio de Zagottis, minister for science and technology in Brazil, delivered a speech before the Tenth Session of the Intergovernmental Committee for Science and Technology for Development in which he listed the items that he believed necessary to facilitate industry-university interaction in Brazil. While his list focuses on one country, Brazil, many of the items have broad applicability:

- Universities need to obtain information about industry's existing, potential, and future technological demands;

- Universities, and especially engineering schools, must create a feedback mechanism with industry to enable academia to keep track of existing knowledge in industry;
- Industry must pay adequately for consulting services provided by university researchers; and
- Interaction should focus on preparing and updating the skills of R&D personnel, acquiring and generating technology, and technology transfer.[27]

A number of studies support pieces of de Zagottis's observations. In one study dealing with building science capacity in nine developing countries, Behrman and Fischer concluded that the traditional triangle model of what is necessary to build science infrastructure lacked a number of factors. To the triangle consisting of government, industry, and universities and research institutes they added three components: (1) "a *science community* oriented to industrial research coming out of the three previously mentioned groups"; (2) "a body of industrial *users*, who apply the technology"; and (3) "a market that elicits and utilizes S&T [science and technology] results, making the effort profitable."[28]

The key to this system functioning properly is that strong linkages exist among all six components. Across the countries they studied, the principal gap that Behrman and Fischer found is the lack of market pull. Specifically, they noted that there was insufficient competition among local firms in all countries studied, which resulted in little desire to upgrade technology. This was due largely to an inadequate appreciation by industry of the role of technical innovation, as available technology seemed to fill existing needs. Nonetheless, a weak market signal often conflicted with governmental programs requiring local R&D activities. In many countries, this was exacerbated by a lack of trust within the industrial sector of the ability of academic researchers.[29]

Factors Contributing to Success

People engage in or encourage industry-university research collaboration for many reasons, including income generation and

Industry-University Research Collaboration   111

economic development. The parties involved may have notably different reasons. Similarly, each party may define success quite differently. For the sake of simplicity, a "successful collaboration" will refer to a productive relationship in which all parties are satisfied with the way people and organizations work together and with the results of their joint efforts.

Incentives to Collaborate

In most developing countries, at least in the earlier stages of development, industries conduct little if any R&D. This is a major barrier to fruitful industry-university relations. Moving beyond this situation may involve interim steps, such as firms contracting with universities for R&D assistance. However, if market signals are weak, positive experiences with this type of small-scale collaboration may not provide enough stimulus for firms to begin developing their own R&D capability. In the case of Thailand, removing government controls over the industrial environment is necessary before competition can develop in the private sector and the role of technological improvement becomes evident to individual firms.

Unlike some developing countries, a number of Central and Eastern European countries have had the necessary human resources for expanding S&T capacity, but the lack of market competition with its incentives for improving products and production methods kept those with research training from working on projects with industrial application. These countries were not involved in the technological innovations that characterized the 1980s and provided a vehicle for a number of East Asian countries to become newly industrialized countries (NICs).[30]

It appears that setting a high limit for the income that academic researchers can earn through contracting does not guarantee that they actually receive much remuneration. In the case of Turkey's revolving funds, participating faculty members have not received nearly as much income from their involvement with industry as the program allows. In countries where faculty salaries are low compared with those in industry or other countries, inadequate reimbursement of faculty researchers for services rendered to industry may not only discourage individual collaborations but contribute to brain drain that may already be a problem.

The revolving funds experience suggests another lesson. The program was intended to support research, but a significant proportion of contracted work has been for pilot testing. As long as the program allows this to continue, firms will have no incentive to establish their own testing facilities, and no one will be inclined to collaborate on true research projects.

Building Partnerships

The single most important factor in the success of any industry-university collaboration is the existence of one person who initiates and nurtures the project. Such a person is energetic and views the success of the project as crucial for his or her professional development. Equally important, beyond excellence in science, is that this individual have superb management capabilities. While there is certainly need for strong leadership, true collaboration can occur only if individual researchers make it happen. Formal agreements made by administrators are likely to fail.[31, 32, 33, 34] Where there is little tradition of interaction, starting small, e.g., with individual research contracts, and then expanding into larger collaborative mechanisms in time, makes sense.[35, 36] Starting small is also a good way of overcoming concerns stemming from uninformed perceptions. Academicians who have had little or no contact with industry assume that collaboration requires that they adapt what they do and how they do it to industry's needs.[37] While companies need short-term applied R&D to solve problems, they can also profit from academic researchers serving as short-term consultants. Institutions and researchers geared toward basic research can benefit companies by conducting long-term strategic research.[38] Those in industry who have been successful promoting collaboration have found that the most fruitful ventures come about when the university participants do what they do best and are not forced into the industrial mold.[39,40]

Project Selection

In examining the Southeast Asian NICs to determine which factors had contributed to their progress, Ranis found that one factor was the process by which researchers chose projects. Taking as his example the S&T institute, common in developing countries, he found that successful Southeast Asian countries and Japan (shortened to EAJs) "force such institutes to be useful to the market place either by only providing a partial subsidy and/or one that is being reduced over time, as was the case with the Korean Advanced Institute of Science and Technology (KAIST), or by policies designed to encourage firm level R&D through tax provisions that permit the current costing of R&D." In other, and less successful, developing countries, the governments tended to be the main financiers of institutes whose researchers were motivated more by the "hot" research topics in international academic circles than by translating technologies for market use. Ranis concludes that the EAJ emphasis on private sector contracts rather than governmental subsidies played a large role in the choice of research projects.[41] Choice may be affected not only by the source of funding but also the terms of the financial agreement.

South Korea has several examples of how a government can stimulate development of research capacity and the economy simultaneously. KAIST (reorganized in 1989) is notable not only for incentives to work in areas that have applications in the market place but also for combining graduate training, research tied to economic needs, and measurement and standards development in the same institution. The two new centers' programs, SRC and ERC, illustrate a similar approach to combining incentives with an organizational framework that also focus on doing several things simultaneously in one institution. One of the key features underlying the centers programs and KAIST is that no component is intended to function independently of the others. It is not surprising, therefore, that a notable number of SRCs and ERCs were awarded to KAIST.

Support for S&T activities, be they performed in universities or industry, should be focused on the country's or region's highest priority areas.[42, 43] Identifying and occupying a niche that reflects local conditions, resources, and comparative advantages should be the goal.[44] Porter points to Japan as an example of a country that also recognized the role of *disadvantage* in determining priorities and spurring innovation.[45] Identifying and compensating for disadvantages makes it possible to put comparative advantages in better perspective. This approach is probably as valid for universities and individual companies as it is for countries.

Institutional Factors

In addition to those directly involved in relationships with industry, two institutional factors are significant. First, if the collaboration is to involve more than one-on-one relationships between university and industry personnel, the character of the university's culture is important. Specifically, the question is whether the culture can be characterized as "entrepreneurial."[46] In the absence of this feature, a strong leader, especially during periods of external financial pressure, can influence the culture and direction of the institution. This was discussed earlier, but it applies as much in developing countries as in their developed counterparts.

One indicator of entrepreneurialism within university departments is the development of "spin-off" companies, or academic start-ups, in which faculty members start a company to commercialize an idea that has resulted from their research. The practice is clearly controversial and not always allowed. While there can be definite financial benefits for the researchers and economic benefit from the success of a new product, university administrators are concerned about the effect of the time spent working on commercial ventures on the quality of researchers' teaching and their availability for graduate students. Some universities require that faculty members who establish their own firms give up their academic appointments.[47]

University administrators are looking more closely at the possibilities and ramifications of spin-off corporations. From the standpoint of income generation, university patenting and licensing offices should make certain that intellectual property rights are protected to clear the way for income generation through licensing discoveries to larger firms. Universities have a stake in taking an active stance of this sort because their facilities provide the launching ground for spin-off corporations. Sometimes, institutions put up part of the startup capital, so their interest is even more substantial. Finally, universities with extensive research activities take kindly to the supplementary research funds that can accrue from spin-off corporations.[48]

Another institutional factor is the match between what universities can provide and what companies need. Academic researchers should be aware of the expectations of their industrial counterparts, as well as the role that collaborating companies believe that universities are best suited to play. In a study conducted jointly by the Government-University-Industry Research Roundtable of the U.S. National Academy of Sciences and the Industrial Research Institute, senior research managers in a variety of companies had clear ideas about which party should be responsible for what in industry-university research relations. Specifically, they felt that it was a mistake for universities looking for revenue to reorient their research toward project discovery, as they are not appropriately equipped to handle this role. Furthermore, the industrial researchers did not look favorably upon collaboration programs such as university-based research centers in which individual companies were affiliates of centers. "Generally, industrial affiliates programs are not profitable . . . and generally, companies are less and less interested in participating. Those that continue to support such programs tend to do so either as good will gestures or to have access to students and faculty for recruitment." The industry research managers concluded that "the primary role for universities is as educator and provider of talent. This function is universities' greatest contribution to the process of innovation. . . . Providing in-depth, fundamental understanding of scientifically and technologically new or emerging ideas is another significant role for universities."[49]

The British Department of Trade and Industry developed a list of factors that contributed to the success of winners in the Industry Year 1986 competition. Experience has shown them to be important in other developed countries as well:

- combine the right people with the right structure. One without the other is insufficient;
- personalities matter. A driving force at the operational level is essential;
- Top-level commitment gives strategic clarity to the project and creates an environment in which successful collaboration can take place;

- Collaborative projects need structural or facilitating mechanisms that give them freedom to evolve;
- The real benefits for collaborators derive from the process of collaboration;
- All involved need sustained motivation and commitment; and
- Benefits accrue for both sides and knowledge is transferred in both directions.[50]

The Role of Proximity

Proximity of university laboratories and industry is critical if collaboration is to take place.[51] Close proximity encourages personal contact, personnel exchanges, equipment gifts, and sharing of facilities.[52] According to Porter, it also leads to the development of entire systems, or clusters, of collaborators. These industrial clusters include universities that create specialized programs, research institutes that are established to meet certain needs, specialized infrastructure, and suppliers who become interested in being involved.[53]

Ease of access of partners to each others' facilities is the essence of many collaboration models. With long distance transportation and communications being difficult in many developing countries, collaborative ties are easiest to arrange if the partners are near each other. This is particularly true when collaboration includes students working at industrial facilities. Proximity is also likely to be important for the success of science or technology parks. Similarly, proximity may also encourage firms near science parks to become partners. One technopark in Turkey located in an area with a strong industrial base had eighty-nine sponsors at the outset, most of which were industrial firms nearby.

There are at least two schools of thought about the desirability of proximity in developed countries. Segal found that local linkages are convenient and frequently beneficial, but not always appropriate or sufficient. Stretching horizons may provide more intellectual stimulus for institutional growth that would not come about with a parochial partnership.[54] There are undoubtedly circumstances under which this is true. However, Porter points to Rochester, New York, and Memphis,

Tennessee, as examples where proximity of collaborators was responsible for the development of technology-based regional strengths.[55]

Sources of Difficulty

It is possibly more difficult to identify unsuccessful collaborations than successful ventures. In fact, defining what is unsuccessful is murky. Some use the designation for collaborations that were intended but never took place. Others deem a collaboration unsuccessful if one party (usually industry) stops supporting the activity. The latter may be misleading. Industry can pull out for a variety of reasons, including deciding: (1) to develop the product another way; (2) that nothing will come of the project; and (3) that the work of academic colleagues is unsatisfactory.[56]

An underlying assumption in any discussion of industry-university relations is that both parties are ready for such interaction. Both need to have achieved a certain amount of performance capability in order for there to be a basis for collaboration. A university with research facilities and faculty trained in Western universities can do little for firms that have no technological orientation and are unable or unwilling to adopt more sophisticated techniques. Conversely, firms that seek to move from importing technology to producing it themselves have little to gain from relations with universities that have poor research facilities and no faculty members with the necessary research skills. At the most basic level, universities need to have something to offer industry and industry needs to be in a position to benefit from university assistance.

Many collaborations that might have been successful only last a short time or never reach their potential. One common reason is that not all the necessary linkages were made to translate the result of the collaboration into application. It is not enough for those directly involved to have a productive relationship. If the industrial partner is not able to move the results of the collaboration into use, the firm may be no better off than it was before the collaboration. There would be a gain, however, if the industrial partner acquired skills or knowledge in the process of working with academic colleagues. If the new knowledge or skills are put to use, the collaboration would be a partial success. Seen as discrete, unconnected activities, collaborations cannot produce significant payoffs within an industry or for the economy. They must be a part of larger efforts to meet industrial and economic needs.

Lackluster success, as well as actual failures, can be the result of poor or incomplete implementation of a plan. Personnel, government, and policy changes during any stage of a project can affect implementation, or a program can be implemented differently from the way in which it was envisioned during the planning stage. An example is Turkey's revolving funds program. The legislation establishing the program allows participating faculty researchers to receive a significant stipend. As mentioned previously, only engineering faculty members receive close to the remuneration for which they are eligible. Thus, the way in which the program was implemented failed to create incentives to participation for some who are eligible.

Lack of appropriate skills or foresight can also impair project progress. Complex collaborative arrangements, such as research centers and science parks, can be less than successful if equipment is allowed to deteriorate beyond repair or maintenance. Lack of trained technical expertise is usually the biggest problem. While providing technician training should be a part of the job of university research centers and science or technology parks, it may not come about. Companies wishing to upgrade their production standards may be unable to do so because they lack technicians with the skills necessary to implement any upgrade.[57] Thus if the facility, be it a research center or science park, has an objective of improving production standards via a formal program, the entire activity can be sidelined if another component program, e.g., technical training, is not implemented as planned. The more complex the overall effort, the more success depends on the timely and successful implementation of each part.

Another reason that some collaborations seem to go nowhere is inadequate support for the activities over time. Waffling support is a sign that initial commitment may not have been especially strong. If the activities are not valued by the participating universities and industries, incentive systems may be changed to make them less attractive for researchers to participate. Similarly, a short-term view on the part of those paying for the collaboration can lead to support being reduced or eliminated if results are not produced in a limited amount of time.

Large government-sponsored projects can meet their demise if political (and therefore financial) support is not dependable. A good example is the saga of a number of U.S. science parks for which state support was not nearly as stable as anticipated at the outset. To minimize the possibility of failure, large, expensive collaborative ventures should, from the beginning, be viewed as high political and financial priorities by all involved and commitments for long-term support should be firm. In the absence of these conditions, such ventures are risky and suggest that the partners are not entirely ready to undertake a large, complex activity.[58]

Finally, establishing good working relations is not enough for success. People may be able to work together without being productive. Conditions may be good for collaboration, but no tangible results may appear from the activity. The missing component is entrepreneurism. At least one member of a partnership must have entrepreneurial skills. Building a technology-based economy involves awareness of markets and what niches competitors are pursuing, be they in the same region, or global. To the extent that industry-university R&D collaborations are intended to contribute to economic development, collaborations must focus on what is useful for participating firms. Figuring out what is useful and how to create innovation as a result of collaborations involves entrepreneurship. Planning, developing strategies, determining comparative advantages and disadvantages, identifying opportunities, taking intellectual risks, and convincing potential partners of the advantages of entering into collaboration are all part of entrepreneurship. Knowledge of the importance and role of these factors is often weak.

Conclusion

This chapter has concentrated on what is known about making industry-university collaboration work, not how to raise as much income as possible from such endeavors. The reason is simple. Experience from around the world suggests that, in focusing on the former, an institution has a much greater chance of raising significant amounts of revenue. The British and Turkish examples illustrate what can happen if the alternate approach is taken. In concentrating on raising revenue, the University of Salford altered radically its mission and priorities to the point where it is debatable whether the institution remains a university. Turkey's revolving funds program demonstrates that ignoring whether a university's contribution adds value to industry's efforts, or substitutes for capabilities that companies should be developing internally, underutilizes highly trained faculty members and sets a poor example for students of what private sector research entails.

The Slovenian and South Korean research centers illustrate that academic priorities, particularly basic research and the training of graduate students, do not necessarily interfere with the needs of cooperating businesses when there is an emphasis on developing successful linkages with industry. These centers also illustrate several fallacies regarding industry-university collaboration:

Fallacy 1: Engaging in industry-university research collaboration necessarily results in a reduction in "standards" for faculty research and graduate education. Reality: Designed and implemented properly, collaborative research can enhance both.

Fallacy 2: Gearing academic research towards the needs of industry reduces academic freedom. Reality: The process by which companies and ICCS select research projects not only maintains academic freedom but also gives academic researchers the upper hand in analyzing and recommending project options.

Fallacy 3: Universities cannot provide significant contributions to industrial R&D activities because they are not oriented toward, or are not interested in, the needs of industry. Reality: The South Korean centers and ICCS cannot be successful if they are not attuned to what companies needs, both in terms of research and marketable products. In fact, ICCS seems to be leading, rather than following, the companies with which they collaborate with their project selection process.

Fallacy 4: Graduate education suffers if academic researchers engage in industrial collaboration. Reality: Graduate programs can be enhanced if the collaborative research seeks to develop new, useful knowledge and students work with industrial researchers on collaborative projects.

There are many models of industry-university collaboration around the world and many success stories. The key to making any of them successful from the standpoint of generating revenue is concentrating on making collaboration work for both the collaborating college or university and the participating companies. To do otherwise invites disappointment.

NOTES

*Any opinions, findings, and conclusions or recommendations expressed in this publication are those of the author and do not necessarily reflect the views of the National Science Foundation. The report on which this chapter is based, *Industry-University Collaboration in Developed and Developing Countries,* was prepared by the author for the World Bank, PHREE Background Paper Series, Document No. PHREE/92/64.
  1. N.S. Segal. "IHE Links: The Need for Institution-Specific Approaches." *Industry and Higher Education* (Sept. 1987): 15.
  2. B. Bollag. "University-Industry Collaboration in Europe Called Mainly Positive and Likely to Expand." *Chronicle of Higher Education* (Nov. 7, 1990).
  3. J.S. Fairweather. "Education: The Forgotten Element in Industry-University Relationships." *Review of Higher Education*, 14, no. 1 (1990): 33–45.
  4. National Science Board. *University-Industry Research Relationships.* (Washington, D.C.: National Science Board, 1982). NSB-82–2.
  5. J.N. Behrman and W.A. Fischer. *Science and Technology for Development: Corporate and Government Policies and Practices.* (Cambridge, Mass.: Oelgeschlager, Gunn, & Hain, 1980).
  6. National Science Board. *Op. cit.*
  7. R. Van Dierdonck, K. Debackere, and B. Engelen. "University-Industry Relationships: How Does the Belgian Academic Community Feel About It?" *Research Policy*, 19 (1990): 551–566.
  8. R.A. Blais. "From Research to Production: Reflections on Technological Development Strategies and Relationships Between University and Industry." Paper presented at the International Seminar on the New Political Context of Scientific and Technological Development, Montevideo, Dec. 6–8, 1990.

9. C.J. Dahlman and P. Brimble. *Technology Strategy and Policy for Industrial Competitiveness: A Case Study in Thailand.* (Washington, D.C.: World Bank, 1990).
10. *Ibid.*
11. National Science Board. *Op. cit.*
12. K.W. McHenry. "Five Myths of Industry/University Cooperative Research—and the Realities." *Research-Technology Management*, 33, no. 3 (1990): 40–42.
13. R. Van Dierdonck, K. Debackere, and B. Engelen. *Op. cit.*
14. R. Lalkaka, "Turkey: Industrial Technology Development Program," (1990). Mimeo.
15. *Ibid.*
16. *Ibid.*
17. Segal Quince Wicksteed. *Universities, Enterprise and Local Economic Development: An Exploration of Links.* (London: Her Majesty's Stationery Office, 1988).
18. Segal Quince Wicksteed. *The Cambridge Phenomenon.* (London: Brand Brothers, 1985).
19. A. Kornhauser. *University-Industry Cooperation Under Constraints.* (Washington, D.C.: World Bank, 1993). Forthcoming.
20. *Ibid.*, 14.
21. *Ibid.*, 57.
22. *Ibid.*
23. KOSEF, SRC/ERC 1991. (Daejun City, Korea: KOSEF, 1991).
24. KOSEF, KOSEF. (Daejun City, Korea: KOSEF, 1990).
25. J-C. Kyung, director general for manpower policy, ministry of science and technology, Korea. Personal communication, 1992.
26. *Ibid.*
27. D.L. de Zagottis. "The Brazilian Experience in Shaping a Science and Technology System in Support of Development." Statement at the Tenth Session of the Intergovernmental Committee for Science and Technology for Development, New York, Aug. 21, 1989.
28. J. N. Behrman and W. A. Fischer. *Op. cit.*, 101. All italics in original text.
29. J. N. Behrman and W. A. Fischer. *Op. cit.*
30. E.W. Thulstrup. *Improving the Quality of Research in Developing Country Universities.* (Washington, D.C.: World Bank, 1992). PHREE Background Paper Series No. PHREE/92/52.

31. K.W. McHenry. *Op. cit.*
32. National Science Board. *Op. cit.*
33. D. Osborne. "Refining State Technology Programs." *Issues in Science and Technology* (Summer 1990): 55–61.
34. R. Van Dierdonck, K. Debackere, and B. Engelen. *Op. cit.*
35. K.A. Blais. *Op. cit.*
36. J.S. Fairweather. "Education: The Forgotten Element in Industry-University Relationships." *Review of Higher Education*, 14, no. 1 (1990), 33–45.
37. R. Van Dierdonck, K. Debackere, and B. Engelen. *Op. cit.*
38. N.S. Segal. *Op. cit.*
39. K.W. McHenry. *Op. cit.*
40. J. Vleggar. "Getting Research Off to a Fast Start—The University Route." *Research-Technology Management*, 34, no. 3 (1991): 19–20.
41. G. Ranis. "Science and Technology Policy: Lessons from Japan and the East Asians NICs." *Science and Technology: Lessons for Development Policy*. Edited by R.E. Evenson and G. Ranis. (London Intermediate Technology Publications, 1990): 172.
42. C. Freeman. "New Technology and Catching Up." *Journal of European Development Research*, 1, no. 1 (1989): 85–99.
43. J.A. Muskin. *World Bank Lending for Science and Technology*. (Washington, D.C.: World Bank, 1992). PHREE/92/51R.
44. C. Freeman. *Op. cit.*
45. D. Morgan. "Think Locally, Win Globally: Harvard's Porter Pushes Regions Clusters as the Key to Industrial Competitiveness." *New York Times*, (Apr. 5, 1992): H1, H5–6.
46. N. S. Segal. *Op. cit.*, 18.
47. H. Etzkowitz and L.S. Peters. "Profiting from Knowledge: Organisational Innovations and the Evolution of Academic Norms." *Minerva*, 29, no. 2 (1991): 133–166.
48. *Ibid.*
49. Government-University-Industry Research Roundtable and Industrial Research Institute. *Industrial Perspectives on Innovation and Interactions with Universities*. (Washington, D.C.: National Academy Press, February 1991): 13, 20.
50. Department of Trade and Industry. *The Industry Year Award: Nine Case Studies in Collaboration*. (London: Department of Trade and Industry, 1987).

51. R.R. Nelson. "On Technological Capacities and Their Acquisition." *Science and Technology: Lessons for Development Policy.* Edited by R. E. Evenson and G. Ranis. (London: Intermediate Technology Publications, 1990): 71–80.
52. National Science Board. *Op. cit.*
53. D. Morgan. *Op. cit.*
54. N.S. Segal. *Op. cit.*
55. D. Morgan. *Op. cit.*
56. National Science Board. *Op. cit.*
57. J.N. Behrman and W.A. Fischer. *Op. cit.*
58. G. Blumenstyk. "Pitfalls of Research Parks Lead Universities and States to Reassess Their Expectations." *Chronicle of Higher Education* (July 5, 1990): A19, A24.

PART 2
Case Studies

HIGHER EDUCATION FUNDING IN OPEN DOOR CHINA

Richard A. Hartnett

"Education should be geared toward modernization, the world, and the future," proclaimed Deng Xiaoping as he launched China's drive for economic modernization over a decade ago. In Deng's plan, Chinese education would no longer serve the narrow ideology of "proletarian politics," but would become the engine for building China into a powerful and modern nation.[1] Education's principal task would be to produce *rencai* (manpower or talents for society) to meet the goals of modernization.

During the Third Plenary Session of the Eleventh Central Committee of the Chinese Communist Party in 1978, the objectives for economic development were intoned under the rubric of the Four Modernizations (in Agriculture, Industry, Science and Technology, and Defense). By the year 2000, China was to quadruple its agricultural and industrial output, and by the middle of the next century, it was to reach the economic levels of the developed countries. Accompanying these ambitious production goals were a series of sweeping economic policy changes including the separation of ownership from managerial authority, an incipient market-oriented system, and the development of plural ownership. Gradually, China's hyper-centralized system was beginning to take on some of the characteristics of local initiative and market regulation.

Deng Xiaoping targeted higher education with the task of training specialized personnel to meet his goal of economic revitalization. Correspondingly, substantial changes took place during the decade in the structure, management, curriculum, and financing of higher education, including unprecedented increases in student enrollment and the number of institutions. In addition to describing the basic features of the Chinese higher education system, this chapter examines some of the key issues affecting the funding of Chinese higher education and presents some strategies for improvement in the decade ahead.

Enrollment Trends in Chinese Higher Education

At the birth of the People's Republic of China in 1949, there were only 205 regular higher education institutions and 116, 500 students. Since 1960, Chinese higher education enrollment has taken a "V" shape. Total enrollments decreased from 962,000 in 1960 to 48,000 during the mid-point of the Cultural Revolution (1970). By 1989, the numbers soared to 2,082,000 students and 1,075 institutions.

These dramatic shifts are a result of several factors. First, the "Great Leap Forward" movement took place in the late 1950s and propelled the growth in higher education from 229 institutions in 1957 to 1, 289 in 1960. Student enrollment rose as well from 441,000 to 962,000. Such unparalleled expansion caused several systemic problems, particularly an unbalanced structure and unplanned development; poor instructional quality and inadequate training and preparation; the proliferation of many small, highly specialized institutions with concomitant diseconomies of scale and low internal efficiency; and exceedingly high financial costs to operate this expanded system.[2]

Secondly, during the next five years, the higher education system was reorganized to provide a more rational structure for subsequent development, and the number of colleges and universities was reduced from 1,289 in 1960 to 434 in 1965; the total enrollment decreased from 962,000 in 1960 to 674,000 in 1965. However, the Cultural Revolution broke out in 1966, transforming the higher education system. Not only did the size of the system decline but a new type of student dominated the colleges and universities: the worker-peasant-soldier student (*gongnongbing xueyuan*), who lacked proper qualifications. Furthermore, all entrance examinations were eliminated.

Thirdly, in the late 1970s, the Deng Xiaoping government embarked on an open door policy with the West and a policy of economic reconstruction and development. As the government looked to higher education for trained manpower and specialized personnel,

**Table 1. Chinese Higher Education Institutions:
Basic Features Since Liberation**

Year	No. Reg. Insts. H.E.	Enrl.	No. Grads	No. Entrants	No. Full Time Faculty	Fac./Stud. Ratio	Av. Inst. Size	Adm. Stud. Ratio	Adm. Pers.
1949	205	116,504	21,353	30,573	16,059	7.2	568	11.0	12,841
1950	193	137,470	17,607	58,330	17,319	7.9	712	10.9	14,979
1955	194	287,653	54,466	97,797	42,066	6.8	1,483	9.0	26,006
1960	1,289	961,623	136,138	323,161	139,142	6.9	746	9.7	93,316
1965	434	674,436	185,521	164,212	138,116	4.9	1,554	10.6	71,741
1970	434	47,815	102,672	41,870	128,617	0.4	110	N/A	N/A
1975	387	500,993	118,955	190,779	155,723	3.2	1,295	3.3	165,395
1980	675	1,143,712	146,635	281,230	246,862	4.6	1,694	9.2	105,186
1989	1,075	2,183,450	613,474	625,682	397,365	5.5	2,031	7.6	167,230

Source: Figures extracted from PRC Ministry of Education, *Achievement of Education in China 1949–1983* (Beijing: People's Education Press, 1984); 1989 data are from *Achievement of Education in China*, 1990.

the higher education system expanded to 805 institutions of higher education and 1,207,000 students by 1983. By 1989, there were 1,075 institutions and 2,183,000 students. (See Table 1 for figures on higher education from 1949–89.)

Concerning field of study, engineering is clearly the largest discipline, representing about 50 percent of the total enrollment in the early 1960s and about 40 percent in the late 1980s. This is a consequence of the government's emphasis on engineering to spur national development. The second largest field is education, representing 25 percent of the total enrollment—a reflection of China's vast need for teachers, especially in the rural areas. As of 1989, the next largest fields were business administration, medicine, arts and humanities, science, and law.

Despite the rapid expansion of the last decade, the percentage of the Chinese college cohort has remained quite low by world standards. As presented in Table 2, the ratio has remained rather constant at about 1.6 since 1960, a consequence of the rapid growth of the college age population throughout the thirty-year period. At the same time, the percentage of female students has increased noticeably from 25 percent in the early 1960s to about 33 percent in the late 1980s.

As of 1989, there were 397,300 full-time faculty, an increase of 38 percent over 1980. At the same time, across all types of institutions, the student-teacher ratio (STR) was only 5.5, one of the lowest in the world, and the average student enrollment was 2,031, up slightly from 1,694 in 1980.

Table 2. Higher Education Enrollment in China: Selected Years

Year	Total Enrollment in Regular Higher Institutions (in thousands)	As percentage of age group (% of 20–24 year olds)
1960	961.6	1.62
1965	674.4	1.30
1970	47.8	0.07
1980	1,143.7	1.35
1985	1,703.1	1.67
1989	2,082.1	1.66

Source: PRC State Statistical Bureau comp., *Statistical Yearbook of China*, for 1985 and for other years cited (Hong Kong: Economic Information Agency, 1985).

During the period of rapid expansion, a national reform of higher education took place to allow the universities to respond to changing societal requirements. The objectives of the 1985 education reform policy were "to change the management system of excessive government control of the institutions of higher education, expand decision making in the state, strengthen the connection of the institutions of higher education with production organizations, scientific research organizations and other social establishments, and enable the institutions of higher education to take the initiative and ability to meet the needs of economic and social development."

Overview of the Finance of Chinese Higher Education

In terms of type of control and funding (Table 3), there are three types of Chinese higher education institutions. (1) Thirty-six *key* institutions are governed directly by the State Education Commission (SEdC), which is responsible for the overall guidance of the higher education system in China through formulating policies, decrees, and plans. The SEdC replaced the Ministry of Education in 1985, and it is parallel (at least in theory) to the State Planning Council, the State Economic Commission, and the State Commission for Science and Technology. The SEdC group accounts for about 11 percent of the total enrollment. The average size is 6,683 students. (2) Three-hundred and seventeen institutions are under the control of central ministries like the Ministry of Agriculture, Ministry of Public Health, etc., representing about 33 percent of the total. The average size is 2,124 students. (3) There also 722 *provincial* institutions administered by provincial educational commissions, accounting for 56 percent of the total, but averaging only 1,618 students per institution. The SEdC and central ministry institutions are funded from the budget of the Ministry of Finance in Beijing. The allocation is based on head-count enrollment. The provincial institutions are funded by the department of finance in each province.

Table 3. Higher Education Institutions by Affiliation, 1989

Affiliation	No.	Enrollment	Avg. Size	# of Teachers	STR
SEdC	36	240,578	6,933	52,605	4.6
Central Ministry	317	673,263	2,124	145,421	4.6
Provinces	722	1,168,270	1,618	199,339	5.9
Total	1,075	2,082,111	1,937	397,365	5.2

Source: Department of Planning, State Education Commission, 1989.

Although it accounts for only 1 percent of the total educational enrollment, China allocates about 22 percent of its resources to higher education. By comparison, primary and secondary education accounts for 89 percent of total enrollment, but receives just 54 percent of the funding.

As Table 4 shows, the public expenditure on higher education has increased more than five times from 1978 to 1988, increasing from Y 1.5 billion to Y 8.1 billion (about 25 percent of the total expenditure on education). In terms of per capita GNP, higher education expenditure in China is 199, compared to 231 in India and 149 in Asia.

Table 4. Public Expenditure on Education, Selected Years (in billion yuan)

Year	Total expen. on ed.	Expen. on high ed. expen.	%	Expen. on general ed. expen.	%	High ed. expen. as % of public expen.	%	High ed. expen. as GNP	%
1960	3,963	1,362	34.4	2,601	65.6	64,514	2.11	146.40	0.93
1967	3,373	0.529	15.7	2,844	84.3	44,185	1.20	178.44	0.30
1975	5,193	0.830	16.0	4,363	84.0	82,088	1.01	300.36	0.28
1980	11,319	2,817	24.9	8,502	74.1	121,273	2.32	447.00	0.63
1985	22,435	6,082	27.0	16,353	73.0	184,480	3.30	855.76	0.71
1988	32,356	8,174	25.2	24,182	74.7	266,830	3.06	1,398.42	0.58

Source: *Statistical Yearbook of China for 1985* and other years cited.

With respect to total recurrent expenditure in higher education, personnel expenditure represents only 42 percent, a consequence of relatively low faculty and staff salaries (Table 5). The average salary of a full professor in China is less than Y 400 a month, or about 80 U. S. dollars. On the other hand, non-personnel expenditure is relatively high because it reflects the costs of running an institution which conducts itself more like a city than an academy of higher learning. Chinese higher education institutions must provide for housing, affiliated schools, and hospitals for university staff and their families. Similarly, capital expenditures are relatively high (Y 2.93 billion), reflecting the rapid expansion of higher education during the open door period.

Table 5. Structure of Higher Expenditure and Unit Cost, Selected Years (in billion yuan)

Recurrent Expenditure

Year	Total Expen. of High Ed.	Sub Total	Pers. Expen.	Non-Pers. Expen.	Capital Expen.	Units/ Recurrent cost (in yuan)
1980	2.81	1.91	0.82	1.09	0.90	1,752
1981	3.21	2.23	0.92	1.31	0.98	1,753
1982	3.44	2.39	0.98	1.41	1.06	1,922
1983	4.30	2.78	1.18	1.60	1.52	2,186
1984	5.22	3.27	1.26	2.01	1.95	2,229
1985	6.08	3.62	1.45	2.17	2.46	2,477
1986	7.51	4.29	1.71	2.58	3.30	2,564
1987	7.54	4.54	1.82	2.72	3.00	2,314
1988	8.17	5.25	2.33	2.82	2.93	2,521

Source: *Statistical Yearbook of China for 1985* and other years cited.

Funding Issues in Chinese Higher Education

The predominant problems facing the higher education since the rapid expansion of the system after 1980 have been excessive unit costs and diseconomies of scale, ineffective organizational structures and management practices, and high student subsidies and limited revenue sources. As higher education expanded in the 1980s, the state failed to pay attention to several aspects of efficiency and effectiveness.

High Unit Costs and Enrollment Expansion

Higher education expansion in the 1980s was accomplished by means of institutional multiplication as opposed to institutional enlargement. As noted earlier, the total number of institutions soared from 675 in 1980 to 1,075 in 1988, but the average size remained below 2,000 students. In fact, there are still 381 institutions with less than 1,000 students. Despite some fluctuations over the years, the average unit recurrent cost of Chinese higher education (presented in Tables 6 and 7) is quite high: over two times the per capita GNP in China compared with 1.0 in East Asia and the Pacific and 0.5 in developed countries. The reasons for this are manifold, but chief among them is the extremely low STR, the low student-administrator ratio, and the low student-total staff ratio. Other contributing factors are the over-specialization of programs and courses, the low utilization of equipment and facilities, and the the socialist conception of higher educational institutions referred to above as the "city" phenomenon. This accounts for 23 percent of total recurrent expenditures in provincial universities, for example.

Table 6. Unit Cost of Public Higher Education,
China and Other Asian Countries (c. 1985)

Asian Countries	Unit Cost[a]	STR
China	330	5.2
India	231	15.9
Indonesia	106	14.0
Korea	105	42.2
Malaysia	190	11.4
Nepal	249	13.2
Philippines	50	16.0
Sri Lanka	111	10.7
Thailand	178	8.3

Source: J. Tan and A. Mingat. "Educational Development in China." Technical Department, Asia Region. (Washington D.C.: World Bank, 1989).

[a] Unit cost is defined as per-student recurrent cost as a percentage of per capita GNP.

Table 7. Unit Cost of Education in China (in yuan)

				(In 1985 yuan)		
Year	Higher	Secondary	Primary	Higher	Secondary	Primary
1980	1752.38	60.13	23.19	2075.82	71.23	27.47
1985	2477.29	128.54	47.30	2477.29	128.54	47.30
1988	2314.70	141.15	59.96	1717.40	104.74	44.49

Source: Author's compilations.

Higher Education Funding in Open Door China 135

Unit recurrent cost is closely related to enrollment size and student-teacher ratios, and low average enrollments in China produce diseconomies of scale. According to some calculations, increasing the average size of Chinese higher education institutions to about 8,000 or 10,000 students would yield substantially lower costs and substantially improve the economy of scale. Keeping in mind the special needs of science and technical fields, the larger the university (up to a certain point), the more efficiently it can be operated.

It is not likely, however, that the average Chinese institution of higher education, which currently enrolls about 2,000 students, will quadruple or quintuple its size in the near future. But even more modest expansion in enrollment coupled with increases in student-teacher ratios would yield significant reductions in unit costs (Table 8).

For example, the agriculture-related colleges currently have an enrollment of 1,888 students, and the simulated projections for colleges with an enrollment of 2,000 and an STR of 3.2 indicate an average recurrent cost of Y 1,372. If the enrollment doubled, the cost declines to 1,146, a savings of 16 percent. If the STR alone is increased to 8.0, the cost is Y 1,186, a savings of 13 percent. However, if both the enrollment and STR are increased to these levels, the cost falls to Y 961, or a 30 percent savings. Similarly, if the science and technology colleges (average size is currently 2,604) were increased from 2,000 to 4,000 and the STR nearly doubled from 4.1 to 8.0, the savings would be 30 percent. If the enrollment were expanded to 6,000 with the STR at 8.0, the savings would 36 percent. For normal schools, the costs would be reduced by 29 percent by raising the size from 2,000 (average size is currently 1,922) to 4,000 students and extending the current average STR of 6.3 to 8.0. In each of these simulated cases, increasing the STR to 12.0 would realize savings in the range of 45 percent. Cost reductions continue as the size of the institutions increases to 8,000 and 10,000 students, but fall off after that.

By fields of study, the expansion should target science, technical, engineering, management, health, and education. Currently, the rates of technicians and engineers in the labor force in key sectors such as manufacturing, energy, and transportation are quite low (.56 percent) by world standards. If China is to meet its challenges in a rapidly expanding service economy, it will require preparing between 5.5 million to 9.6 million technicians and engineers (the number is

Table 8. Simulated Cost Projection for Selected Types of Universities (in yuan)

Avg. Enrl.	Agriculture-Related STR			Science & Technology STR			Economics, Finance, Law, Political Science STR			Comprehensive STR			Normal STR			Medical STR		
	3.2	8.0	12.0	4.1	8.0	12.0	8.3	8.0	12.0	6.5	8.0	12.0	6.3	8.0	12.0	5.0	8.0	12.0
1,000	1,823	1,637	1,483	1,712	1,562	1,407	1,274	1,286	1,132	1,441	1,383	1,228	1,449	1,383	1,228	2,734	2,618	2,464
2,000	1,372	1,186	1,032	1,261	1,111	956	823	835	681	989	932	777	998	932	777	2,282	2,167	2,012
4,000	1,146	961	806	1,036	885	730	598	609	455	764	706	551	772	706	552	2,057	1,941	1,787
6,000	1,071	886	731	960	810	655	523	534	380	689	631	476	697	631	477	1,982	1,866	1,712
8,000	1,033	848	693	923	772	618	485	497	342	651	593	439	659	594	439	1,944	1,829	1,674

Source: Data extracted from World Bank, *China: Management and Finance of Higher Education.* (Washington, D.C.: World Bank, 1986), pp. 38–40.

[a] Student-Teacher Ratio

smaller, between 2.3 million to 4.0 million, using more conservative approaches).

For professional personnel in economics and finance, the needs are similar, requiring an increase of 27 million workers at the minimum, that is, increases from a minimum of 1.5 percent of the labor force to 2.3 percent or as high as 4.3 percent depending on the projection model. Shortages of graduate trained economists and finance professionals are even more acute, and even with high rates of growth at the undergraduate level, it is not likely that China will meet its target of producing a million graduate degrees in these fields by the end of the decade. Instead, companies and government agencies will have to rely on more informal alternatives like on-the-job training and non-degree continuing education.

In any case, it is clear that in terms of recurrent unit costs, larger universities can be operated more efficiently than smaller ones, and China should use the institutional expansion rather than the institutional multiplication model for increasing enrollments. Also, mergers and consolidations should be considered, especially for small colleges and large institutions in the same locale.

Reorganization and Institutional Innovations

To support higher education's key role in the pursuit of economic rejuvenation, the CCP announced in its 1985 *Decision on the Reform of the Educational System*:

> The key to success in the reform of the higher educational system . . . is to change the management system of excessive government control over the institutions of higher learning, expand the powers of decision-making of the institutions of higher learning in school management . . . and enable the institutions of higher learning to have the initiative and ability to meet the needs of economic and social development.

Between 1985–1989, the momentum was shifting gradually toward institutional autonomy, but this was interrupted in the aftermath of June 4. Currently, organizational decision making remains highly centralized in China, with the presidents of the national universities reporting to the state education commission, the presidents of the specialized institutions reporting to the line ministries, and the presidents of the provincial or local universities reporting to the provincial or local authorities. Despite some recent loosening of vertical control, the institutions' prerogatives in teaching and research, financial management, and personnel administration are tightly circumscribed, stifling innovation and impeding institutional responsiveness to China's rapid socioeconomic transformations.

On campus, authority lines are often unclear and organizational structures and communication systems are informal and overlapping. Roles and responsibilities of university administrators are often ambiguous, causing personnel redundancies and other organizational inefficiencies. With the growth in size and complexity of Chinese universities, new organizational structures are needed to define authority and responsibility more clearly and make the institution more responsive to societal directions.

In particular, greater differentiation of executive authority under the office of president would improve organizational effectiveness, and at least three vice-presidential offices of academic affairs, administration, and university development should be considered.

Since the mid-1980s, lateral cooperation between the higher education institutions and other sectors of Chinese society has increased remarkably. Not only have universities and colleges increased cooperation with one another, but they have taken major initiatives to develop consortia with production units and the growing private sector in China. They have developed training programs for production units to meet various manpower needs, conducted contracted research, and provided various types of consultation services. Dozens of universities are engaged in new technology-based research and development projects. For example, Beijing University, Qinghua University, Beijing University of Technology, and Beijing Aeronautics and Astronautics University have established the Zhong-Guan-Cun New Technology Development Area. Sichuan University and Chengdu University of Science and Technology have set up the Chengdu New Technology Development area, and Southeast University in Jiangsu province has participated in the establishment of the Pukou Development Area.

Currently, nineteen Chinese higher education institutions have also established joint venture companies with communities by providing technology and key technical personnel. For example,

Beijing Aeronautics and Astronautics has established an automobile testing and inspection system with the Dongsheng township of Haidian district (Beijing). And Beijing University of Science and Technology set up a joint venture for a steel rolling mill with the local community in Shunyi county (Beijing).[3] These arrangements have enhanced the budgets of the universities. For example, Chengdu University of Electronic Technology generated Y 12,420,000 in 1989, which is 84.7 percent of its total income besides state appropriation. According to SEdC statistics, Chinese universities and colleges generated Y 505 million in 1986, Y 693 million in 1987, and Y 823 million in 1988 by providing these services. These activities have also significantly enhanced the earning power of the faculty, many of whom work as consultants for the private companies in their spare time. The potential for making substantial sums of money "moonlighting" is so strong, whether one in involved in one of these formal consortia or is simply freelancing, that some of the more enterprising professors have made enough to purchase private automobiles, even though their regular university salary is only about Y 5,000 per year (less than $1,000 U.S.).

Student Support

Before the enactment of the 1985 reform plan, the government provided full support for a student's university education, including tuition, fees, and lodging. In some fields, students even received free meals. This support totalled about 20 percent of the total higher education recurrent expenditure. In an important reform decision five years ago, the state proclaimed that it would no longer be "responsible for all cash outlays for universities and colleges."[4] Accordingly, state subsidies were reduced and moderate tuition charges were introduced (about Y 400). Students were expected to help pay part of their educational expense in work-study programs, and a new scholarship and loan program was set up to reward students with superior academic accomplishments, or those enrolled in teacher training or other high demand fields, or those pledged to work in the poorer, more remote regions. Also, "self-supported" students who obtained scores slightly below the minimum for acceptance on the admission examinations were admitted under higher tuition charges. Recently, students are now expected to contribute toward the cost of lodging, as the tendency toward declining state support becomes inexorable. Some report that these measures have had disproportionately adverse effects on the country's most needy students, for whom the costs of attending a university, especially one of the key institutions in the large cities, are become increasingly burdensome. Whether this will widen the gulf further between groups and regions is a growing concern.

Under a new policy effective in 1993, the government is encouraging Chinese universities to enroll more enterprise-sponsored and self-supported students for master's degree programs. Under the existing policy, 80,000 postgraduate students are supported entirely by the central government and are enrolled mainly in basic science research studies. The aim of the new policy is to shift the focus to more applied and professional areas of studies commensurate with the government's emphasis on technology and economic development. Until recently, graduate education has been gravely neglected in China, causing great shortages in manpower and talent. During the Open Door era, for example, Chinese universities have graduated less than 200,000 master's degrees and only 7,000 Ph.D.s. For the vast majority of university students the principal avenue for further specialization has been study abroad (*chuguo*), and the phenomenon of "brain drain" troubles many Chinese educational leaders. Many of the expatriates are top of the line scholars who have delayed their return to China indefinitely for both economic and political reasons. In any case, it remains to be seen whether recent initiatives will increase the mobility of university graduates, make further university study in China more attractive for China's most gifted scholars, and meet the country's critical need for trained professionals in engineering and business.

Another important innovation has been the emergence of private institutions of higher education in China (all private institutions were banned by Mao after 1949). The first was apparently Yanjing Huaqiao University which was established in Beijing in 1982 by an association of overseas Chinese. It admitted 140 students who paid about Y 250 for tuition and were enrolled in English language studies. Today, there are about 1,000 students who pay about Y 1,000 for tuition and major in English, tourist management, and clerical studies. Altogether, there are now seventeen private colleges and universities in Beijing alone. Elsewhere, well-known Hong Kong businessmen have established new private institutions like that of the new university in Shantou (Guangzhou province), founded by Li Ke-shing, which features more than 500 faculty. A new private college also opened in Shanghai with more than 17,000 students majoring in nine departments. In central Henan province, local officials and Chinese-Americans jointly established Huanghe (Yellow River) University, offering courses in economics, computer science, and American studies. Consistent with government's tendency to reduce the ratio of public expenditure for higher education, it is likely that "privatization" will become a major force during the decade ahead and provide the model for institutional autonomy and innovation.[5]

Improved Management of the Campus

Most Chinese universities are "self sufficient" organizations replete with faculty and staff apartment buildings, dining halls, schools for children of the employees, clinical and hospital facilities, factories, printing shops, motor pools, etc. Faced with running these enormous auxiliary enterprises, it is no wonder that Chinese university presidents typically describe their role as that of a "mayor" of a city rather than the leader of an academic enterprise. The president of Qinghua University, Liu Da, put it this way:

> My energy has not been spent in directly organizing teaching and scientific research in the university, but has been spent in dealing with administrative affairs relating to the housing, clothing, food, transportation, childbirth, retirement, sickness and death problems of the teachers, staff, workers, and students in the university. . . . It is not society which manages the universities but rather the universities which manage society.[6]

As much as 50 percent of the total useable space on many campuses is devoted to faculty housing and communal facilities. With the vigorous growth of the Chinese economy, alternatives to self-sufficiency exist in the form of new primary and secondary schools, health care facilities, and municipal housing, allowing the universities to convert communal space to classrooms and laboratories.

Another major problem concerns the maintenance and repair of facilities. Too frequently, maintenance of university buildings is deferred or, in some cases, totally ignored. Not surprisingly, new buildings (like libraries and classroom buildings erected with funds from Hong Kong benefactors) age so rapidly that they appear to be twenty years old rather than two years old. The backlog of maintenance and repair often runs as high as 12.5 percent of the university's plant replacement value, twenty-five times greater than that of comparable U.S. institutions. In sum, maintenance deferral represents a serious long-term problem in Chinese universities, creating exponential repair costs in the future. Each university should immediately establish a management maintenance schedule including preventive maintenance, facilities inspection, productivity standards, and work planning systems to prevent an impending crisis.

In addition to problems in facilities management, there are critical shortcomings in general management skills and management systems at Chinese universities. Besides lacking training programs in fiscal management and a higher education management preparation for middle-level and top-level leaders, the system of internal and external auditing of university accounts has not been implemented in China. Internal audit reports are critical for managers to review in detail the fiscal health of the institution. External audits are necessary for the SEdC, line ministries, and provincial bureaus for similar purposes.

Disparity in Funding by Regions

The contrasts are vivid between the most developed areas and the undeveloped areas. These disparities are reflected in the finance and support of higher education institutions in these regions. For example, the recurrent expenditure per students in Beijing is about Y 3,200, Y 3,283 in Shanghai, and Y 3,550 in Guangdong. By contrast, the expenditure per student in Jiangxi province is Y 1,905 and Y 2,122 in Anhui province. The regional disparities are also revealed in the number of students enrolled in higher education. In the country at large, there were 18.7 students per 10, 000 enrolled in higher education. In municipalities like Beijing and Shanghai the average was 136.5 and 98.8 respectively, compared to only 11.8 in Anhui, 9.1 in Guanxi, and 8.7 in Guizhou provinces. The incongruities are also geographic. In the "eastern region," which includes fewer provinces than the "non-eastern region," there are 579 institutions (out of 1,075 total) and 1,149,000 students, with a 55 percent share.[7]

At the same time, the rates of participation in higher education by males and females are not equal. The proportion of female students has fluctuated from about 27 percent in 1965 to 24 percent in 1978 to 34 percent in 1989, matching the highest ratio of 34 percent in 1974 (Table 9). Correspondingly, the proportion of female faculty has increased slightly from about 21 percent in 1965 to 25 percent in 1978 and 29 percent in 1989 (Table 10). Not surprisingly, the disparities are even greater by academic rank, with females accounting for only 4 percent of all full professorships in China as compared with 34 percent of lectureships. They hold 35 percent of administrative positions, but no data are available on the ratios by level of authority.

Table 9. Female Students in Regular Institutions of Higher Education in China

Year	Number	% of Total Enrolled
1947	27,600	17.8
1949	23,200	19.8
1965	181,300	26.9
1978	206,500	24.1
1983	324,900	26.9
1989	702,000	33.7

Source: Author's compilations based on *Achievement of Education in China*, 1949–83, and other years cited.

Table 10. Female Faculty in Chinese Higher Education

Year	Number	% of Total Enrolled
1950	1,900	11.0
1965	28,400	20.6
1978	52,400	25.4
1983	78,300	25.9
1989	114,000	28.8

Source: Author's compilations based on *Achievement of Education in China* 1949–83, and other years cited.

Low External Efficiency

External efficiency indicates the degree to which universities and colleges serve the labor market and the larger socioeconomic needs of Chinese society. In market economies, this can be measured by rate-of-return analysis, but in a social commodity system like China such measures are not applicable. In China, the job assignment process is controlled by the government and a centralized plan is used to assign college graduates to different jobs. In 1988, there was an experiment to change the system from a "one-way system" to a "two-way system" in which employers were asked to specify requirements and choose graduates. In 1990, however, the one-way system returned. The highly centralized planning system produces a mismatch between demand and supply. In some fields of study, supply of graduates exceeds demand, while the reverse is true in other fields. In sciences, basic science has too large a proportion, applied science too little. In engineering, there are far too many heavy engineering programs and too few light industry ones. In the humanities and social sciences, there are too few graduates in journalism, communication, library science, and management science. For example, in Guizhou, there is a surplus of almost 4,000 teachers of Chinese, mathematics, physics, and chemistry, but a shortage of 4,000 teachers of biology, English, history, and geography.

Declining Allocations

Although the total expenditure on higher education has increased faster than the increase in total public expenditure, the allocation in constant price has declined from Y 5.14 billion in 1986 to Y 4.40 billion in 1988. Inflation has further exacerbated the situation. Even in the early 1980s when the inflation rate was low (when the retail price index was 101.5 percent and cost of living index 102.0 percent), the cost of instructional materials rose rapidly. In Beijing, according to Min, from 1980 to 1985, the price of stationery and paper increased by almost 64 percent, laboratory materials by 66 percent, books and periodicals by 91 percent, and building maintenance materials and labor by 55 percent.[8] By 1985, the retail price index was up to 198.9 percent and the cost of living index was 111.9 percent, both of which soared to 118.5 percent and 120.7 percent in 1988. The inflation rate greatly reduced the purchasing power of university and college budgets and the real amount of funding available to the higher education system.

Strategies for Improvement in the 1990s

1. In light of the current climate of economic austerity and financial retrenchment, high priority should be given to improving internal efficiency to make the system more cost efficient and cost effective. Efficiency would be promoted by internal reorganization of universities and colleges in which small departments would be closed or merged, specialities broadened, program duplications eliminated, and more effective use made of staff and physical resources, especially increasing the student-teacher ratio and improving the rate utilization of classrooms and laboratories.
2. Enrollments in most institutions should be expanded (two or three times if possible) and student-teacher ratios raised to a minimum of 8.0 or 12.0 if possible. Furthermore, to improve economy of scale, small institutions need to be consolidated into larger ones. As pointed out earlier, raising the average size of institutions could result in substantial savings and allow the system to serve larger numbers of qualified students—students who are currently denied admission to the regular higher education sector. Such a step would require, however, unprecedented cooperation among the three governing structures (SEdC, central ministries, and provincial governments).
3. To reduce the fiscal difficulties, further cost sharing should be initiated in the form of increased tuition charges and reduced subsidies for student board and lodging. This would also allow the system to provide more student places.
4. Higher education institutions should be allowed to generate more funds by themselves. Universities can generate income through research contracts with industries, by providing technical consultation, and by training students at the workplace. Chinese universities are beginning to establish these links with the private sector, and they should be even more aggressive in developing these partnerships.
5. The structure should be rationalized to adjust enrollment quotas to each field of study and increasing quotas to those with higher demands for college graduates. Internally, specialties should be broadened to increase the flexibility and adaptability of graduates.
6. In China, there is a large unmet demand for higher education but a policy limiting the growth of the higher education sector because of financial constraints. Therefore, alternative provisions must be considered such as promoting non-state-run institutions of higher

education and further expansion of distant higher education and the TV university system.
7. Consistent with the 1985 education reform policy, institutions should be granted more autonomy and the power of the presidents increased to allow them to respond more quickly and creatively to societal priorities, improve efficiency and morale, and strengthen the intellectual foundations.
8. Management training is needed to improve maintenance of facilities and promote sound accounting practices, including internal and external audits of institutions. A higher education leadership institute should be formed in cities and regions to train administrators and their staffs in educational administration.

Coda

Since China embarked on its Open Door initiatives, Chinese higher education has shifted from a rigid state control model to a state supervision model. Organizationally, if not politically and academically, universities enjoy more autonomy than they did in the wake of the Cultural Revolution, particularly in student admissions, financial management and revenue enhancement, personnel administration, and multi-lateral relations and international linkages. Relaxation of state control has been accompanied by increases in non-governmental forms of support for higher education. In 1990, support from private enterprises was 6.9 percent of all higher education revenues, up from 6.2 percent the previous year, and the ratio from fees and taxes stood at more than 10 percent. At the same time, however, the higher education system faces enormous challenges. The growth rate in higher education is not commensurate with its size (despite recent stabilizations), or with its expectations for leading China's economic advance into the next century. University graduates face uncertain job prospects as better paying jobs in the so-called private sector are filled by those with much less academic preparation. On many campuses, a malaise infects student behavior and attitudes about the future, sublimated momentarily perhaps by dreams of economic success or study abroad. Moreover, paths to advancement for younger faculty are blocked by archaic seniority policies and an academic career has lost a good deal of its Confucian luster. Academic inbreeding (*jinqin fanzhi*) and patronage among faculty act as an impediment to the flow of new ideas and innovation. Similarly, the organizational structure remains excessively stratified, stifling modern management practices and impeding strategies to promote greater cost efficiency.

Nevertheless, commensurate with the country's vast yet untapped potential, Chinese higher education possesses the ingredients to meet these formidable challenges. Chinese universities must maintain the dynamism of the reforms and innovations that emerged in the late 1970s and continue to modernize the funding system and the organizational configurations without sacrificing the distinctive features of their magnificent intellectual and aesthetic heritage.

NOTES

1. Ruiqing Du. *Chinese Higher Education: A Decade of Reform and Development (1978–1988)*. (New York: St. Martin's Press, 1992), p. xi.

2. From materials prepared by Weifang Min for the forthcoming book by Richard Hartnett and Weifang Min, *The History and Development of Chinese Higher Education*.

3. From information provided by Weifang Min in "Higher Education Institutions and Community Development in China." Paper presented at the International Conference on Education, Social Change, and Regional Development, July 23–25, University of Hong Kong.

4. *Beijing Review*, 34 (Aug. 24, 1987): 6.

5. Ruiqing Du. *Op. cit.*, pp. 39–40.

6. Jurgen Henze. "Higher Education: The Tension Between Quality and Equality," *Contemporary Chinese Education*. Edited by Ruth Hayhoe. (Armonk, N.Y.: M.E. Sharpe, 1984), p.132.

7. Leslie nai-Kwai Lo. "The Irony of Reform in Higher Education in Mainland China." *Issues and Studies*, 25 (Nov. 1989): 29–32.

8. Weigang Min. "Higher Education Finance in China: Current Constraints and Strategies for the 1990s." *Higher Education*, 21 (1991): 151–161.

ADDITIONAL SOURCES

Achievement of Education in China: Statistics, 1949–1983. Department of Planning, Ministry of Education of China. (Beijing: People's Education Press, 1984).

Achievement of Education in China: Statistics, 1984–1989. Department of Planning, State Education Commission. (Beijing: People's Education Press, 1989).

Keyong Cai and Wei Zhao. "Dui woguo gaojiao cunci jiegude tansuo" [Explorations of our country's higher education structure by level]. Edited by Keming Hao and Yongquan Wang. *Zhongguo Gaodeng Jiaoyu Jiegou Yanjiu* [Studies of the Structure of Chinese Higher Education]. (Beijing: People's Education Press, 1987).

Keyong Cai. *Gaideng Jiaoyu Jianshi* [A Short History of Higher Education]. (Wuhan, China: Huazhong College of Science and Technology Press, 1982).

John Fairbank and Edwin O. Reischauer. *China: Transition and Transformation*. (Boston: Houghton Mifflin Company, 1978).

K. Hao and L. Zhang. "On the Reform in the Structure of Chinese Higher Education." *Jiaoyu Yanjiu* [Journal of Educational Research]. (December 1987): 3–17.

K. Hao and Y. Wang. *Research on the Structure of Chinese Higher Education*. (Beijing: People's Education Press, 1987).

Keming Hao and Yongquan Wang, eds. *Zhongguo Gaodeng Jiaoyu Jiegou Yanjiu* [Studies of the Structure of Chinese Higher Education]. (Beijing: People's Education Press, 1987).

Ruth Hayhoe. *Chinese Universities and the Open Door*. (Armonk, New York: M.E. Sharpe, Inc., 1989).

Juergen Henze. "Higher education: The tension between quality and equality." Edited by Ruth Hayhoe. *Contemporary Chinese Education*. (Armonk, New York: M.E. Sharpe, Inc., 1984).

Huang Shiqi. "Contemporary educational relations with the industrialized world: A Chinese view." Edited by Ruth Hayhoe and Marianne Bastid. *China's Education and the Industrialized World*. (Armonk, New York: M.E. Sharpe, Inc., 1984).

Li Li. "Higher education: Reforming and restructuring the system." *Beijing Review*, 31, no. 24 (1988): 25–30.

Y. Li. "Research on Economics of Education in China in the Past Ten Years: Review and Future Prospect. *Jiaoyu Yanjiu* [Journal of Educational Research]. (November 1988): 23–29.

Leslie Nai-Kwai Lo Lo. "The Irony of Reform in Higher Education in Mainland China." *Issues and Studies*, 25 (November 1989): 12–54.

Statistical Yearbook of China 1988. (State Statistics Bureau. Beijing, 1989).

J. Tan and A. Mingat. "Educational Development in Asia: A Comparative Study Focusing on Cost and Financing Issues." (Washington, D.C.: Technical Department Asian Region. The World Bank, 1989).

Y. Wang. "The Structure and Governance of Chinese Higher Education." *The Role of Government in Asian Higher Education.* (Hiroshima, Japan: Research Institute of Higher Education, Hiroshima University, 1988).

TOWARD UNDERSTANDING THE ECONOMICS OF AFRICAN HIGHER EDUCATION

Teshome G. Wagaw

Introduction

Higher education in Africa for the purpose of this chapter is defined as those postsecondary institutions of four years or more duration or their equivalent. Sub-college institutions are not included unless otherwise specified. The term "economy" goes beyond the budgetary and financial components to include issues of quality and efficiency of facilities, equipment, and personnel utilization, enrollment, admission, and graduation rates of students, as well as the extent of deployment of the graduates of these institution in the development programs of the respective societies.

Institutions of higher learning in Africa, as anywhere else, are considered to be the nerve centers of modernization. They represent the highest expression of a society's search for continued renewal, enlightenment, growth, and fulfillment. Among other things, these institution train, certify, and otherwise equip some of the sharpest minds for leadership roles in government, business, industry, the professions, the arts, and literature. The number of people thus equipped and certified is still relatively very small, but their potential and actual power and influence in society are disproportionately very high. It is not, therefore, surprising that these centers of higher learning are looked upon with hope, admiration, awe, fear, and even with suspicion by young and old, and particularly by actual and aspiring politicians.

For Africa, such sentiments and high expectation are summed up in the words of Julius Nyerere, the highly respected former president of Tanzania. As the first chancellor of the then East Africa University he sought to outline as clearly as possible the missions and practices of the young institution. He said:

> We must, and do demand that this University take an active part in the social revolution we are engineering. I am not telling the University to become a center of opposition to the elected Governments. On the contrary, the University belongs to the people and must serve their wishes. But if the University is to be of any benefit to the people or their government, then it must be a center of objective thinking; and it must accept all the responsibilities which go with that position.

Nyerere goes on to add that the university must maintain:

> ... the spirit of truth; it must be as objective and scientific as possible, and must fight prejudice of all kinds, at all times, and at all places.... The University must think, and force us to think in terms of humanity—not any sectorial interests. Its members must guard against their own prejudices as well as ours.[1]

These are formidable responsibilities for the emerging institution to think about—responsiblity, loyalty to the nation, truthfulness, objectivity, involvement, inclusivity, and humanness. Other African leaders of the time more or less expressed similar sentiments for their respective institutions of higher learning.[2] Thirty years later we can observe the progress they have made, the roads they have traversed, and the new challenges they have confronted as they sought to maintain the ideals set out for them. It is not a perfect record that we find, but that is not grounds for pessimism either.

In societies such as those found in much of Africa where most of the governance is nondemocratic, some African institutions, through the students and teachers, have taken it upon themselves to analyze and criticize the shortcomings of politicians from time to time. Often these actions are held against them, and sometimes the host institution pays a heavy price in the form of budget cuts or worse.

Higher education in its present form is new to the African scene. However, ancient models are not entirely lacking. The University of Sankore in Timbuktu flourished in the sixteenth century as a center for scholarship and learning in the areas of law, philosophy, and theology. Another institution of similar importance which may be considered as part of Africa is Al-Azhar University in Cairo, which has been in existence for more than a thousand years. This institution became well known for the study of Islamic religion and law and still continues to function even as it expands and modernizes its scope by embracing other branches of study. In Ethiopia, another ancient land, there were centers of higher studies sponsored by the Ethiopian Orthodox Church, the national church, under its system of monasteries, scattered over the highlands where specialists in religious and canon law as well as some of the high-level state functionaries were trained, and where traditional scholarship was nurtured and supported. In recent times, in Sierra Leone, the Church Missionary Society of London founded Fourah Bay College in 1827 as a center for Christian religious studies. In the aftermath of World War II, that institution formed the basis of a state university. Other institutions of higher learning included two in Nigeria and another in Uganda. These latter institutions were established under the tutelage of colonial powers and provided rudimentary instruction in law and the humanities as well as some vocational fields.

For the most part, however, the more than eighty colleges and universities now operating in Sub-Saharan Africa came into being after political independence was attained beginning in the late 1950s. From 1961 to 1982, the development of African institutions of higher learning, both in numbers and structural program complexity, was very significant.[3] By 1980 the number of universities increased from thirty-two in twenty-three countries to eighty in forty-three countries. Fifty of these institutions are located in Arabic and English speaking countries, and the rest are found in francophone, lusophone, and other countries.

By world standards, because of their short history, enrollment rates in African universities are still very small, under one percent on the average. However, taking 1965 as the first year of deliberate expansion of university education, the rate of growth since that time has exceeded that of any other region of the world and has progressed at a much faster rate than the lower levels of the continent's education systems. The number of university students per 100,000 inhabitants doubled or tripled in two-thirds of the countries over the period 1970 to 1980. In most of the remaining countries there was not significant change, and in four of the smaller countries there was a decline. In terms of regions within the continent, the North African countries, led by Egypt, rank first, followed by West Central, and East Africa in that order. At this writing, eight of the fifty-one African countries do not have universities. Recent censuses indicate that the number of university students as a proportion of the relevant age group in each country is one percent for more than half of the countries in 1980, while in 1970 this proportion was exceeded in only about nine countries. Egypt, Libya, Congo, Tunisia, and Morocco (except for Congo, all of these are North African countries) lead the rest of the countries in this comparison with 13.7, 5.8, 5.2, 4.8, and 4.8 percent respectively. Many of the countries of the region would expand enrollment, and there is obviously a demand for it, but financial constraints have become severe. It is to the economic aspect of higher institutions that the rest of the analysis of this paper is directed.

Financing Higher Education

In Africa, most of the responsibility for the control, financing, and maintenance of higher education comes under government purview. At the beginning this was intentional. In most of the countries on which African universities were modeled, that was the way it was done. In addition, African countries had just come out from long domination under the colonial yoke, and they would not have trusted non-government institutions with shaping the highest level of intellectuals and future leaders. At the time the policies were laid out in the 1960s, much of the thinking at the world level was in support of welfarism, and African policy makers did not particularly feel they were out of bounds in this regard. This is understandable. Whether developed or underdeveloped, in all societies, governments support higher education because doing so is in the national interest. The amount, manner, and purpose of subsidization varies from country to country, but the national government must always stand behind the training of the leaders in society, with some provision for non-governmental bodies to contribute whatever they can.

Further, since there was a dire need for a highly trained workforce at all levels of national life, there was little alternative than for these countries, with the cooperation of their international allies, to

The Economics of African Higher Education

commit themselves to providing access to free higher education, at home or abroad, to qualified young people. In the course of a relatively brief time, the provision of free education resulted in a relative enrollment explosion, for higher education came to be perceived by the individuals as a sure passport to government employment opportunity, high salary, prestige, and social mobility. Increasingly, successful matriculants came to view university admission as a matter of right rather than privilege. Tuition, fees, board, and lodging facilities were provided free to the student. In most countries, even faculty housing was provided free.

Another precedent was established at that stage. Due to the way that the educational systems were structured at the grade school levels and the nature of the examination systems that led to university or college admission, most successful matriculants came from urban-based, wealthy segments of society. As a rule, the better primary and especially secondary schools were located in the major towns and cities. Whether public or private, the graduates of such schools, whose families were often relatively well off financially, had a much better chance of getting admitted to colleges and universities. On the other hand, people from the rural-based schools (where the vast majority of the people live), which by definition were less endowed with qualified teachers and adequate facilities, and women and other traditionally suppressed linguistic or religious minorities, were left out of the universities.

This phenomena, in addition to making colleges and universities enclaves of the elite and privileged who are destined to rule over the majority, has, economically speaking, a regressive effect since it subsidizes the education of the wealthy. It is also questionable whether such graduates of the universities will be the ones who will dedicate their lives to the uplifting of the poor, rural African population out of the tremendous economic, political, and cultural abyss in which they find themselves. Thus, in terms of equity and suitability for development, the system of financing higher education remains very poor by indirectly discriminating against the majority of society. The merit of such practice, if there is one, must be found elsewhere in terms of creating a highly qualified workforce for social development.[4]

There are a number of other difficult problems. While enrollment growth is expanding (eight-fold between 1960 and 1980), the economies of most of the countries remain stagnant or, relative to demographic growth, have regressed. The universities' share of government budgetary allocations is declining generally in all but a few West African countries. In terms of per-student costs relative to percentage of gross domestic product (GDP) per capita, the economic burden of higher education in African countries is substantially higher than in any other developing region. For instance, the 1979 per capita GDP was $480 for countries in Sub-Saharan Africa. The cost per student per year of higher education was $4,185 which translates into costs that are 872 percent per student of the GNP per capita income. Contrast this with costs that are 22 percent of GDP for a primary school student. It has been estimated that in Sub-Saharan African countries the incomes of more than nine workers with average annual earning are required to support one student in an institution of higher learning per year. To put it another way, forty-eight children are deprived of places in primary schools for each student attending a higher education institution. This gross imbalance can hardly be tolerated for long.[5]

These unit costs of higher education are, as pointed out earlier, higher than the average for developed countries and much higher than the average for Asian and Latin American countries. At the same time, while many of the other developing nations are increasingly improving access to higher education for high school graduates, African countries, with the exception of northern Africa, lag substantially behind all developing countries. Projection to the year 2000 shows an even more troubling prospect. If African countries are spending beyond their limit even for relatively few spaces in higher education, and the social and personal demand for expansion is increasing, how should they respond to meet these challenges?

Diversifying the Sources of Financial Support

Not surprisingly, institutions of higher learning have received sharp criticism from both external and internal sources. Some criticism is uniquely applicable to the African realities, but other criticism has been leveled at institutions of a similar nature. Criticism includes: elitism, isolation, encouraging or supporting an attitude of self-importance among the students rather than fostering the ideals of

The Economics of African Higher Education 157

humility and a desire for community service, encouraging the transfer of Western ideology at the expense of indigenous ideology, facilitating social stratification, operating as if they are grafted onto the societies rather than growing out of them, and the like.[6] The institutions are also blamed for contributing to political instability, being academically oriented at the expense of being practically involved in solving the problems of society, being driven by the "diploma disease" on the part of students and their parents rather than being driven by societal or national needs, draining scarce resources from the lower sector of education which is supposedly more important and cost effective, and the like. We will not spend much time here analyzing the merits or lack thereof of criticisms such as these. Suffice it to say that even though some of these accusations may be true, for a young institution trying to function in the framework of traditional, undeveloped societies, such criticism is often unhelpful. In this kind of critical climate, attracting additional moral and financial resources from government or outside is very difficult.

There is no denying that higher education institutions are very expensive; their unit costs are high compared with the lower grades in the education system. But once again the question may be raised, would the enduring interests of society be better served without such institutions? The answer at least for most thoughtful persons is a resounding "no!" At the same time it must be granted that the institutions must be ever vigilant to see to it that the dollars entrusted to them are well spent and that other than traditional sources of financing are identified, cultivated, and utilized. We will turn to this later.

Whether expressed in aggregate (GNP) terms or on the basis of per capita income, the economic condition for most African countries has not been very healthy over the last couple of decades. The economies of most are either stagnant or regressing, even as demands for increased budgetary allocation from other sectors of national life than higher education are growing. Foreign aid in the form of loans, grants, or concessions are dwindling fast. Most of the students themselves are not able to pay for their education; in most of the region, the population continues to grow at a very unacceptable rate. Drought, famine, and disease (including AIDS) contribute to the problem of resource shortage. The past has been hard, but the future looks even harder unless some drastic action is taken.

Institutions of higher learning and their governments must take strong measures to stop the erosion and downward slide of financial support. The measures that need to be taken may include identifying new sources of income and a more efficient use of those already available. It is not going to be easy to make significant progress in both areas, but progress must be made. Internally, the institutions can maximize efficiency if they take actions to curtail student wastage in the form of dropouts or class repetitions. There are differences from country to country, and improvements have been noticeable in some instances, but according to a World Bank report, student wastage in African countries remains unacceptably high. [7]

At the next level, the teacher-student ratio as well as class size and student contact hours need to be significantly increased, the quality and quantity of research accelerated, and the service to the community by students and faculty improved. Additional measures that need to be taken in order to improve the internal efficiency of the institution include: intensive utilization of facilities, equipment, and if necessary, use of these throughout the calendar year.

Other measures, sometimes known as external indicators of efficiency, include the impact these institutions make on the economy and society as a whole. The instrument used to measure this efficiency is cost-benefit analysis. In spite of the many constraints that may be leveled at this kind of approach, there is no denying it has some value when used wisely. At any rate, the indicators for this instrument include full employment, unemployment, under employment, workforce shortages, quality and efficiency of graduates at work, the amount and relevance of research to national needs, and the like.

The measures enumerated are valuable and should be considered in the search for institutional efficiency. But they have significant shortcomings. For instance, in the broad arenas of teaching and research, the universities must be held accountable. But how in the world are they going to control the employment policy of the country? Productivity in work is in part determined by the motivation of the individual, the general work environment prevailing in the office or plant, and the reward system provided. In other words, worker productivity is a function, not only of the quality of training, for which the universities are responsible, but also of the working environment and the reward system, whose locus of control is outside the universities. In other words, the tools of measuring efficiency by external criteria may be useful in as much as they provide some notion regarding the utilization of trained workforce. But they have as much limitation as utility. Let us now try to relate these measures to the African realities.

In spite of the rapid growth in enrollment over the past twenty-five years, the absolute number of students is still low, except perhaps in Nigeria. In thirteen of the twenty-three countries surveyed in the 1980s, for instance, enrollment was below 4,500 in many of the universities surveyed. The proportion of total enrollment in science subjects, contrary to government desire, was very low—22 percent or lower. Still, the determination to increase enrollment in the sciences, engineering, and subject studies persists. But again, these subjects are more costly, and they require students with strong mathematics and science backgrounds.[8]

As far as the labor market is concerned, there is evidence of growing unemployment and underemployment.[9] Some countries, such as Ethiopia, Egypt, Mali, Somalia, and Guinea at one time had low unemployment due to government guarantee of employment for all graduates. Here again, the picture is complicated by the mix of the graduates, by the high salary that graduates demand, by the weak economy, and by individual motivation levels.[10]

African institutions of higher learning have recently been suffering for lack of sufficient resources. A visit to some of the libraries, classrooms, and laboratories, and a talk with some of the responsible faculty and administrators can convince one that they are in dire difficulty.[11] But demand for expansion continues. This pressure for expansion is coming from two sources. As the school system expands, more youth will graduate from the high schools. Many of these are going to seek admission to postsecondary schools, including universities. For the government, it will be politically impossible to control this very successfully. Social demand will also continue to grow because there is real need for more highly trained, educated people in administration, technical, and industrial fields. So for these combined reasons the universities will have to expand rapidly. But from where will the funds come?

The governmental sources are taxed to their limits even as more demands are made on them from other sectors of the economy. The government, of course, can make across-the-board cuts in funding and spread the result thin over larger areas. But this will further weaken the capability of the institutions to produce quality output.

The remaining option, the ardent quest of practically all institutions of higher learning of developing and many developed nations, is to increase revenues from non-government sources.[12] For Africans, this includes imposing user fees on students and their parents; initiating loan schemes where students may borrow and then pay back once they begin working or pay back at least in part in the form of services in critical areas of national priority; asking non-public institutions and organizations to contribute directly; convincing international organizations to continue or even increase their level of support, and running business ventures that produce income. Some of these have already been tried in a number of African countries.[13] Levying user fees on those who can afford it or on their parents and guardians is desirable and makes economic and moral sense. But it has proved extremely difficult to implement. Countries such as Ethiopia, Nigeria, and perhaps others have tried and failed.[14] In all such instances, students resisted and went to the streets to demonstrate their displeasure. In all cases the governments backed down.

The loan schemes have been talked about a lot among governments, and among bilateral and international donors. So far, loans have proved very difficult to implement. Corporation and business people have the means to contribute, but so far they have not done so to a meaningful extent.[15] Perhaps in the future they may do so if it is in their corporate interest and the government provides some kind of incentives such as tax deductions. It needs hard selling. I do not think the international community will increase its contribution to this particular sector in the foreseeable future. If anything, contribution from this source will shrink.[16] Product selling is possible, but it requires a lot of commitment to initiate and administer. Whether in the foreseeable future the universities and their governments will have the vision, the drive, and the tenacity to initiate and carry out some of the activities remains to be seen. In the meanwhile, due to lack of adequate financial support, the institutions of higher learning in Africa are hurting very deeply.

Institutional Economy and Public Relations

Part of the success of attracting moral or financial support from all possible sources is a function not only of how the universities perform but also how they are perceived to discharge their function. The former is substantive, the latter is appearance, but in the final analysis and for the good health of the institution, both areas have to be addressed. The African universities are still young and are not well understood by the mostly rural public community of their respective societies, and this lack may make them vulnerable to attack; the international community has its own agenda, and expectations which are not always in congruence with the goals of the institutions; and the educated class which is supposed to be sympathetic is still a tiny minority. The politicians have their own agenda, which is not always in line with the enduring interest of the institution. There is, therefore, a balancing act required of the leadership of the institutions. The enthusiasm that prevailed in the early 1960s and 1970s in support of higher education is changing in the 1980s and 1990s. Unless there begins to be a regeneration of support from many quarters, institutions of higher learning may be relegated to a second place position or starved out to the point of being useless and be replaced by other, inferior types of institutions.

Even now, the institutions are being told by economists that investment in primary education yields greater economic return than does investment in secondary education, and that higher education is the least cost effective of them all. It is argued, for instance, that investment in primary education is relatively cheap and is justifiable from the point of view of equity because it reaches the poorest of the population inexpensively; it overcomes the major weakness associated with investment in higher education by contributing to enormous economic growth, equity, and the alleviation of poverty. Governments, with the advice of international agencies, are now shifting their policy priorities and budgetary allocations to support of primary, secondary (technical-vocational or comprehensive education), and postsecondary non-university institutions.

While such a change is fraught with grave methodological and philosophical problems and may not be taken at face value by reasonable people, it may be used by some as ammunition to withhold support. These arguments in favor of such a program are misleading.

While the desire of governments to search for better alternatives to higher education in a quest for economic or human resources development is understandable, there is the danger of overlooking the long-term interest of societies for short-term gains. It must be kept in mind that it is the universities which can develop the intellectual pool for all sectors of life by establishing regular departments, by providing outreach services to business, government, and the peasantry, and by leading in research and dissemination of knowledge in the physical as well as social sciences and technology. Universities also set the intellectual, cultural, as well as ethical tone of their countries. Therefore, societies need institutions of higher learning, but they cannot write them blank checks. Institutions of higher learning must be ever sensitive to the other legitimate societal concerns including equity of access, efficiency, and cost effectiveness.

While seeking additional moral and budgetary support from all sources is necessary, institutions of higher learning need to take effective measures to make themselves as cost effective as possible and must appear as such to their publics. There is need to improve upon the effective utilization of physical and human resources at their disposal. Wastage in the form of student dropout and class repetition are very high. Other areas that need improvement are class size (by and large an optimum enrollment must be maintained to realize savings), teacher contact hours, and the intensive use of classrooms, laboratories, and other physical facilities.

A number of African countries still maintain the colonial legacy of providing dormitory facilities not only for students but for faculty and staff as well. Some even provide for periodical leaves of absence for faculty which can be spent in England or France as a matter of course. While it may be considered desirable from a personal and even professional point of view to provide such amenities, the practice is too costly and totally insupportable given the existing financial conditions of the continent. Further, higher education must assume that it works in close cooperation and understanding with national goals regarding the training of a sufficiently high-level workforce with the appropriate mix of skills.[17] This entails, among other things, close involvement of faculty in the planning activities of governments. But it is a two-way road here. Government bureaucrats must realize that the universities and colleges are a reservoir of rich human talents which await full utilization. As often happens, some people in government are often

The Economics of African Higher Education 163

unwilling to invite these talents to be involved. There seems to be some suspicion or fear on the part of these officials lest the faculty take over their operation or expose to the world some of their bureaucracy inefficiencies, and even corruptions.[18]

Equity of access to higher education is a real problem in Africa. In the years immediately preceding 1980 (latest figures available), the proportion of women students exceeded 20 percent in only about half of the countries. For the rest, the percentage of women students was between ten and twenty. In addition, female students tended to drop out earlier than men, and in terms of choice of field of studies, they tended to concentrate in the social and teaching sciences, followed by the health professions. In universities that offer both graduate and undergraduate programs, the number of female students at the graduate level remains very low. Considering the enormous role women play in the African economy in general and in the family in particular, the neglect of this vital segment of the population is inexcusable.[19]

Nearly 80 percent of the African people still live in the rural areas. Young people from the rural areas are still underrepresented in the universities. There are many reasons for this, such as the poor quality of the secondary or primary schools, the need for rural youth to stay home to help out the family, and the like. But such problems are not impossible to remedy. It is important to add here that one aspect of the economy of higher education is the extent to which it endeavors to develop the talents of all segments of society in a fair and equitable manner consistent with the established criteria of excellence. It is also axiomatic that talents exist among the rural youth—males, females, and people of all religious and ethnic backgrounds. In fact, it has been shown that people of rural background are the ones most likely to go back to their home areas to help once they have completed their training.

Still another area of economic life the institutions of higher education must attend to is the desire of society to produce more educated people in the technical and scientific fields. While we may question the methods of arriving at certain figures, it is obvious that there is a need to produce a workforce capable of carrying out challenging responsibilities in vital technical and scientific areas of development. The 1961 plans for African higher education had recommended a ratio of 60 to 40 percent in favor of the technical and science fields, a goal for the most part still unrealized by 1992. Over the last three decades there has been a noticeable shift from the social sciences and humanities into the desired technical and scientific areas. Still, because of deficient backgrounds at the earlier levels of education due to lack of scientific equipment, facilities, and qualified teachers, the natural sciences and engineering fields attract relatively few students in most of these countries. African states have yet to come to grips with the fundamental causes underlying this problem. Perhaps one solution would be to let the free market operate by rewarding graduates differentially according to their field of interest. Another way, perhaps the better way, is to strengthen the curricula and the teaching skills in the sciences and in technical fields at the lower levels of the education system.

Together with the efficient use of resources, mention must be made of the brain transfer, brain overflow, or brain drain phenomenon. In 1963, the Tananarive Conference on higher education recommended that, as African universities developed, most students be trained in their home countries, or at least within Africa. According to that plan, by 1980 only 5 to 10 percent would be studying abroad. However, in 1979–80, an estimated 159,800 students were pursing their studies overseas. This was a dramatic increase over 1974–75 when the figure was 99,700. That number of Africans studying abroad in 1979–80 represented about a quarter of the total student body, indicating that for a variety of reasons—prestige, better study facilities and academic environment, attractive monetary rewards upon graduation, etc.— African students, whether supported by their governments, international or private organizations, or individuals, continued to proceed abroad. The concern of the home governments, as noted elsewhere, is whether these students will return home, and if they do, whether they will be over-qualified or unqualified to fulfill the urgent development needs of their countries, and whether their training will lead to long-range political implications. Definitive answers to many such questions await further study. Suffice it to say that increasingly the vast majority of graduates are either forced or choose to stay outside of their own countries.[20] Their eventual return at a later date is very doubtful.

Mention also needs to made here regarding the brain drain among those highly educated individuals who are leaving Africa in search of better economic opportunity, to escape political persecutions, or in search of professional fulfillment. There is also evidence that those who leave the continent are some of the most ambitious and better qualified who are able to sell their skills in the international market. It is unlikely that the trend will reverse itself soon. What this means, among other things, is that the countries thus affected will be further impoverished in many ways—economically, culturally, and politically. Remedies should be found to stop the drain.

In concluding this section, it must be noted that in general, the enrollment growth in African institutions of higher learning, although still low by world standards, has been significant. African states are deservedly proud of their commitments of vast amounts of precious resources to this venture. But it is clear also that because of social and student demand, the institutions will be forced to expand, and that present financial outlays are becoming inadequate to cover the expenses of a fast expanding system, especially when the economies in many of the countries remain stagnant or are regressing.

Conclusion

African institutions of higher learning have been accused of being rigid, unimaginative, and imitative, following the metropolitan approaches designed for other societies at other times under different socioeconomic and political conditions. These and similar charges contain some elements of truth. However, most African institutions of higher learning, after drawing their initial inspiration from European or North American models, have built their own traditions, values, and approaches while remaining mindful of their obligation to global standards of excellence in scholarship and the dissemination of knowledge. This is a natural and highly desirable development, for the interests of Africa and the world will, in the long run, be better served by African research and teaching conducted by educated Africans rather than by perpetuation of the "dark continent" myths that have been spread for centuries by those external to African conditions.

Nevertheless, the qualitative aspects of African and other systems of higher education should be continually examined. In the African context, the qualitative question may be assessed by examining the role of the institutions in (1) the development of high-level personnel for the various sectors of national life, (2) the development of indigenous science and technology, (3) the safeguarding and expansion of African cultures, and (4) the revitalization of the educational system.

As anywhere else, the primary role of African institutions of higher learning has always been the imparting of knowledge, skills, and attitudes at the highest level. It is from the resulting pool of qualified people that the political, economic, cultural, and spiritual leadership has been drawn. For too long in Africa, however, such leadership has been imposed from Europe by Europeans with little regard for the wishes or interests of the local people. As a result, when African countries gained their independence there were only 142,000 university students in the whole continent, and many countries had only twenty or so university graduates. In addition, even as late as 1960, the few African universities, which were then often little more than faculties or institutes in the early stages of development, confined themselves to the teaching of the humanities and the law. Even after independence this imbalance persisted for some time despite accusations that the universities were ivory towers, unresponsive, even irrelevant, to the urgent development needs of the respective societies.

In the industrialized countries, higher education developed in step with social and economic evolution, which was accelerated first by the industrial revolution, then by scientific and technological breakthroughs. In most instances, these countries were fortunate enough to find themselves equipped simultaneously with academic training facilities on the one hand, and political, administrative, and socioeconomic infrastructures, and production potential on the other. So, for the most part, the primary question for these countries was, and still is, matching training needs to socioeconomic requirements or correlating the needs of the production sector with the educational system. For African institutions of higher learning, the problem of correlating the production sector with education is more complex and problematic.

As far as training is concerned, the institutions of higher learning should not only ascertain the whole range of African development needs, based on solid knowledge of local and national environments, but also their educational programs should correspond to development goals that help communities solve their basic and practical problems. The primary aim, then, of the universities and other institutions which are more specifically designed to address practical problems is to develop a new breed of dedicated high-level personnel which breaks

The Economics of African Higher Education 167

away from the traditional, primarily academic education inherited from the colonial past. At the same time, African institutions of higher learning realize that the requirements of Africa do not absolve them from their obligation to maintain their fair share of the world currency of excellence in the creation and dissemination of knowledge. Thus, the multiple responsibilities of these institutions are that they must respond totally to the development needs of Africa in the area of workforce development, in the revitalization the economy, in the revitalization of the education system, in researching and developing the African cultures, and in sharing the results with the global community.

Governments rightly expect institutions of higher learning to train the professionals, technicians, and managers required by their respective societies for economic growth. They expect training to be done through the design of relevant curricula and with a high degree of efficiency. In addition, governments expect higher education to contribute to other social and economic goals, to provide consulting services to public and private organizations, and to provide extension programs for farmers, business, and professional groups. Governments also consider institutions of higher learning as potential or actual sources of international prestige. Because of these multifaceted roles and expectations, governments tend to get involved in university activities. However, the relationships are inevitably delicate.

If institutions of higher learning are to carry out quality work, they need a fair measure of autonomy in the design and control of policies relative to admissions, curricula, examinations and graduation, and the selection and promotion of faculty and staff. They also need freedom to teach and freedom to research and disseminate information.

However, being the most articulate groups of any society, faculty and students presume themselves to be catalysts of thought and leaders in social and intellectual criticism and action. In doing so they usually draw the wrath and hostility of governments to themselves and their institutions. Weak governments are threatened by such activities, and rightly so. Many coups d'état have been precipitated or aggravated by universities, which contributes to instability in government. Faculty and students tend to be idealists and at times impatient. Maturity on both sides in administering institutions of higher learning and in handling and channeling views, ideas, and concerns appropriately may eventually contribute to better understanding and mutual support. Perhaps involvement of faculty in planning and implementation of governmental activities as well as in national services may provide some means for mutual understanding.

The number of African institutions of higher learning has expanded rapidly since the early 1960s. Qualitatively, too, they have shown significant progress, especially in the preparation of high-level personnel for the various segments of the economy, including government and quasi-government organizations. They have been instrumental in providing the requisite environment for critical thinking, dialogue, and discussion of the enormous problems facing African countries.

Due primarily to fiscal, political and attitudinal constraints, however, institutions of higher education have yet to develop the crucial understanding and loyalty of the masses of people and the political and business leadership, without whose moral and financial support they will not survive as entities capable of discharging their critical roles in social development. They have yet to convince those in political authority that the quest for objectivity in research and the dissemination of knowledge require freedom from fear of persecution by those in power, whose current views, political or otherwise, may not be supported by academic inquiry. The cultivation and nurturance of a tradition of tolerance, understanding, and support for universities requires sustained effort on the part of those who are in a position to render it—members of the academic community as well as political authorities.

African institutions are called upon to expand in every direction. These calls for expansion are driven by social and student demands and they are real. At the same time, their fiscal support is dwindling, and they cannot count on the government to continue to bankroll them. This dilemma requires resorting to non-traditional sources of support including charging students for at least part of the costs, encouraging private organizations to contribute, and being otherwise very efficient in operating the institutions. Only to the extent that they take such measures do institutions of higher education have any hope of continuing to discharge their responsibilities.

NOTES

1. Julius K. Nyerere. "An Address by the President of Tanganyka at the Inauguration of the University of East Africa." *Education and Nation-Building in Africa*. Edited by L. Gray Cowan et al. (New York: Fredrick A. Praeger, 1965), pp. 309–13.
2. Teshome G. Wagaw. *The Development of Higher Education and Social Change*. (East Lansing: Michigan State University Press, 1990), pp. 9–27.
3. The expansion rate declined beginning in 1983. See UNESCO, *Development of Education in Africa*. (Paris: UNESCO, 1982), pp. 84–112.
4. Teshome Wagaw. "Access to Haile Silassie I University." *Ethiopia Observer*, 14, no. 1 (1991): 31–46.
5. These and other comparative analyses are well documented in a World Bank report. See Keith Hinchliffe (consultant). "Higher Education in Sub-Saharan Africa." (Washington, D.C.: The World Bank Education and Training Department, November 1984), pp. 62–86.
6. *Ibid.*, 19.
7. The dropout rate for most of the countries is 35 percent and more. For detailed accounting of this, see *Ibid.*, 75–80.
8. *Ibid.*, 38.
9. In 1969–70, in collaboration with a man from the Netherlands, I made a study of the development and utilization of high level workforce in English and Arabic speaking African countries for the United Nations Economic Commission for Africa. The conclusion we drew was that even at that early stage there too much unemployment and underemployment of this category of people.
10. Hinchliffe. *Op. cit.*, 40, 54, 63.
11. In the summer of 1991, I had occasion to revisit some of the these institutions. I came away convinced that in so many areas of staff development, quality of instruction, library acquisitions, and the like they are worse off at this time than they were twenty years ago when I had made a systematic survey of these institutions for the United Nations Economic Commission for Africa.
12. At this writing, there is a team of Brazilian university presidents visiting the University of Michigan. Their priority: to learn how to raise funding from non-government sources. So is Pakistan. The

University of Michigan itself just this month launched a drive to raise one billion dollars within five years. The Africans are not the only ones that are thinking in this fashion.

13. Charging user fees of students or their parents has been tried repeatedly in many institutions and has invariably failed. It is only consultants from overseas that seem never to tire of bringing the subject up again and again. But then they have a home to go to.

14. In 1968, as dean of students of the Haile Silassie University system, I was pressured into appointing a committee to screen students that were able to pay from those unable to do so. The students demonstrated in the capital city. The prime minister was soon on the radio to let the nation know that his government had abandoned the plan. Politically it was hot and it has never been tried by successor regimes since. Other African nations have tried to levy user fees too, but as far as I am aware, they have all abandoned the effort, primarily for political reasons.

15. To my knowledge, so far only in South Africa have business organizations shown interest in contributing toward the training of students at university level.

16. Most of the donor nations and international organizations have concluded that the universities are not their priority. Even the World Bank helps primarily in the physical aspects, not in the development of curricula or programs.

17. The science of workforce planning has never been error free for a number of reasons. Until the technique is perfected universities are advised not to follow the plans slavishly. At the same time in their curricula and admission and graduation policies they should let the public know that they are not uninterested in approximating the national needs in this vital area.

18. I found this out in my days as a faculty member of the Haile Silassie I University in the 1960s and 1970s, and later as consultant to the United Nations Economic Commission for Africa. There was a feeling of insecurity on the part of the government officials, perhaps in some instances justifiably so, to invite faculty to participate in planning deliberations at the national level. In some instances they seem to prefer expatriates to nationals.

19. In my extensive experience in different parts of Africa, issues of low women participation in higher education and many areas of national life has been raised on numerous occasions at national and

international forums. In such discussions the men dominate, of course, while the few women present tend to be very shy or intimidated. The men think all is fine. They insist, "leave the women alone. They are doing all right." Until the women themselves are better organized, progress is going to remain painfully slow.
20. I have argued this in detail in Teshome G. Wagaw. *Op. cit.* 1990, pp. 2–4.

ALLOCATING BUDGETS USING PERFORMANCE CRITERIA

Michael A. Brown and David M. Wolf

Introduction

De Montfort University has a current enrollment of around 14,500 students, so is a large institution by British standards. Over the next decade it is planned to double in size via a distributed system of campuses and associated colleges, which will make it large even by international standards. Budget management in such a large and increasingly complex organisation therefore represents a considerable undertaking. De Montfort is a new university (formerly part of the so called polytechnic sector) and has well-developed systems of budgetary control that distinguish teaching funding from research funding. It has (up to now) received very little general funding for research, so nearly all its research income (around £10M in the last fiscal year) is associated with specific project budgets. Staff working on these projects are wholly or partly financed from these budgets, as are related non-staff costs. All other staff and non-staff costs are met from the main revenue budget, which is almost entirely made up of teaching funding and tuition fees. Tuition fees comprise 60 percent of the total income available for teaching. Thus, although all academic staff are expected to engage in research and other scholarly activities, the costs of this time must, in most cases, be supported by the base of teaching income. Teaching income largely consists of a block grant from the funding council plus tuition fees. The fees of most students are in effect also paid by the government, although this is routed through local education authorities. What follows concerns the management of this budget, currently totalling some £50M of public funds.

The funding of universities in the UK comprises separate allocations for teaching and research. Research funding is separately allocated by the Higher Education Funding Council (HEFC) on the basis of quality ratings produced for each subject area within each university. In addition, a large part of government funding for research is distributed via research councils on a project basis. All of this research funding is subject to separate accounting and must be quite clearly distinguished from funding allocated for teaching.

Context

There have been significant changes in UK higher education over recent years as the system has shifted rapidly from the education of a relatively small elite towards a mass higher education system with much higher participation rates and wider access. This has been, and will continue to be, accompanied by a significant reduction in unit funding per student. There is also, in the UK as elsewhere, an increasing requirement for universities to be more accountable for the public funding they receive. This is accompanied by a funding system which encourages competition between universities and a more direct relationship between funding and student population. The phenomenon of reducing unit funding and increasing accountability is now apparent in most countries.[1]

At De Montfort University, 1991–92 enrollments were up by approximately 50 percent compared with 1989–90, and over these two years unit income per student was degraded by about 8 percent per year in real terms, which indicates the scale of the problem to be faced in budgetary control. In 1989, the institution adopted a new organisational structure designed to manage its teaching and research activities within a framework of the financial responsibility imposed by the stringent commercial controls and accountability required by the government. Academic departments were grouped into ten schools, designated as cost centers. These were established on the basis of academic coherence, and to be of sufficient size to manage a devolved budget. A school/cost center which was too small would be in danger of becoming too parochial, there would be a loss of economies of scale, and it would be difficult to cross-subsidize new developments and other activities within the school and in general have the flexibility desirable within a cost center. On the other hand, there are dangers in a school

Allocating Budgets Using Performance Criteria

being too large. The head of school has to balance the academic aspirations of the departments within the school against the resource realities within which the school must operate. This becomes increasingly difficult if the head is too remote with too large a span of control. Some adjustments have been made to the original composition of schools, but their sizes have been maintained within these notional upper and lower limits.

Before describing the budgetary allocation processes which have been developed, it is worth noting some of the principles underlying the approach. The cost center philosophy adopted means that heads of school have considerable flexibility in managing their budgets. These are now two line budgets, staff and non-staff, and the only restriction imposed is that money cannot be moved from the non-staff budgets to the staff budgets. This is agreed by the head of school at the beginning of the financial year, without the approval of the senior executive. Otherwise, the school has, in effect, complete freedom of action within university guidelines. All financial transactions are implemented via a financial management computer system and are subject to the usual monitoring and regulatory framework of a commercial system, but with a commitment accounting overlay. It would be possible for the senior executive to intervene rapidly if any unusual spending pattern or other irregularity were detected.

As well as having a devolved budget, another important principle is that amounts under-spent against budget can be carried forward to the next year; of course, the same applies to any small budget over spends, although the system makes the creation of over spends very difficult. Short of an institutional financial crisis, it is intended that this principle should be maintained, and furthermore, unless a school were building up an unjustifiably large accumulated surplus, their budget allocation is not affected by any such carry-forward. In general, the intention is to be as consistent as possible in budgetary management to maintain continuity and build confidence in the system. It must be said that this is not easy in a context where there have been and will continue to be so many significant external changes in the methods determining the funding received by higher education institutions in the UK.

A third principle is that over time, the budgets allocated to schools should be broadly in line with the income generated by their activities. As will be seen, a major part of the methodology that has been developed in support of the budgetary allocation process is concerned with measuring the income derived from teaching that can be attributed to schools. Furthermore, this is done in a way which does not encourage too much insularity of schools, i.e., does not discourage them from cooperating and "trading" with each other, since the results of this are reflected in the income attributed to each school. As already mentioned, research income is subject to separate accounting. Finally, the process has been designed to enable both long-term and short-term objectives to be addressed both at institutional and school level in the allocation and deployment of resources. This mitigates against too formulaic an approach in the allocation of budgets.

It should be stressed that resource management within the institution has to be viewed in the context of its academic purpose. A framework has been developed to ensure that the quality of the university's academic activities are maintained and enhanced in accordance with explicitly defined objectives and standards at all levels within the institution. All courses are validated by a thorough process involving both internal and external peer review. In addition, the institution has been regularly subject to inspection and quality rating by government inspectors, who thoroughly scrutinize all aspects of operations, including classroom performance and facilities provided for student learning. This latter role will in future be taken over by new external quality assurance bodies, including one being formed in conjunction with the new funding council. During the last few years, as the institution has managed a diminishing unit income per student, the quality accolades have increased appreciably. Finally, an extensive system of monitoring, review, and audit continues to be developed within the institution in terms which allow actual and planned performance to be compared, and in ways which will facilitate continuous quality improvement.

Performance Evaluation Methodology

Having adopted a devolved financial management system, the modelling of performance used to inform the budgetary allocation process presents a considerable challenge. Figure 1 represents diagrammatically the system flow of funds and information during the main revenue budget allocation process and the modelling of school performance. Three key models are used in these processes. Current student enrollments from the central student record system and targeted enrollments from the strategic plan are input to the student allocation model. This assigns students proportionally to each school in a manner consistent with the school's contribution to the teaching and administrative requirements of each course year. Since there are many courses, each with up to four or more years, and a considerable degree of joint teaching (where more than one school contributes to a course), this model, while straightforward in principle, is large and requires a considerable data collection and maintenance effort.

In Britain, as is common in Europe, a "course" is defined as a complete programme of study leading to a higher education qualification (diploma, degree, or postgraduate qualification). Traditionally, courses have each had their own specific study programme, with few elements of communality between courses. However, it is now increasingly the case that courses share elements, and more flexible modular structures of course provision are becoming common. The income attribution model uses the output of the student allocation model to distribute the funding provided for each course and student fees to schools. This model is quite complex, since funding levels vary according to the nature of the course, as do fees. Funding varies according to which subject area and mode of study (e.g., whether full time or part time) a course falls in. Additionally, within each of these categories there is an element of core funding, marginal funding at a different unit rate (up to this year gained through a competitive bidding system), and students for whom no funding is provided (i.e., fees only are received). There are also two fee bands with different fees also applying according to whether the student is classified as overseas or home. A fuller description of this funding system and the approaches developed within the institution to bidding can be found in Wolf and Wilson.[2] The determination of a course income is, therefore, by no means simple. There is also the question of the "transfer price" to be used in allocating income from a course based in one school where another school is providing a teaching input. The income attribution model supplies a theoretical income at school level for budgeting allocation use and performance evaluation purposes. Although declared "theoretical," the figure is considered to be, in practice, the closest

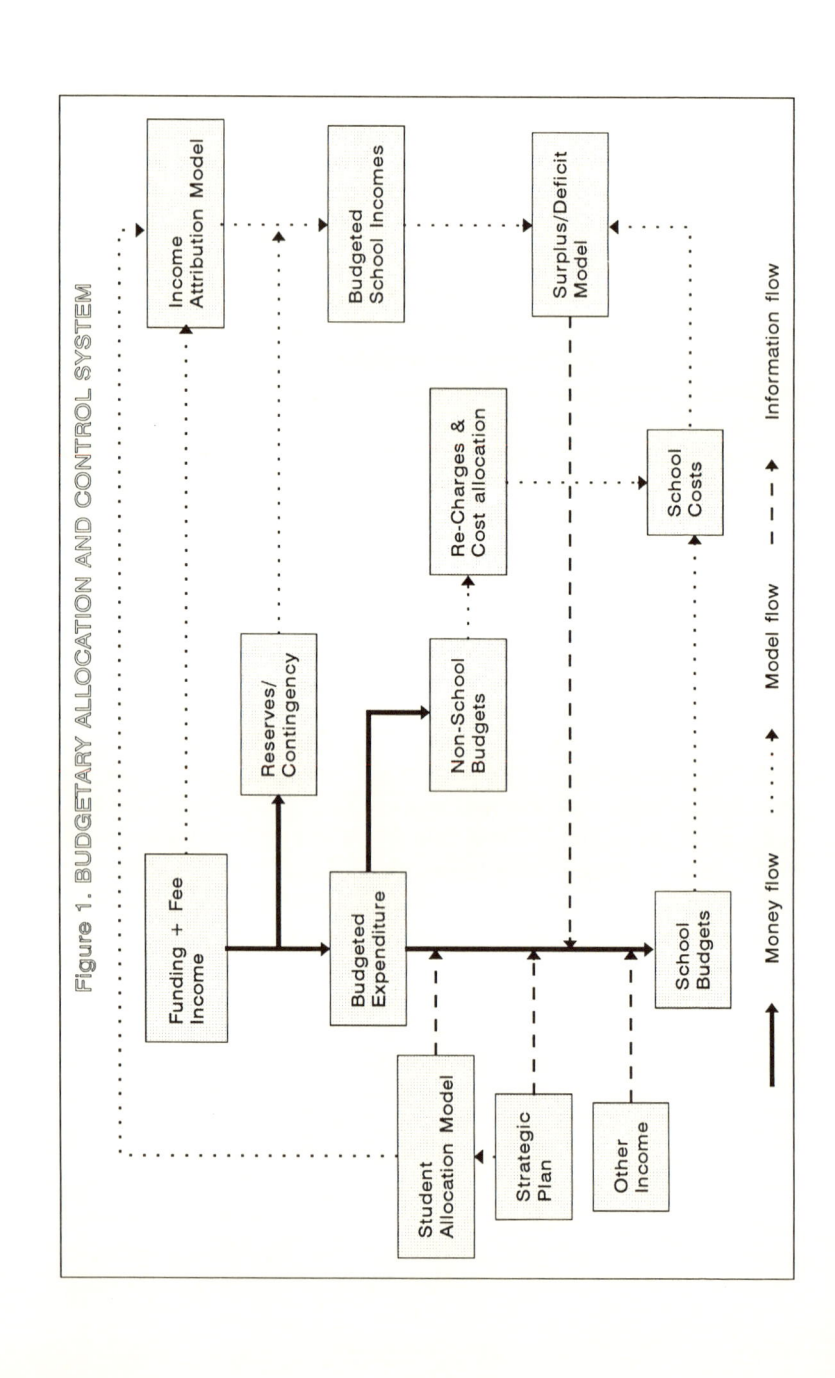

Figure 1. BUDGETARY ALLOCATION AND CONTROL SYSTEM

Allocating Budgets Using Performance Criteria

obtainable to a true school teaching income figure. However, it needs to be stressed that this is not a straightforward accounting exercise, and as indicated earlier a number of rules and matters of policy influence the result of this process.

Institutional expenditure which falls outside the control of schools is managed via a number of cost centers covering the support and administrative areas of the institution. Some of these costs are recharged to schools according to their usage, e.g., reprographic and telephone costs. The remaining costs are allocated in various ways. The major components are a central services charge allocated in proportion to FTE (full time equivalent) student numbers as determined by the student allocation model, and a space charge allocated according to the square metres of space "owned" by the school (its specialist laboratory and studio teaching space, offices, etc.) and its usage of common teaching spaces. The space charge covers all space-related revenue costs such as maintenance, heating and lighting, caretaking, cleaning, etc. It is not related to capital charges.

The merging of the income attribution model and school costs is provided within the surplus/deficit model, which produces absolute and relative performance measures for senior management use in decision support. Essentially, the output of such a model provides the equivalent of a source and application of funds statement for the course provision activities of the institution. It has extensive applications inperformance appraisal, but for the purposes of this paper, its application to the budgetary allocation process will be highlighted.

The Budgetary Allocation Process

Referring again to the principles on which budgetary management is based at De Montfort University, it can be seen that the annual allocation of revenue budgets to schools must meet several primary objectives:

1. Budget allocations are essentially two-line, with the split between staffing and non-staffing agreed at the beginning of the year, leaving the schools to disperse their budget over a range of spending categories. The allocation process, therefore, only needs to

determine these two numbers. Heads of school are responsible for setting and managing budgets at the more detailed line-item level.
2. Over or under spends carried forward from the previous year's budget are not taken into account in determining these allocations.
3. Budgets should reflect the performance of the school as indicated by the performance evaluation models described in the previous section. Thus, the amount allocated in a year will reflect the school's current surplus/deficit position, its targeted surplus/deficit (which is not necessarily break-even), and the planned changes in workload as indicated by the student allocation model applied to strategic plan numbers.
4. The annual allocation should take into account long-term factors, as determined in the institution's strategic plan, as well as short-term factors. An annual budget might, therefore, be agreed that would temporarily worsen a school's surplus/deficit position for a longer term advantage. In general, strategic factors can include judgements of long-term financial advantage, the maintenance of the university's subject profile, and the possibly indirect benefits resulting from external (e.g., governmental) pressures and incentives.

The allocation process begins with a budget request submission from each head of school which estimates the needs of the school for the coming year in the light of its existing commitments and any new activities which form part of the agreed strategic plan. This submission must specify budgets for different options and indicate priorities for any spending proposals. This is considered by the executive pro vice-chancellor (a member of the senior executive), with responsibility for resources, in conjunction with the director of finance. There follows a process of detailed discussion with each head of school, informed by the performance evaluations described in the previous section. As illustrated in Figure 1, the budget will take into account the school's surplus/deficit position (both current and targeted) and projected changes in student workload. The total budget will be set so as to move the school nearer to its target surplus/deficit, other things being equal. This process results in an overall budget which is agreed on after discussion and possible amendment by the senior executive as a whole, which then submits it to the finance committee of the board of governors. Further consideration results in the final budgets, which are ratified by the board of governors.

The budget that might be determined purely on surplus/deficit grounds may be varied by longer term considerations, as outlined in 4 earlier, and shown on the diagram as the influence of the strategic plan. Before considering this and other factors that may influence allocations, it is worth referring to Figure 2. An overall objective has been to bring school costs and attributed income into line over a period of years. Figure 2 shows how the position has changed over the period since 1989. As can be seen, there has been a considerable change over this period, where at the start, one school (7) was effectively subsidising the large deficits of three other schools (1, 3, and 9). This large surplus has been substantially reduced (by relatively favourable budgetary treatment) and two of the three schools (1 and 3) in substantial deficit are now in a break-even or better position.

A major change in the composition of schools 8 and 9, made to optimise academic growth, has resulted in one school (8) displaying a deteriorating position. However, this should be improved in the medium term by the advantages available from the restructuring and rationalization resulting. The deficit also reflects, to some extent, the fact that School 8 has courses which are relatively expensive to deliver compared to the subject average. For strategic reasons, the university wishes to maintain this range of provision, and in any case, there is some prospect of funding levels improving in this area in the future. This illustrates the fact that surplus/deficit targets are not necessarily to break even, although this will generally be the case. The position of School 5 reflects the influence of longer term factors on budget allocation. Its target is to break even, but its budget allocation has allowed for a temporary deterioration. Specifically, it was given an increased staffing budget to allow for the development of a planned new range of course provision which will generate medium-term gains in efficiency.

Finally, there are some other factors that may be taken into account. These are summarised in Figure 1 as the influence of what is loosely described as "other income." The allocation process that has been described relates primarily to the main revenue budget, which largely consists of public funds and tuition fees for teaching. This factor summarises the effects of other accounts—principally capital accounts and research and consultancy income. School 1, for instance, can be seen from Figure 2 to have moved from a substantial deficit position to a substantial surplus position, but this was in part achieved by a

Figure 2. SURPLUS/ DEFICIT OUTCOMES

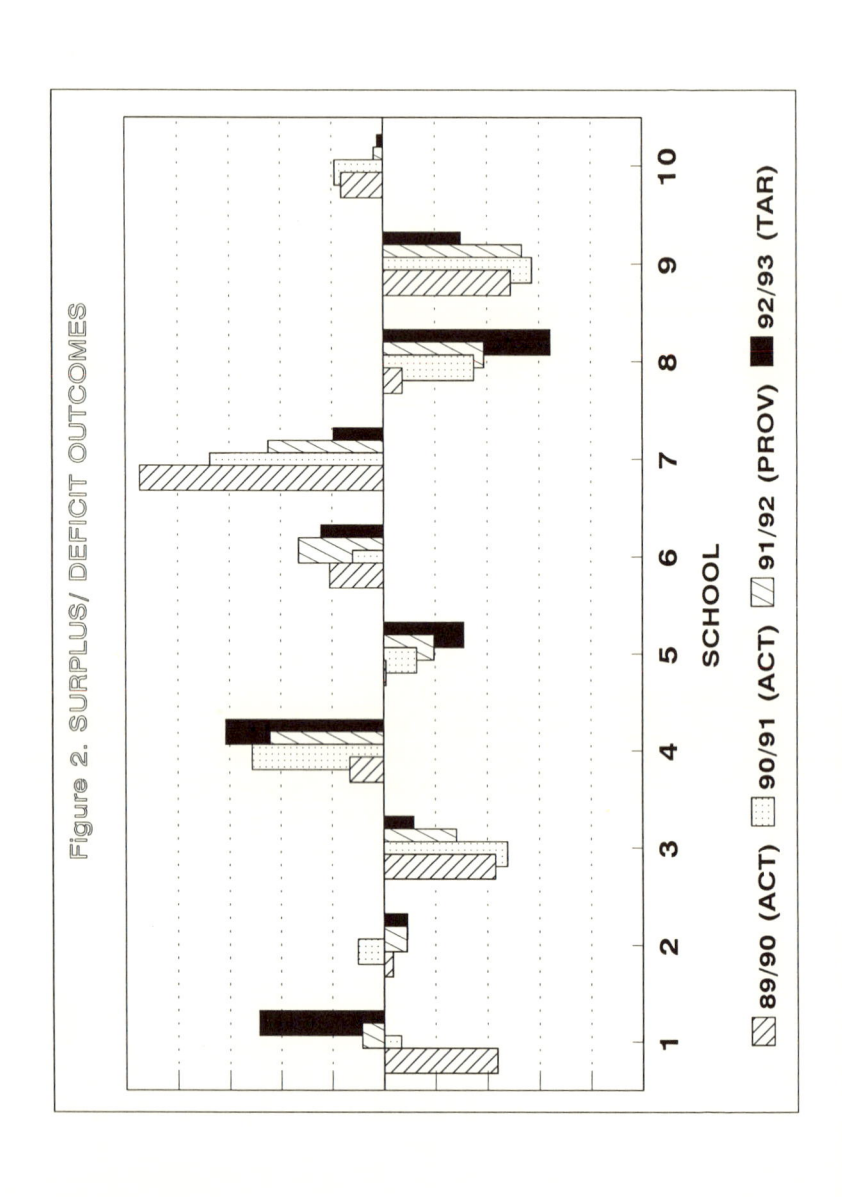

89/90 (ACT) 90/91 (ACT) 91/92 (PROV) 92/93 (TAR)

considerable capital investment in building adaption to allow it to make significant changes in the way its course provision was delivered. Its budget has been set to generate some payback of this investment to allow for necessary investment in the future in other areas. School 3 is planned to go through a similar process. Also, School 4, although generating a surplus, is currently receiving a substantial investment in capital equipment. As mentioned earlier, School 8 is not expected to break even, given the current level of funding for its area of work. Its deficit reflects the operation of both strategic factors and the influence of "other income." The university wishes to maintain its provision in this area for strategic reasons, and is therefore prepared to carry some deficit for this school, albeit rather less than that currently shown. However, this school is producing a growing surplus on its research and consultancy earnings which can be offset against this deficit, and this is taken into account in expenditure allocations for the year.

The Impact of Performance-Related Budgetary Control

The process of budgetary control that has been described has had very significant effects within the university. In general, it has promoted a very thorough examination of activities throughout the institution, with the emphasis on maintaining and enhancing effectiveness and quality while increasing efficiency. Of particular interest has been the effects on course delivery, which is and will remain a major part of the university's mission. The close examination of any process is almost certain to bring benefits, no matter what prompts it. Although the motivation for examining the design and delivery of courses was initially largely financial, there have been other, academic, factors prompting such an examination, and it is the university's belief that the result has been to produce courses that are both academically excellent and efficient in their use of resources. There is certainly no evidence of any significant deterioration of quality, and indeed, much evidence of courses being substantially improved. The institution has been regularly subject to external inspection and in 1991–92 its quality ratings were significantly increased to make it one of the highest-rated institutions in what was the polytechnic sector—86 percent of students were on courses rated as being of "outstanding quality."

When the approach to budgetary control that has been described was introduced, a thorough programme of assessing the costs of course delivery was also instituted. A methodology was developed to establish these costs, which has been described in Wolf and Wilson.[3] A "design to price" philosophy has been introduced throughout the institution; this does not mean that the objective is to design cheap courses. The objective remains to design academically effective courses, but subject to the constraint of the available resource envelope. In some areas, this has resulted in modifications to existing courses, but more significantly it has resulted in the complete redesign of whole areas of course provision. A case study will illustrate this.

Referring to Figure 2, it can be seen that School 1 was in substantial deficit in 1989. This was already an improvement from its position in the previous year and reflects some increase in efficiency obtained from the modification of its then range of course provision. A debate within the school reached the conclusion that what was in danger of happening was a worsening deficit with a steady deterioration in the effectiveness of its course delivery. It was decided, therefore, to meet the challenge by completely redesigning its whole range of provision and developing a new course structure. This process was managed by a team of academics from within the school with advisors from the central management team. The resource envelope that could be afforded was determined, and guidelines were produced for the academic staff on what could be afforded in terms of staffing input, and how to cost required resource inputs. A modular structure was arrived at where each course consisted of a coherent set of modules as a core with other modules chosen from the total pool available, subject to various practical and academic restrictions (prerequisites, corequisites, etc.). A complete resource model of the whole scheme was developed, and academic staff groups designed the modules in their subject areas using the resource guidelines provided. Some standard module designs emerged as well as a number of special cases resulting from the wide range of subjects covered. The resource model evaluated the effects of different designs. After several iterations through this process a design emerged that met the overall resource constraints and satisfied the academic objectives of staff. The new course structure satisfied the university's rigorous validation procedures and was introduced in 1990. Since then the management team has continued to monitor its development and improve on the original design as a result of experience. As can be seen from Figure 2, the fortunes of the school have changed dramatically as a result of this. Furthermore, all indications are that this new structure is satisfactorily meeting the aspirations of both staff and students within the school, and on the whole the response has been enthusiastic. Such a large scale change is bound to cause some problems and some initial concern, but this has been more than offset by a marked increase in quality in some areas of the school's provision, an increase in new developments in areas that had remained untouched for many years, and a very sharp increase in student applications reflecting the attractiveness of the new more interesting and flexible course structure.

It is hoped that other similar exercises currently under way will produce equally good results, but it is worth stressing, once again, the quality assurance framework within which such developments are taking place. This year will see the introduction within De Montfort University of a more extensive system of quality management based on the explicit identification of objectives and standards for a quality service (aligned at all levels). Strategies and plans for achieving those objectives, and mechanisms for the measurement and evaluation of performance against the objectives and standards set, will be audited. Thus, the academic objectives of the institution remain paramount in its exercise of budgetary control.

Conclusion

This has been a description of the response of one university in the UK to the climate in which it is now operating, but it is worth, in conclusion, underlining some of the lessons learned at De Montfort University in developing its budgetary control and management processes and relating these to a wider international perspective. D. Bruce Johnstone raises what he terms the "mega-issues" of costs confronting higher education in almost every country.[4] These include the questions of how much of a nation's resources can be devoted to higher education, and what the unit costs of the process should be. One conclusion is clear: in most countries of the world, especially in the present economic climate and with the growing competing claims of other social priorities, there is (and will continue to be) severe pressure on universities to control and reduce their unit costs. As he rightly points out, the appropriate measure here is unit of output, or putting it another way, it is not just cost efficiency that is sought at the expense of effectiveness. At De Montfort University, we have found that there are two crucial adjuncts to the budgetary control process. One is the need for a rigorous application of quality management principles, the other is the need to redesign educational provision with the objective of maximising effectiveness subject to resource constraints—a "design to price" philosophy. This is in contrast to an approach which sets cost cutting as its objective; "efficiency versus mere parsimony," as Johnstone describes it. It is always possible to reduce costs in the short term by wielding an axe; programmes can be cut, staff released, maintenance budgets degraded, etc. A much greater challenge is to really examine the processes involved in delivering higher education and positively change the way we do things. At De Montfort University, we believe we have achieved some success in doing this, and if faculty are given the information with which to work, positive and innovative responses result. It must also be said, as Johnstone also points out, that an essential prerequisite is a governmental approach to public sector budgeting and control that allows institutions the freedom to adopt the kinds of approaches that have been described. For all the criticisms that can be leveled at the government's approach to higher education funding in Britain, it has certainly given universities considerable freedom to develop innovative approaches to management.

Associated with the points made earlier are some key aspects of the appropriate mechanisms for implementing an appropriate budgetary control system. William Massy has vividly described the upward pressures on university costs, driven by what he describes as "The Academic Ratchet," and "The Administrative Lattice." [5] His proposals, although set in a somewhat different context, bear some marked similarities to the approaches we have found to be successful at De Montfort University. To summarise, there is the need for a considerable degree of decentralisation to what he terms "responsibility centers," without abdicating the role of central management. Associated with this is the idea of "revenue attribution budgeting," which means, essentially, managing streams or segments of revenue rather than line items, and making appropriate decisions on which streams to devolve and which to hold centrally for block distribution. Massy also highlights the need for information systems and decision models to guide the allocation process. At De Montfort University, considerable effort has been put into developing such systems and models, with positive results. Although the models described inevitably have their limitations and will no doubt continue to need refinement and further development, they have established a climate within the institution of open information, more transparent decision processes, and an acceptance of the need for judgements to be grounded more on rational and objective analysis based on data readily available to faculty rather than assertive and elegantly expressed rhetoric, as more often used to be the case.

NOTES

1. D. Bruce Johnstone. "The Costs of Higher Education: International Trends and Issues." *International Higher Education: an Encyclopedia,* vol. 1. Edited by Philip G. Altbach. (New York: Garland Publishing, 1991).
2. D.M. Wolf and R.T.J. Wilson. *Surviving Competitive Tendering: An Institutional Perspective.* ICHE Conference, Edinburgh UK, August, 1991.
3. D.M. Wolf and R.T.J. Wilson. *Decision Support Systems for Financial Planning and Control in a UK Polytechnic.* (The Association for Institutional Research Conference, Louisville Ky., May, 1990). Published in Resources in Higher Education, ERIC Clearinghouse on Higher Education, George Washington University (Washington, D.C., December 1990). ED 321699.
4. D. Bruce Johnstone. *Op. cit.*
5. William F. Massy. "Rebuilding the Fiscal Bridges to the Twenty-First Century." *Building Bridges for the Twenty-First Century.* General Session Presentations 31st Annual Forum. Edited by Jean J. Endo. (Florida: Association for Institutional Research, 1992).

CHANGING PATTERNS IN THE FUNDING OF UNIVERSITY EDUCATION AND RESEARCH: THE CASE OF THE NETHERLANDS

Cornelius A. Hazeu and Peter A. Lourens

Introduction

The Netherlands can best be defined as a social-democratic welfare state: that is to say, it is governed according to social and democratic principles, it is prosperous and relatively egalitarian. No single political party has a majority in Parliament, making coalition government a permanent necessity. The need for the various parties to engage in consultation and to strive for a consensus is reflected in many areas of society. Central government is seen as having key responsibilities: this is not only its own view, but accords with the expectations of most of society. Occasionally, public expenditure seems to be getting a little out of hand, and the country experiences a period—as in the 1980s—characterised by cutbacks and decentralisation. But time and time again we discover that this has been a temporary "blip," leaving the roots of the structure of our society quite intact.

Leaving this snapshot image of the Netherlands political situation, we shall examine a close-up of the university landscape. In our country, higher education and academic research are to a large extent viewed as part of overall government responsibility. It is government that must ensure that as many students as possible are able to pursue their studies, by providing the necessary system of grants and loans, and that funds the lion's share of university research. Some statistics may be useful here:

Population:	15 million
Number of university students:	188,000
National income (1992):	US$ 285 billion
Government budget (excl. social insurance):	US$ 120 billion
Government budget for education:	US$ 20 billion
Government funding for universities:	US$ 2 billion

The government provides the necessary funding for the Netherlands universities in two ways—through direct and indirect channels. Direct funding is provided by making an annual sum of US$ 2 billion available (for both education and research), and indirectly by making an annual sum of approximately US$ 235 million available to the national science council (the Netherlands Organization for Scientific Research, NWO), which uses a large proportion of this money (US$ 140 million) to finance university research projects and programmes (while the remaining US$ 95 million of the science council's budget is allocated to its own institutes). At present, higher education in the Netherlands consists of a so-called binary system, with around ninety institutions for higher vocational education and fourteen universities. The latter number includes the Open University, which is funded by a separate allocation model, and the Agricultural University of Wageningen, which is directly funded by the ministry of agriculture.

Viewed historically, the Netherlands universities are set up according to the German model for which the name of Humboldt has become a byword. Universities are not only—or not even in the first place—centers of education, but also function as havens for academic research. The major distinction between universities and institutes of higher vocational education is that university teaching is done by people who are themselves engaged in research. University education and research are regarded as two sides of the same coin.[1] Until the 1980s, this ideology even penetrated the funding structure of the universities. Government funding did not treat university research as a separate category, but merely as an additional item in the teaching budget. More money for every student that joined a particular faculty automatically meant more money for research in that discipline. In other words, the funding of university research was calculated on the basis of educational input—student numbers—and output did not play a role. Since the 1960s these universities have traditionally received their block grants from the government through formula funding. In

Funding University Education and Research: the Netherlands

principle, they are able to spend these grants as they see fit once they receive them.

In this chapter we will examine the pattern of change in the allocation of government funding by the ministry of education and science to the twelve "regular" universities.

Some Basic Data Concerning the Development of Higher Education Finance

Since the end of World War II, the funding of Dutch universities has basically been targeted towards the supply side. The allocation was initially based on input and demand, and any norms were more or less loosely connected to notions about costs per unit. In the period between 1960 and 1975, the flow of government funds to higher education in general almost trebled in real terms. Compare the following table which relates higher education spending to the national income in millions of Dutch guilders indexed for the year 1985.[2]

Table 1. Government Funds to Higher Education, 1965–1985
(in millions of guilders)

Year	National Income	Higher Education	HE as % of NI
1965	189,536	2.072	1.1
1970	278,700	4.727	1.7
1975	327,754	6.553	2.0
1980	374,852	7.337	2.0
1985	418,860	6.136	1.5

Source: Ministry of Education, Government of the Netherlands.

As can be seen, in terms of the percentage of national income (NI), the funding of higher education nearly doubled over that period. This was mainly due to the rise in the number of students. Moreover, in those years the funding of research was still directly linked to the number of students. This resulted in a kind of financial multiplier for the universities. In 1980, the percentage stabilised to drop back to 1.5 percent of NI in 1985. In real terms, government funding of higher education fell back to the level that was initially attained during the 1970s. At this point it should be noted that this drop-back in government funding is the overall result of an ongoing increase in the funding of the higher vocational institutions and the introduction of a so-called budgetary ceiling for the university sector. The universities, therefore, bore the brunt of the reduction in the growth of the budget.

Yet, during the 1980s, the intake of students at Dutch universities showed a marked increase, as is indicated by the following table:

Table 2. Enrollment Trends, 1983–1990

Year	Intake of Students
1983	28,181
1984	28,400
1985	28,436
1986	30,427
1987	33,938
1988	34,223
1989	35,731
1990	36,728

Source: Ministry of Education, Government of the Netherlands.

These figures show a rise between 1983 and 1990 of 30 percent. Taken together the tables indicate that Dutch universities had to face growing stress during the 1980s between increasing enrollments, and budgets which decreased when looked at from the point of view of costs per unit. It therefore became increasingly necessary to develop a new funding model which could cope with this stress and the budgetary ceiling in particular. Coupled with changes in the steering system, this resulted in the new model introduced in the budget for 1993.

Developments in the Funding of University Education

This section seeks to outline how the first generation formula funding model for universities in the Netherlands, which dates from the 1960s, gradually developed into a fourth generation allocation model which has been introduced for the budget year 1993. In describing the development, we shall make a distinction between the allocation of funds for education and the funding of research.

Funding University Education and Research: the Netherlands 193

The changes between the first three generations of university formula funding were (albeit with the benefit of hindsight) comparatively small and incremental. All three featured in some way the following basic formula:

volume × price → budget

In other words, the required budget was basically generated by multiplying a number of students and a volume of research in some way or another with the actual (or normatively perceived) costs. At least that is how these models were intended to function at the time of their development. They left the basic idea of a claim model based on (factual or presumed) costs per unit intact.

Since the 1960s, student numbers at universities have dramatically increased, and the present number is three times the total in 1965: 188,000 instead of 64,000. This growth also brought pressure to bear on the funding formula. Government funding of the universities was forced to stop meeting the rising financial claims at the end of the 1970s. Due to both the vast increase in the number of students and new social needs requiring the government's financial attention (the environment, the greying of the population, the national debt), it proved no longer possible to match the budget increases that appeared to be called for on the basis of the outcome of the claim-models. For more than a decade now the national budget available for the universities has remained fixed at a level of approximately $2 billion (education and research).

With the budget allocation for 1993, the Dutch government introduced a distribution model. The basic concept remains formula funding. However, the new model will no longer be based on notions about costs per unit, but instead will allocate premiums for clearly defined outputs within the framework of a given and stable overall budget for all twelve universities. So the basic formula will now become:

given budget = (fluctuating) volume × (fluctuating) price

Here is the main reason why the fourth generation model marks a major and important change-over to a new generation of allocation models: the fact that the allocation of government funding to Dutch universities is progressing from a claim model to a distribution model which, incidentally, in the near future may also be used to integrally allocate government funding to the whole of the Dutch higher education system (excluding the Open University).

The Four Generations of Allocation Models

The development of the four generations of allocation models for the Dutch universities shows a tendency towards an output lump-sum funding system. As will be seen later, this tendency is closely related to a corresponding tendency in the steering system.[3] First, however, the differences between the first three generations will be briefly described.

The First Generation: Input/Declaration

It is not easy to think of the Dutch first generation model as a model at all. It became known as the so-called Piekaar-keys, named after the director at the Dutch education department who formerly authorized the distribution of the available funds over the universities. He made use of "keys" (norms) which were related to the number of students and the scale of the university. These keys were applied within the framework of a declaration system. Their application was based on incremental calculations made whenever a university applied for more budget. Most remarkable is that the keys were only known to a limited number of people at the ministry. This of course gave rise to questions regarding the accountability of their application.

The Second Generation: Input/Norm

Naturally, the covertness of an allocation process triggered by secret keys met with growing antagonism from the universities, basically because no one knew what to expect. In response to initial efforts by the ministry to define more public norms, the universities took it upon themselves to investigate their own actual cost structure. On the basis of their findings the ministry gradually developed an intricate and more sophisticated model which aimed at publicly relating the so-called tasks to the means. This model was in fact the first to

Funding University Education and Research: the Netherlands

feature the three statutory functions of the universities (education, research, social services). The model basically involved more or less precisely calculating the actual costs of given curricula, then generalising them so that they could be used as the norm for allocation to all universities.

Teaching in particular was funded by establishing normative workloads for students in six different groups of curriculum profiles (arts, sciences, social sciences, medical, technical, and agricultural studies). Based on assumptions about timetables, staff hours, etc., these profiles generated the basic norms in terms of the amount of teachers required for a given number of students. These basic student-staff ratios were further differentiated to allow for economies of scale and differences in the amount of ancilliary staff considered necessary for the different profiles and different universities. Add further differentiating norms for the amount of equipment, space, energy, etc., and the result was an already fairly complicated model which required a powerful computer and the logistics of the APL programming language to generate results.

The Third Generation: Output/Norm

The allocation of funds in the second generation model was still essentially based on the number of students, so essentially on inputs. Due to expectations (based on estimates) of a possible future shortage of funds (through an expected decrease in the number of enrollments as a result of the end of the postwar birth-rate increase), it was considered necessary to introduce more output orientation into the model, partly as a means of defending the overall budget against possible competition from other governmental departments. For this reason the early 1980s saw the introduction into the existing model of a sub-model for the allocation of funds for teaching which has become known as the education/demand model. This third generation development involved, among other things, the incorporation into the existing model of further differentiating factors. In order to measure the teacher workload required, the yearly intake for each university by profile was multiplied by a specific factor representing the estimated output of graduates by that university in that particular profile.

The Growing Need for a Fourth Generation Model: Information-Problems

The introduction of the education/demand model took place in 1982. By its very nature it caused a huge increase of the already existing complexity of the model. Moreover, the first straight-through calculation of the new model, based on the actual output of graduates, led to a budget claim which was still higher than the existing financial ceiling for the universities. To retain the integrity of the model (which aimed at relating tasks to means), it was necessary to reduce the tasks. At the time, the policy of the Dutch education department was such that necessary cutbacks were orchestrated directly from within the ministry itself. This meant that on such occasions the minister would eventually decide which university departments would have to cut back or even close down, basing his decisions on whatever (sometimes scanty) information he possessed. Of course, this caused a lot of external turmoil. In the end, however, the financial contractions needed were indeed achieved in this way, basically by reducing the basic grants through decreasing the differentiation factors for economies of scale.

However, as one would expect, by doing so, the usefulness of the model was further reduced, even in such a way that only a few experts were still able to discuss the model's intricacies. Because of this, the model could certainly no longer function properly as a vehicle for discussion between the minister and the universities. The history of these departmentally orchestrated reductions (which took place in 1982 and again in 1985) clearly indicated that the government would at least have to cope with huge information problems were it to continue to repeat such direct intrusions into what the universities considered to be the prerogative of academic liberty. In the wake of information problems follow political problems, so a new approach was called for.

In the period from 1985 to 1988, while the government brooded over this problem, further cutbacks, necessary each year to make the tasks fit within the means, were usually realised by reducing any number of the several different norms that would ensure the budget generated by the claim model would not exceed the amount of money available. Only a few technically minded people could follow what this meant in terms of the allocation model. Needless to say, there was hardly any further discussion about reduction of tasks. Though this third generation model purported to be a claim model, it was in actual fact being used as a distribution model. The universities were simply forced to increase their efficiency further and further by cutting back on any financial slack that might still exist within their internal arrangements. Of course, this approach did in fact continually reduce the costs per unit, but it was certainly not a very satisfying development from the quality point of view.

Since the budget for 1989, a simple budget reduction factor has been used to fit existing tasks within the available means, basically in order to ensure that boardroom discussions over the result of the model did not get lost in technical details. For the year 1992, this reduction factor amounted to more than 6 percent of the overall government grant (around US$ 100 million). According to the universities, the actual budget reduction (on a fixed costs per unit basis) amounted to even more than US$ 300 million, if the reductions since 1982 are also taken into account.

As with most formula funding systems, the universities had always in principle been able to spend the money generated by the formula as they pleased once they received it. Early in 1986, this was taken a step further when the Dutch parliament approved a policy document called *Higher Education, Autonomy, and Quality*. This document, which forms the conceptual basis for a new higher education bill to be put into effect in August 1993, marks an important turning point in Dutch higher education policy. The document redefines the role of government, which hitherto had been more like that of a conductor, to that of an equal partner and mediator or catalyst for the universities. In it, planning through dialogue on an equal basis is a crucial concept. Here are some of the reasons for this change.

Increasing consumer sovereignty demands constant and adequate adaptation of the supply side of higher education. This makes it of paramount importance to provide incentives for self-regulating and entrepreneurial institutions of higher education. The information problems connected with this need for adaptation are such that the role of a government can no longer be like that of a conductor. Surely, the government is an important shareholder, but it cannot adequately fill a seat on the board of directors.

Attention also became more and more focused on the higher education system as a whole and the demand side in particular, thereby raising the issue of the binarity of the existing system. For a time, the voucher-concept was discussed as a possible new means of allocating the government block grant. However, this debate has so far borne no fruit.

Key to changes is the increase of the autonomy of the institutions. This will be achieved basically by a reduction of the rules and regulations, particularly where they prescribe the institutions *ex ante* how to act. Instead there will be a system of *ex post* quality control with funding based more and more on actual performance, i.e., output, both from a quantitative and a qualitative point of view. This is one of the main reasons why the Netherlands takes so much interest in the development of performance indicators.[4]

The Fourth Generation: Output/Lump Sum

Thus, the stage was set for a totally different allocation model. It was clearly recognized that there would probably always be budget constraints. There seems to be a limit to what Dutch society is willing to invest in higher education now that a relatively high level of participation has been reached. Though estimates indicated a possible fall in the number of students applying for higher education, this fall has so far not materialised. Instead, the actual numbers (and even the estimates based on them) seem to keep on rising (the participation rate is now at around 30 percent). Against this backdrop it was decided that at any rate claim models would no longer be adequate for the allocation of funds to the institutions of higher education. Instead a small but robust distribution model was considered necessary. It should cover the whole of higher education (excluding the Open University). Its main functions should be the allocation of any given amount of budget in such a simple way that there can be a fruitful dialogue at boardroom level about the important issues in higher education.

To conclude this section, we provide a brief overview of the main demands for the new model and, where necessary, a brief description of the way in which they have been made operational. Together they constitute the main features of the new Dutch integral allocation model governing both the universities and the institutes of higher vocational education:

1. Transparent, easy to understand and easy to validate.
   This demand resulted in the simple basic algorithm: given budget = (fluctuating) volume x (fluctuating) price. Operationally, the model contains three separate main compartments:
   for education: about US$ 500 million will be directly allocated on the basis of each university's performance with regard to the new education parameters (see 3);
   for research: around US$ 1.2 billion will be allocated on the basis of each university's performance with regard to the new research parameters;
   The remaining US$ 300 million will be allocated indirectly on the university's aggregate performance in both education and research, reflecting the idea that for universities, education and research are two sides of the same coin.
2. Practical, involving easy data retrieval based on counting the number of students rather than using estimates. Datasets should be easy to assemble and validate and should be fraud-proof.
3. Further increased output orientation.
   This will be achieved by counting only the number of students during a period limited per individual student to the actual duration of the normative curriculum (i.e., four years for most studies). The results of this yearly count will be the main volume parameter in the educational compartment. The second volume parameter will be the number of succesfully passed doctoral diplomas per annum.
4. Cost effective.
   For allocation purposes only, the educational costs per unit are postulated to be the same both for the universitites and the institutes of higher vocational education. This is intended to enable students to switch easily between the constituting parts of the binary higher education system without causing undue extra costs to the government. The higher education premium per unit of allocation will be determined yearly by the minister on the basis the available budget divided by the relevant outputs (the result of 3).
   The available educational budget will be divided by university by multiplying the number of relevant students and the number of successfully passed doctoral exams (see 2) with this premium.
5. Offer a more or less stable macro budget perspective to the institutions to enable them to plan ahead.
   This will be achieved on the one hand by the minister of education and science making long-term agreements with the minister of finance about the amount of money available for higher education, and on the other hand by clearly and in advance defining the outputs

which will be the basis for the allocation in years to come so that the institutes are well aware of the intended financial incentives.

Developments in the Funding of University Research

As seen before, since the 1960s, student numbers at universities have dramatically increased. This growth also brought pressure to bear on the funding formula of university research. At the beginning of the 1980s, government concluded that the passive funding of research (in certain disciplines which might happen to be in fashion) was no longer a viable option. A fundamental choice was made in 1982 by abolishing the system of funding university research as part of the teaching budget. Only a certain proportion of the research remained dependent on student numbers, while for the remaining research a new "conditional funding" system was introduced.[5] Presently, the number of university research places (in full-time equivalents) amounts to 10,500 (65 percent from the first and 15 percent from the second flow of funds. A further 20 percent comes from a third flow of funds earmarked for contract research).

An Earlier Attempt: Conditional Funding

Under this new system, universities were obliged to develop research programmes that met certain criteria: they had to be of a reasonable size (at least five years' work, expressed in full-time equivalents); they had to exhibit cohesiveness; and their quality would be liable to five assessments per year by external committees. The objective of conditional funding was to promote the quality and cohesiveness of research, and to enable it to be subjected to better, more explicit evaluation from the point of view of scholarship and relevance to society than it had been before. This also reflected the fact that the total budget for university research had gradually grown to such proportions that the government, which is after all responsible to the taxpayer, was obliged to exercise more control over it.

The original point of conditional funding had been that differences in research quality might lead to reallocations between universities—that is what "conditional" was intended to convey. But the minister, succumbing to pressure from the universities (who were not at all enamoured of a "zero-sum-game" of this kind), decided at a later stage to abandon this plan. The research volume that each university had in the year the conditional funding system was introduced was frozen. This took the edge off the new instrument, and the minister cast about for other ways of steering university research by way of the funding system. But the universities, too, found the situation unsatisfactory; they regarded the conditional funding system as bureaucratic and saw the whole system of funding as impenetrably complex. These are the circumstances that have led up to the minister's present, second, attempt to introduce a more dynamic factor into the funding of university research.

Social Relevance and Priorities of Science Policy

In 1991, it was decided not only to introduce a new allocation key for the funding of university education but also to find new models to allocate the funds for university research. Here, too, a trend is emerging whereby funding is based more on figures related to output (i.e., numbers of Ph.D.s and such like). Of the about US$2 billion with which the universities are directly funded, the model allocates over about US$500 million directly to teaching and about US$300 million indirectly to both education and research. The US$1.2 billion which the model allocates directly for research is made up of four components.

The first of these—more than 180 million (15 percent)—is a basic fund. It expresses the fact that research is a prerequisite for university teaching. The allocation of this component accordingly depends on where teaching is concentrated in each particular establishment. The second component, totalling more than US$ 90 million (8 percent), is related to doctoral work, resources being divided among the universities as a premium on the number of graduates completing their doctoral theses at each university. Twice the premium is paid for doctoral theses in the exact, technical, and medical disciplines compared with those in the social sciences and humanities. The third component consists of a premium for every research school a university has. This component will not be introduced until the system of research schools presently being phased in has been completed.[6]

The fourth and most important component of research funding (an annual sum of almost US$ 1 billion, almost 80 percent of the total) is related to what is dubbed "relevance to society." The minister and the universities have agreed that quality and social relevance are to play an important role in allocating this component. Amicable and even obvious though this may sound, the universities still regard it as a major intrusion—or potential intrusion—into their autonomy. They were, after all, used to government making these resources available without earmarking them beforehand. In order to limit budget reallocations between universities, it has therefore been agreed that the annual reallocations may not exceed 3 percent of this part of the university research budget. This means that a maximum of US$30 million may be redistributed among universities annually. The pool needed to make reallocations among universities possible, is being created initially by cutting 3 percent of each university's share of the "social relevance" component.

Research Foresight Studies

Now we come to the question of how the government intends to introduce the necessary dynamic principle into the funding system, and the mechanism by which reallocations are to be made. The Netherlands being a democracy that operates on the basis of consultation, government has to advance sound reasons for allocating a budget, or for making changes in the yearly allocation of a budget.

To this end, the government is setting up a system of research foresight studies as an instrument intended to mold strategy in the field of research. In principle, this process will focus on all research that is state funded, inside and outside universities. The idea is to enable national research priorities to be formulated and make it possible to decide what changes are necessary in resource allocation both within and among academic disciplines and research areas. Where such decisions are related to university research, they will be implemented through the funding system, but universities may also choose to anticipate this by incorporating the set priorities when shaping their research plans. The proposed system constitutes a significant innovation in relation to Netherlands research. Although the

Funding University Education and Research: the Netherlands

government has conducted a number of research foresight studies in the past, no fixed framework existed for implementing their conclusions. Furthermore, it has been customary to date that the government's science policy was shaped with additional incentive funds in addition to the main stream of funds for university research. Now we are going to attempt to set up an integral approach combining research foresight studies and mainstream university research funding.

The government does not wish to dictate research priorities to scholars, so there are various means to obtain the views of the academic community concerning priorities and programs.

An important step in this process is appointing a committee of top researchers and board members and representatives of research and other organizations. The brief of this consultative committee is to promote the conducting of such studies and to produce an options paper providing arguments to help the minister justify the priorities of science policy. To this end a limited number of fields (around twenty) have been pre-selected on which the committee makes proposals. These proposals include recommendations on the substantive organization of research (forming of special-emphasis fields, weak points, gaps where new fields need exploring or new forms of collaboration establishing, or conversely, where areas can be cut back etc.).

Every four years the committee will make recommendations to the government, which will respond by drafting a strategy policy document. Then, having received further recommendations on this policy document, the minister will discuss it with parliament. The desired result is consensus on a national research strategy. Once such a consensus has been achieved on the main decisions, consultations with the universities and others will follow on how best to implement them. The final stage in this decision-making process is for the government to make concrete decisions on which areas—and which universities—are to receive the extra resources.

As far as the universities' funding model is concerned, this means the end of non-selective allocation, with resources being earmarked to a certain extent. The government is then faced with the problem of how to check whether universities have complied with these requirements; the universities will have to adjust their modes of reporting to clarify this point.

Conclusion

The fourth generation of formula funding as outlined earlier has been introduced with the budget for the universities for 1993. The introduction of the new formulae for education for the institutions of higher vocational education will gradually take place in the next couple of years, thus facilitating a gentle phasing out of differences which at present still exist between the old allocation models for the universities and the higher vocational institutes, respectively. In a couple of years' time, Dutch formula funding of higher education will thus have developed to one integral allocation model for both the universities and the institutions of higher vocational education. Concerning the funding of university research, the attempt made ten years ago to introduce a dynamic factor into university funding (the conditional funding system) proved unsuccessful. A second effort is presently under way: the use of foresight studies to steer research funding. This is a complex process involving many factors and extending over a long period of time. We do not yet know whether it will work.

An obvious question to ask is whether the whole thing could not be done more simply. The answer is that it could. After all, both the direct funding of the universities and that of the national science council (NWO) come from the budget of the ministry of education and science. What could be more obvious than to switch a share of the resources from one to the other? It is easier to make agreements with the national science council, which would then be receiving a larger proportion of the means for university research, than with all the universities together. Furthermore, it is easier for an organisation such as the national science council to select strictly on the basis of quality, partly because it is not in the position of having to appease several faculties all together. Adopting this method also would bring the ratio between the first and second flows of funds more into line with that in other countries. In short, there is ample reason to aim for a simpler way of controlling research.

When the present minister of education and science took office in 1989, he began by moving in this direction. But the universities are powerfully placed within the Netherlands consultative democracy. Their power has two distinctive features:

- the law safeguards equality of development opportunities among universities;

- certain universities—those founded on denominational principles—occupy a special position under the law, as well as having strong ties with the Christian Democrats, the largest political party.

These political and legal facts of life make it hard to devise generic measures. Their powerful position has enabled the universities to stave off any further attempt to switch resources from the first to the second flow of funds. Agreement has now been reached, however, on the introduction of a steering mechanism into the first flow of funds, by way of the process described earlier.

Is this new effort to introduce a steering mechanism into the first flow of funds more likely to succeed than the effort made ten years ago? A cautious optimism would appear to be justified here. Although it is true that conditional funding did not lead to reallocations, it did lay the foundations for university research programming, intra-university research policy, and so forth. University administrators are now better equipped to respond to external demands. In that respect, conditional funding was not a complete waste of time.

NOTES

1. C.A. Hazeu. *Science Policy: A Behavioral Approach.* (Aldershot, UK: Gower-Avebury, 1990).
2. A. J. J. Spee and F. J. De Vijlder. "From Formula Funding to Financing Demand; the Case of the Netherlands." Paper prepared for the International Course on Higher Education Funding, Institute of Education, University of London, July 1–5, 1991.
3. A.A. Jaarsma and P. A. Lourens. "Patterns in Financing Education, part one." *Proceedings of the Solenice Conference on Innovation of Education.* Solonice, Czechoslovakia, April 26–29, 1992, Hobeon Group, The Hague, the Netherlands, 1992.
4. C.A. Hazeu and J.F.A. Spangenberg. *University Research Performance: Measurement, Management and Optimization.* (The Hague, the Netherlands: SDU, 1991).
5. J. Spaapen. "External Assessment of Dutch University Research Programmes: An Evaluation." *International Journal of Institutional Management in Higher Education,* 9, no. 1 (1985): 72–78; and A.F. J. van Raan and J.G. Frankfort. "An Approach to University Science Policy: a New Research-Funding System." *International*

Journal of Institutional Management in Higher Education, no. 2 (1980): 155–163.

6. C.A. Hazeu. "Research Policy and the Shaping of Research Schools in the Netherlands." *Higher Education and Management,* 3 (November 1991): 283–291.

ISSUES IN FUNDING HIGHER EDUCATION IN EASTERN EUROPE: THE CASES OF THE CZECH REPUBLIC AND SLOVAKIA

James E. Mauch and Daniel S. Fogel

For those living outside of Czechoslovakia, it is difficult to understand the current situation and constant change, including the split into two separate republics, one Czech, the other Slovak. Yet, through an understanding of the traditions leading up to today, one can gain some understanding of Czechoslovakia and the changes occurring in post-Communist Eastern Europe. This chapter describes the context of Czechoslovakia's higher education system and analyzes funding issues facing Czechoslovakia and its institutions of higher education.

The Historical Context

The rich traditions reflected in European higher education, reaching back almost a millennium, provide historical legacies that are important factors in the present restructuring of Czechoslovak higher education. Following on the founding of the universities at Salerno, Bologna, Paris, and Oxford, Prague became the site of a great university, which followed in structure and organization the ancient university models of its predecessors.[1]

Founded in 1348, Prague was the site of the first of the great Central European universities, followed by Vienna in 1384, and Heidelberg in 1385. After the founding of Charles University, other important universities were established throughout the Czech and Slovak lands during the next 200 years. The early historical developments of the Czechs and Slovaks led to the present situation of two republics federated in an uneasy alliance always in danger of disintegration. Bohemia and Moravia in the Czech lands united under the crown of St. Wenceslaus while the Hungarian monarchs ruled the Slovaks. Even after the Habsburgs effected a personal union of the kingdoms of Bohemia and Hungary, the regions retained their local administrative agencies.[2]

The Austrian-German university model forms one of the important traditions of Czechoslovakia's educational system and provides a framework for understanding what exists today. By the end of the nineteenth century, institutions throughout the world were emulating German universities. Lord Ashby called the German university model "the nineteenth-century idea of a university."[3] The model influenced the development of modern universities in Japan, the United States, and much of Europe, including Czechoslovakia. German became the language of scholarship, scientists emulated German scientific and teaching methods and degrees, and German laboratories became the world standard.

Modern Czechoslovakia was founded on October 28, 1918, as the Czechoslovak Republic, the predecessor of the Czech and Slovak Federal Republic (CSFR). Tomas Masaryk, the first president of the nation, tried to reduce the power of the church and of German culture in the Czech lands. One of the early struggles in higher education was a fight over the language of instruction, between German and Czech.

The Slovaks, on the other hand, were emerging from Hungarian domination. In Slovakia, Comenius University was established in 1918 and quickly became a premier education facility. At its founding, it was the only Slovak institution of higher education in Czechoslovakia. By 1936, Czechoslovakia had thirteen higher education institutions with fifty-two faculties, more than 23,000 students and more than 3,450 professors, docents, and teaching staff.[4]

World War II devastated Czech higher education. After November 17, 1939, the Nazis closed all education institutions within the territory of the Nazi Protectorate of Bohemia and Moravia. The institutions remained closed for almost six years, after which they slowly reopened. In Slovakia, institutions remained open and grew during this period; the Nazis permitted the formation of the Slovak Technical University (1939) and the Bratislava School of Economics (1940). In many cases, Czech faculty were forced to relocate to Slovakia to provide instruction at Slovak universities.

Table 1. Quantitative Development of Czechoslovak Higher Education, 1936–1990

	# of Institutions			# of Faculties			# of Full-Time Students			Female %		
	CSFR	CR	SR	CSFR	CR	SR	CSFR	CR	SR	CSFR	CR	SR
1936–37	13	12	1	52	49	3	23,435	21,356	2,079	17.3	17.4	16.3
1945–46	11	8	3	44	32	12	54,902	46,203	8,699	18.5	18.5	18.7
1948–49	22	18	4	55	40	15	55,788	46,838	8,950	23.2	24.0	18.9
1960–61	30	20	10	88	61	27	55,567	38,837	16,730	30.7	29.5	33.4
1974–75	36	23	13	103	65	38	113,553	67,307	46,246	40.8	39.0	43.6
1979–80	36	23	13	109	68	41	142,226	87,597	54,629	42.4	42.0	43.0
1984–85	36	23	13	110	68	42	140,971	89,940	51,031	44.2	43.4	45.8
1989–90	36	23	13	112	69	43	137,905	88,751	49,154	45.0	44.6	45.8
1990–91	36	23	13	132	82	50	149,048	96,379	52,669	45.3	44.4	46.9

Source: OECD, *Higher Education in the Czech and Slovak Federal Republic*, 1992, p. 24.
CSFR - Czech and Slovak Federal Republic
CR - Czech Republic
SR - Slovak Republic

Soon after the end of World War II, Soviet-style communism was imposed as the model for Czechoslovakia, as it was for Eastern and Central Europe. While it is too early to analyze all the legacy of this history, some negative features of the system are clear: the failure of central economic planning; the priority given to heavy industry over consumer goods; the bureaucratic control of human rights and freedoms; the ever-present internal security forces and use of informants; an arrogant and powerful bureaucracy; the constant attempts to suppress dissident thinking and activity; the use of groups and organizations in service to the state (including universities and mass media), and the use of Marxism-Leninism as the rationale for all actions.

The imposition of communism affected higher education as well. University research in Eastern Europe suffered from the almost complete isolation imposed on political grounds by the Communist governments. Over the years research, scholarship, teaching, and science were held back by the restrictions on travel or other modes of communication, by the lack of access to research reports, books, journals, and other scholarly materials originating in the West, and the intrusion of the party and government bureaucracy in academic decisions.[5]

For forty years the Czechoslovak Communist party tried to remold higher education in the image and likeness of the Soviet Union and international communism. The party not only funded, but controlled all levels of higher education; it also used institutions as instruments for controlling and reeducating student minds to create the "new Communist man."[6]

Along with isolation, an ideologically defined curriculum, and the loss of outstanding teachers, East European universities were characterized by a widespread system of rote learning, conformity to prescribed programs, and a few widely prescribed texts. Isolation and controlled content became, in terms of content and approaches, more and more remote from reality. The Communist bureaucracy was all too successful in destroying individuality. University personnel, among others, saw the state as punishing risk-taking, initiative, or creativity, and as positively reinforcing conformity to Marxist dogma, following directions, and supporting collective over individual achievement.[7]

The party was paranoid with respect to faculty who might be politically unreliable. Faculty in the sciences were assigned to work at the academies of science to isolate them from university colleagues and students. Government-run science academies (imposed by the Communists in emulation of Soviet higher education) did research while the government limited universities to instruction. The academies were favored in the competition for funds and universities suffered in terms of a lack of funds, autonomy, freedom, and scientific isolation under strict government (party) control. With respect to academic governance, the academies of science were subject to direct control by the party at the highest levels, bypassing the ministry bureaucracies. The Czechoslovak Academy of Sciences emerged as the primary organ for establishing and administering research programs throughout the country.[8]

The "normalization" following the Prague Spring caused many leading scholars and researchers to exchange their teaching positions for menial jobs or to choose emigration. The higher education system continued to be poorly developed because central government control meant that institutions were unable to exercise academic prerogative within their schools.[9] The ministry of education and culture administered higher education for the party, abolished academic senates, and replaced elected academic officials with people appointed by the ministry and political leadership.

The government rigidly centralized and politicized higher education in terms of funding, student access, curriculum, staffing, resource allocation, and planning. Each successive five-year plan was designed to provide the planned state economy with personnel to meet the needs of the state, while at the same time attempting to assure that too many graduates would never appear to swell the ranks of the unemployed. State planning and funding affected university plans for student enrollment and discipline-specific decisions.

This administrative structure resulted in a decrease in Czechoslovakia's international recognition and the reputation and position of higher education in research and science. The party particularly controlled the humanities curriculums to ensure that information was consistent with party dogma. The "nomenklatura system" enabled the party to control, and status positions were acquired by backdoor procedures.[10] New departments of Marxist theory and dogma were established at the universities to make sure students and faculty were instructed in the right way of thinking. Membership in the party was a distinct criterion for the highest academic posts.

Table 2. Breakdown of Numbers of Students and Teachers in Czechoslovak Institutions of Higher Education, 1936–1991

	Students Total	F - T Czech & Slovak	F - T Foreign	P - T	Others	Student/ 1000 Inhabitants	Prof. and Associate Professors	Other Teachers
1936–37	24,965	23,435	1,530	N/A	N/A	1.6	1,469	2,052
1945–46	54,902	54,902	N/A	N/A	N/A	4.1	N/A	N/A
1948–49	62,893	55,788	1,912	5,193	N/A	5.1	1,430	4,495
1960–61	92,260	55,567	1,849	26,740	8,104	6.7	1,723	8,781
1974–75	149,526	113,553	3,400	27,372	5,201	9.3	3,405	13,361
1979–80	196,518	142,226	3,382	44,963	5,947	12.3	4,166	13,697
1984–85	183,911	140,971	3,989	29,344	9,607	11.0	5,670	13,465
1989–90	182,580	137,905	5,098	30,544	9,033	10.9	6,992	13,325
1990–91	193,612	149,048	4,803	28,127	11,634	11.4	6,814	12,536

Source: OCED, *Higher Education in the Czech and Slovak Federal Republic*, 1992, p. 24.

Conforming to the planned system was the paramount means for evaluating the effectiveness of each institution.[11]

To be fair, the Communist legacy has had positive aspects, although they may be difficult to describe objectively so soon after the collapse of the hated and repressive regimes. The state offered free public education from early childhood to the university level and eradicated widespread illiteracy. The educational level of the adult population in much of the region was raised and, up to 1980, the rate of participation in higher education increased. A substantial increase in female participation in education was also very positive.[12]

Nearly 50,000 students were studying full time at the fifteen universities in the Czech Republic and over 9,000 students were studying in the three universities in the Slovak Republic when the Communists took over in 1948. By 1990, the number of full-time students was about 149,000, of which 96,400 were in the Czech Republic and 52,600 were in the Slovak Republic.[13] However, Czechoslovakia lost ground in comparison with the developed countries. By 1990, 16 percent of the 20–24 year-olds were enrolled in higher education, putting Czechoslovakia near the bottom of European higher education.[14]

Thus, the development of Czech and Slovak higher education has paralleled economic and political history. The past has led to today's dilemmas. The Austrian-German tradition and the effects of decades of communism on academic institutions provide the basis for understanding the present as well as current attempts to reform higher education and its funding.

The Present Structure of Czechoslovak Higher Education

Changes in Czechoslovakia since 1989 have been characterized by a movement away from political control of institutions. Decentralized decision making and curriculum reform are now in the hands of institutions of higher education. Yet, tension exists with respect to funding and reforming the system consistent with the country's traditions.

Legal Framework. On May 4, 1990, the federal assembly of the Czech and Slovak Federal Republic passed "Act No. 172/1990 of Institutes of Higher Learning and Universities," thus abolishing Act No. 30 of 1980 that reflected the ideology and control of the Marxist regime. The new act guarantees basic academic rights and freedoms, including the freedom to do scientific research and publish results, the freedom to hold differing views, and the freedom to profess religious creeds and propagate them.[15]

Changes created by the new law were radical, from strong centralism to decentralization; the relationship between the state and institutions of higher education is not precisely defined with respect to funding, planning, governance, or state authority. The breakup of the nation only adds to the uncertainty. There is still a mistrust of the ministries and of strong central government, and there are questions about the ability of the state to coordinate and finance higher education without someday reestablishing control. Institutions are still trying to define their degree of autonomy, and struggling with new internal governance relationships.[16]

The federal legislation places the executive power for education in the hands of respective republican ministries. The new higher education act gives to the ministries in each republic the responsibility for further development of higher education institutions, coordination of their activities, distribution of financial resources earmarked for the higher education sector, and supervision of the proper use of these resources. The act also created two bodies in each republic to link higher education with the respective ministries of education—the accreditation boards and the higher education councils.[17] Both are powerful bodies, but for this chapter it is important to note that the higher education councils advise the ministry on the distribution of financial resources to individual institutions.

The funds allocated to each republic for higher education are distributed by the ministries to the institutions, and their proper use is monitored by the ministry, with the advice of the councils of higher education. Thus, the distribution, accountability, and general policies are set at the republic level.

With respect to funding, Act 190 (Section 6) states that institutions shall be financed by the state, and they and their faculties may obtain funding from other sources both domestic and foreign, as well as through economic activities. In addition, funding from these sources shall be exempt from state and federal taxes.[18]

Thus, the law has created a new higher education structure. It has made possible the entry of new institutions and the reform of old. It puts more power in the hands of institutions, students, staff, and teachers, and provides the opportunity for funding reforms.

Student Access. Student access to higher education has been low compared to other countries. The nine countries within Central and Eastern Europe have an average of 1,389 students per 100,000, while West European countries (sixteen in total) enroll over 2,400 students per 100,000 population. In 1990, Czechoslovakia had about 1,188 students per 100,000 population.

Table 3. Higher Education Enrollments Per 100,000 Inhabitants

Hungary	938
Poland	1,306
Czechoslovakia	1,188
Central/Eastern Europe (16 Countries)	1,389
Bulgaria	1,677
UK	1,913
Western Europe (16 Countries)	2,405
France	2,655
U.S.	5,142
Canada	5,024

Sources: *Encyclopedia Britannica,* 1991; *UNESCO Statistical Yearbook,* 1990.

These low rates are a result of low levels of student participation in the schools which provide higher education preparation for students, and the universities' reliance on traditional selection criteria. Institutions have removed the political and ideological exclusions. The dean and the senate of each faculty of each higher education institution have full authority to admit students and select criteria for those admissions. Despite this freedom, funds are not available to enable any alternatives to the traditional standards.[19]

Institutions. According to the annex of the Higher Education Act of 1990, there are thirty-six institutions of higher education, twenty-three in the Czech Republic and thirteen in Slovakia. Approximately 20,500 professors teach in all Czechoslovak universities, 75 percent of which are in the Czech Republic.

The largest institutions are Charles University, with sixteen faculties and 28,000 students, Technical University of Prague with five faculties and 19,000 students, Technical University in Slovakia with six faculties and 14,000 students, and Comenius University with nine faculties and 13,000 students. Many of the smaller institutions are specialized and differentiated. Substantive domains within institutes are narrow.

Table 4. Czechoslovak Higher Education Institutions, Faculties, and Students

	Czech Rep.	Slovak Rep.	Total
ESTABLISHMENTS	23	13	36
General University	6	3	9
Pedagogical University	4	2	6
Technical University	7	3	10
Economic University	1	1	2
Agricultural University	2	2	4
Fine Arts Institute	4	2	6
FACULTIES	83	50	133
University	36	21	57
Technical	26	15	41
Economic	5	5	10
Agricultural	9	5	14
Arts	7	4	11
STUDENTS	129,777	69,095	198,872
Czechoslovak	96,379	52,669	149,048
Foreign	3,122	1,681	4,048
Postgraduate (all nat'l)	7,285	3,875	11,160
Part-time (CSFR)	18,693	9,434	28,127
Others	4,298	1,436	5,734

Source: Harbison, 1991: 3; Institute for Information in Education, 1991, p.18–Higher Education.

The recent changes resulting from the 1990 act have resulted in five new regional universities, mostly reconfigurations of state-run institutions built around former schools of pedagogy, e.g., the University of South Bohemia and J.E. Purkeyne University in Usti nad Labem. The idea has been to combine faculties and research institutes into new institutions serving regional needs. This is an attempt to reduce somewhat the concentration of higher education in the large centers like Prague, Brno, and Bratislava. The new universities have received new missions but few new funds.

Teaching Staff. Data show many faculty do not have a Ph.D. or the equivalent. The percentage of full professors in Czech universities is 7 percent compared to 30 percent at American universities. In contrast, 60 percent of all Czech faculty are assistant professors compared to only 24 percent in American universities. In addition, at American universities, for all professorial ranks, faculty members are required to hold a Ph.D. or equivalent degree. This is not the case for Czech universities, where 70 percent of full professors and less than half of all assistant and associate professors hold Ph.D. or equivalent degrees.[20]

Table 5. Student-Teacher* Ratios for Selected Universities Teaching Business and Economics

Charles University	28,000/3,100	9.03
Prague School of Economics	11,340/620	18.29
Technical University of Prague	14,150/1,448	9.77
Bratislava School of Economics	5,268/634	8.31
Comenius	13,248/1,994	6.64
Masaryk	3,150/955	3.30

Source: *USIA Directory of Institutes of Higher Education in the Czech and Slovak Federal Republic, 1992.*
* Full and part-time

Table 5 shows the student-teacher ratios for six of the larger and more well-known universities. The ratios in 1989 in all higher education institutions were about 8.5. The more general universities tend toward lower than average ratios, and technical universities toward higher than average ratios. These ratios are comparatively rich, and contribute to the cost of higher education. The higher education sector has been the beneficiary of social employment. Thus, the labor force may decrease unless enrollments are increased to meet social demand. Base salary for a full professor in Czechoslovakia is approximately 8,000 Kcs per month (US $164) for twelve hours of teaching. At these rates, one cannot expect a dramatic increase in faculty desiring full-time university employment, especially in areas of high demand.

Institutional Governance. Changes in higher education law have led to a degree of autonomy unusual even in Western democracies, and are seen by some scholars as a reaction to the policies of the previous totalitarian system.[21] The act enables institutions to set up their own internal structures, including the content and organization of studies, the filling of posts, criteria for admission and, of special interest to this chapter, internal distribution of financial resources.

The new act established representative bodies competent to decide these issues, including academic senates for individual faculties and institutions, and requires student, teacher, administrative staff, and researcher representation. Rectors and deans also serve in advisory capacities. Scientific councils established at each university have important roles in academic matters concerning teaching and research, including the appointment of associate professors and nomination of professors.[22]

Funding of Higher Education

Czechoslovakia was created as a federal state. In 1992, the two republics agreed to separate, although it will take a while for the full meaning and extent of that separation to be clear. Up through 1993, some activities have been the province of the federal government, such as defense, currency regulation, customs and duties, and foreign affairs, but much of the internal governance was left to the Czech and Slovak republics. The federal parliament raises taxes to pay for federal responsibilities, e.g., defense, and foreign affairs, through taxes on income, sales, profits, and imports, but that is expected to change with the separation.

The Czech and Slovak republics have been independent in internal matters, each with spending and appropriation authority. Each has a prime minister, a cabinet of ministers, a full range of ministries, a parliament, and large bureaucracies. Each republic has a ministry with oversight responsibilities for all education, including higher education.

Expenditures per student are generally higher in Slovakia due to additional government funding. In 1990, the amounts were 36,800 and 33,400 Kcs per student in the Slovak and Czech republics. Between-school variation of expenditure per student is great in both republics, from 79,000 Kcs at some art academies to 16,000 Kcs at the least expensive institutions, usually teacher training and the social sciences. In terms of dollars, estimated per student expenditure in Czechoslovakia has been about US $1,000 a year over the past five years.[23]

Under the Communist regime, total budgets for higher education were drawn up by the ministry on the basis of previous years' budgets, and requests submitted by institutions. These requests were commonly inflated to take into account the expected cut from the ministry. There

Issues in Funding Higher Education in Eastern Europe 219

was no incentive in the system for the institutions to do otherwise, and the ministry had no fair, open, and objective criteria to make decisions in any other way.

There were departures from this incremental budgeting. The party was always able to add extra funds as it wished, e.g., to scientific research institutes, to the institutes of Marxism-Leninism, and to military departments. Given the situation, there could be no realistic strategic planning with regard to program review and evaluation. Institutions were not motivated to assess needs realistically, nor to use the state's resources efficiently. Further, all income collected by the universities reverted to the state, thus discouraging any efficiencies in collection or use of income.[24]

About 98 percent of current funding comes from the state, a legacy from the past. Up to now, there has been little experience with charging students any fees at market rates, and indeed, it may be politically unthinkable in the short run. In addition, most students simply do not have the money to pay for higher education. As a result, inefficiencies are legion, again a legacy from the past. Each institution receives what it got before, plus an annual increment in Kcs. Institutional effectiveness or efficiency were not, up to 1991, a part of the budgetary decision-making process.[25]

All higher education institutions are financed this way except for Tomas Masaryk University in Brno in the Czech Republic. Masaryk was the first university to agree to caps on its state subsidy in exchange for retaining income. Essentially this has meant that Masaryk University keeps the income it receives instead of depositing it in the state account, and the state makes up the difference to meet costs. It is a mechanism to encourage the university to become increasingly self-supporting.

The state in 1989 spent 6.5 billion Kcs on higher education, about 19 percent of the education budget, 1.4 percent of the national budget, and about 1 percent of the national income. Of the 6.5 billion Kcs, the operating budget was 5.6 billion Kcs and investment expenditures (mostly capital expenditures) were 918 million Kcs. Operating expenses went to salaries 45 percent, materials 26 percent, scholarships and fellowships 7 percent, and miscellaneous costs 22 percent (half to science and research expenditures and half to subsidized student accommodations and meals). The OECD report indicates that this percentage allocation did not change much since

1989, and for 1992 institutions have obtained about the same amount of financial resources as in 1990, reflecting a restrictive budget and a decrease in sources of revenue.[26]

In 1990 and 1991, the state has had to reopen the budget to increase the expenditures due to inflation. In 1990 alone the budget increased by 19 percent to cover the rising costs of food, fuel, and renovation. In 1991, the budget for higher education increased by 30 percent to help meet inflation. It is hoped that the shortage of funds will lead the institutions to use their resources more efficiently. The intention of the state, given the high unemployment and the depressed economy since 1989, is to gradually reduce the extent of financial aid it passes out, and to gradually increase funds generated by the institutions.[27]

The Higher Education Act of 1990 made changes in the governance and budgeting system. Within each institution, the academic senates of the faculties and universities decide on budgets proposed by the deans and rectors. The ministry now consults with the higher education councils and the registrars association in determining the allocation of resources. In the 1991 budget, resources were allocated as in the past, but in the Czech Republic, 10 percent of the budget was distributed according to a new method of allocating resources among institutions based on the number of students and a cost per student comparison across disciplines.

In 1992, universities prepared for the full implementation of the new method. The budget is divided into three parts: two-thirds normative, one quarter above normative, and about 9 percent reserves. Thus, for the first time, the major part of the budget (normative) will be allocated on a formula based on the number of students times the average cost per student in various disciplines. Part-time students carry an adjustment factor of 0.4. Table 6 indicates the 1992 calculated cost per student by discipline. These calculations were arrived at by the cost experiences and estimates of the institutions and, therefore, reflect past efficiencies and inefficiencies in providing higher education. For example, arts colleges are small, some as small as a few hundred students, and instruction is labor intensive, with many tutorials. Social sciences and pedagogy have been taught to large groups of students within larger institutions, and with little expensive equipment; while

Table 6. State Expenditures on Higher Education in CSFR, CR, and SR, 1970–1989

		1970	1975	1980	1985	1989
Total(Millions of Kcs)	CSFR	2962.9	4030.6	4783.0	5402.3	6515.5
	CR	1869.9	2452.5	2959.3	3287.7	3960.5
	SR	1093.0	1578.1	1823.7	2114.6	2555.0
- Non-investment Expenditures	CSFR	2510.1	3345.6	4148.7	4702.6	5597.4
- Investments	CSFR	452.8	685.0	634.3	699.7	918.1
Expenditures on HE as % of All Education Expenditures	CSFR	20.2	20.5	19.7	18.4	18.8
As % of Government Expenditures	CSFR	1.52	1.47	1.57	1.51	1.38
As % of National Income	CSFR	0.95	0.99	0.98	0.97	1.07

Source: OECD, *Higher Education in the Czech and Slovak Federal Republic,* 1992, p. 60.

Table 7. Application of 1992 Budget for the University of South Bohemia

	Soc. Sci.	Pedagogy	Technical	Agri.	Medicine	Nat. Sci.	Chem.	Vet.	Arts	Total
U. of S. Bohemia	83	1,257		747	67	42				2,196
Ratios by Faculty	1.00	1.25	1.65	1.90	2.55	2.55	2.55	3.00	3.50	

University of South Bohemia Operational Expenditures Budget for 1992 (thousands of Kcs)

	Normative					Above Normative			
1991 Budget	Application of Ratio	Application %	Adjustment %	1992 Budget	Room/Board	Foreign Lectures	Foreign Students	Sport	Total
72,901	56,722	-22.2%	-8.5%	66,693	8,328	420	0	10	75,451

Source: Budget documents from Czech Ministry of Education and Sport, 1992. Normative in Kcs = 16,921.

Issues in Funding Higher Education in Eastern Europe   223

just the reverse may be said of veterinary science, medicine, and the hard sciences.

In 1992, the formula as applied yielded a great variation in the budgets of individual institutions; some were cut in the extreme and others increased, as compared with 1992. Therefore, the state supplemented the application of the formula so that no institution would suffer too great a shock in one year. For example, the University of South Bohemia, as shown in Table 7, had a total of 2,196 students in various disciplines. Using the budget ratios by faculty (discipline) yielded a corrected number of 3,352. The normative amount as determined by the ministry for the 1992 budget was 16,921 Kcs, roughly the average instructional cost per student in higher education. Multiplying that times 3,352 gave the university 56,722,000 Kcs as a 1992 budget, a 22.2 percent cut in the normative budget from the year before. As a result of the application of the ratios, some of the twenty-three institutions received severe cuts and others great increases, so the ministry was forced to apply a correction factor in order that no institution would receive a cut or increase of more than 10 percent for 1992. In the case of South Bohemia, the decrease turned out to be 8.5 percent, yielding a normative budget of 66,693,000 Kcs. Adding in the above normative amount, the total budget for 1992 was 75,451,000, a severe cut over 1992.

The above normative budget is designated for activities above basic instructional costs, e.g., student room and board, stipends for foreign students, sports, and special programs. The proportion of the budget derived from normative or above normative varies greatly by institution. One suspects that one reason for the budget separation may be to enable the state to increasingly restrict the above normal budget by asking the users to pay ever larger amounts until these activities are largely self-supporting.

It is too early to ascertain the effects of this new method, but it could mean that institutions, given increasingly constrictive budgets and a new method of allocation, will find it necessary to admit more students, release superfluous or incompetent faculty members, and attend to social demand. Since the cost to the student may be the same at a number of competing institutions, and admission to several institutions is possible, students may gravitate to higher quality institutions, with important consequences to Czech higher education. Also, the system may lead to heavy admissions to faculties in which the individual institution, for whatever reason, is efficient, i.e., can make out very well on the basis of the normal budget formula. Conversely, institutions might be expected to restrict programs with large "losses," or find ways to make them more efficient.

External Funding. One source of funds for institutions is external. It seems clear that the state will not cough up ever-increasing resources to higher education, given the increasing university autonomy and the poor state of the economy.

On the other hand, there is very little university tradition of external economic activity: 98 percent of the funds for higher education comes from the state. The remaining 2 percent come mainly from sales of publications to students and teachers, small fees for adult courses, and the sale of accommodations during university holidays. According to the new law, institutions will be relatively free to use money earned through economic activity instead of turning it in to the state treasury, although it is not yet clear what those activities will be. Before 1992, most income received by the institution was deposited in a state treasury account, i.e., returned to the state, including fees and donations. Also, up to now there has been no tradition or tax policy to encourage donations to higher education.

It is now expected that institutions will become more aggressive in earning money and seeking donations from individuals, enterprises, or foundations. Institutions may also be able to sell services of a technical nature to enterprises, and even start enterprises related to their mission such as bookstores, conferences, and special programs. One opportunity which has not yet been tapped is pre-collegiate preparation courses or instruction for those who are not prepared to pass the entrance exams. Such additional financial resources, as indicated earlier, are exempt from taxation.[28]

In addition, institutions and the government are becoming more aware of the need to recover costs of providing goods and services to students at highly subsidized rates. One is already seeing a gradual erosion of the subsidies for room and board, books, and supplies. This will force the institutions to pass on the costs to students, and eventually the students may pay market rates.

Fees have recently been imposed by the state, e.g., admission fees, matriculation fees, and degree fees; the number and amount of these fees vary by institution. This has not been external funding for the university, since the money currently flows back to the state treasury, but that could change. In a move to further free the institutions and to encourage competition, the state could allow institutions to set and retain these fees. The same could happen with room and board.

Tuition. Traditionally, Czech and Slovak students have paid no tuition fees and only nominal amounts for room and board provided by the universities. In addition, many students receive stipends. Recently, institutions have been able to charge fees for special programs and to charge foreign students (those not on scholarships) attending degree and non-degree programs.

Tuition charges are even being discussed for short-term adult education of general public interest, such as classes to learn English or German, and special new programs in high demand such as business administration, where instruction is expensive and students are likely to quickly recoup their investment. There is evidence that students are open to the idea of modest charges, accompanied by loans and scholarships for those who cannot pay, and recognize that some of the gain from higher education is personal, and some accrues to the state.[29]

In the case of foreigners, the Communist practice of admitting foreigners from socialist countries and comrades from the Third World has been discontinued. There are now a few scholarships offered to support reciprocal agreements, but for the most part, foreign students are expected to pay an annual study fee (tuition) of $2,500–$10,000, depending on their field of study. In 1990–91, the percentage of foreign students studying at their own or a sponsor's expense increased, and the fees which had been deposited in the state treasury are now kept by the institutions.[30]

Of course, the fact that students did not pay did not mean education was free. Nor was it free to their families in that the tax structure, as well as other parts of the national income, were devoted to these public expenditures. Thus, the money spent on providing free higher education to a relatively few persons in the population could have had alternative uses, e.g., better medical care, better housing, a more advance infrastructure, wholesome food and balanced diets for the poor, more environmental concern, and better public schools at the lover levels, including vocational and technical education.

On the other hand, tuition-free higher education in Czechoslovakia was available to many students who could not have paid the cost, particularly given a Marxist society where inherited wealth, high incomes, and private ownership of the means of production were all but nonexistent. Also, an attempt was made to admit social classes which had been largely excluded, e.g., peasants, workers, and women.

Nationalized Property. The Communists after 1948 expropriated almost all substantial real property. This has affected universities in a number of ways. First, much of the expropriated property belonging to others was given to educational institutions, and previous owners (individuals, institutions, or enterprises) are now claiming them. Even if new owners are not pushing universities out of the buildings, they want rent. For example, the University of South Bohemia's pedagogy faculty has been occupying buildings owned by the municipality, which wants them returned; and the university's faculty of agriculture is losing agricultural fields to previous owners who are reclaiming their land.

In addition, the party built facilities for itself all over Czechoslovakia, for training and instructional purposes, for party headquarters, and for conference centers. Many of these have recently been given to the universities and must be renovated, maintained, and heated. In either case, whether property is lost or gained, there is a cost to the universities which is expected to exceed budget projections.

Value of Physical Plant. Before 1989, universities had to submit to the ministries an estimate of the value of physical plant, although the reason for this was not always made clear. The most plausible explanation is that it was used as a rough basis for allocating repair and maintenance funds. Clearly it was based on fiction, as was so much else under the Communists. Since in most cases the buildings had been confiscated, or had always belonged to the university, there would have been no recent purchase price upon which to base assessed value. Real property of the universities could not be sold, bought, rented, or otherwise offered at market rates, so it is difficult to imagine on what data any assessment was made. Nevertheless, the annual fiction continued up to 1991. In 1992, for the first time, the universities have been provided with new tables to estimate the value of physical plant. These tables take into account the value of buildings by geographic area, based on recent experience with selling or leasing buildings.

The Future of Funding Higher Education in the Czech Republic and Slovakia

Trying to see into the future is best accompanied by a great deal of humility. We do not know what the future will be. We can see trends that may continue, but the breakup of Czechoslovakia adds uncertainty to an uncertain world. What we can say with some confidence is that, as a result of reform, responsibility and authority within the structure of the higher education system is changing and will continue to change.

It is important to remember that communism existed for at least forty years in Czechoslovakia and Eastern Europe. There is almost no one working at the university who worked in any other system, or who remembers working at a university in Czechoslovakia which was not controlled by the Communists. Thus, change may not always come rapidly or smoothly.

If the increase in institutional autonomy and greater independence from state control continues, we would expect it to result in the creation of new and more relevant curricula, in attempts to hire qualified new faculty and retrain present faculty, in attempts to become major contributors to national development needs, and in the provision of greater access for the next generation of students. The power shift may also force a reallocation of resources and result in some competition for students, quality faculty, and new external resources. Thus, institutions may become more attentive to the needs of the community, state and private industrial and commercial enterprises, local governments, and friends, alumni, and other potential supporters.

This type of restructuring is not uncommon in transformations such as that of Central and Eastern Europe. Before reform, organizations were dependent upon the state for decision making and financial accountability. Reform brings with it far greater autonomy and widens the range of permitted activities and thus, redistributes power among competitors, new entrants, suppliers and buyers. Higher education managers may also be given more autonomy as they become more responsible for their organizations and as they face increased competition from aggressive purveyors of higher education internally as well as externally.

Political and economic changes will decrease university access to guaranteed and controlled placements of students. While some established universities will have a competitive edge, new entrants to the system may quickly gain recognition. For example, new M.B.A. programs are placing students in prominent jobs more rapidly than existing institutions. The hiring firms trust the newer programs to provide students with skills needed by these firms.[31]

Higher education may see new institutions enter the market, bringing with them new capacity and new resources. This influx of other institutions may mean that the barriers to entry will decrease as more existing institutions become autonomous. New institutions may be formed initially as small specialized institutions, e.g., offering management education.

A search for economies of scale is likely. Some existing universities probably will join together to take advantage of common facilities, administrative support, and faculty. This merging has already begun with the recent introduction of new universities that were reformulations of existing institutions.[32]

The established universities may have a competitive edge because they have name recognition within Czechoslovakia. For example, if students view the Bratislava School of Economics as a vocational type of school, it will be at a comparative disadvantage with a prestigious institution of higher learning like Comenius. Bratislava School of Economics' adoption of a new image could be costly compared to more prestigious competitors. Comenius could introduce new curriculum and market this curriculum more easily than its neighboring school.

Certain suppliers to the university will gain power by threatening to raise prices or by reducing supply. Faculty members are one supplier group. Qualified faculty members who can teach the new curriculum, e.g., in social science research, English, or business administration, will be in demand. Also, quality faculty members have new opportunities such as employment in joint ventures, foreign universities, consulting firms, or government.

To respond to this need for faculty, we might expect higher education managers to explore new payment systems including differential pay for highly valued faculty, to widen earnings differentials between skilled and unskilled labor, and to provide training and skill enhancement for faculty and administrators.

If an instructional charge for students is recommended, it may be introduced gradually, perhaps 5 percent of the annual instructional cost per student, or about 1,000 Kcs ($15). This is not a huge amount for some students or families, and a portion of it could be put into a fund for those unable to pay anything. The system could be augmented with a loan program, perhaps with forgiveness provisions for service to the state, or in priority areas, after graduation, e.g., as a teacher, nurse, or physician. If the state withdraws gradually from the "above normative" areas of support, some of those funds could be reallocated to scholarships and loans. Eventually, the student portion of the "normative budget" could be increased until there is a balance between the costs and benefits that accrue to the state and to the individual. This would seem to be a reasonable and gradual way to deal with the tuition issue as long as talented students are not denied admission due to the tuition charge.

If it were to become public policy that students (or their families or employers, etc.) should pay part of the instructional costs, several things could be expected to happen. First, students would be more serious about their work and there would be pressure to complete studies on time and to learn something useful, something which would make the students employable. Second, it would exclude a number of students who simply could not pay. Third, it would force all parties to examine the relationship between cost and benefit, and may eventually lead to shortages of professionals and a greater pay differentiation between uneducated and highly educated labor. Fourth, it may accentuate class differences and lead to greater social unrest. Fifth, it may eventually lead to an end of brain drain as salaries rise to become more realistic in terms of international standards. Sixth, it would cause persons of means to help pay for their instruction. Eighth, it would force the universities to search for economies, such as increasing low student-teacher ratios.

At the same time, the universities could be set free by the state to earn money through conferences, tourism, consulting, publishing, research, running profitable university enterprises, bookstores, lecture notes, exams, franchises, and licensing arrangements. The new law exempts university enterprises from taxation. Also, universities could be encouraged by state taxation policies to seek donations and bequests and to set up foundations to continue the work of the university in perpetuity. Such revenues could help the university in meeting expenses not covered by direct instructional costs.

Where would the rest of the revenues come from, assuming students eventually could pay some tuition costs? One large expenditure is investment or capital costs, about 900 million Kcs in 1989. Since the state owns the buildings and capital equipment, and would continue to do so, one might expect the state to continue to provide that budget item, and in fact it may eventually find a way to justify that continued expenditure as a state contribution. After all, higher education is not only a consumer good, the fruits of which are enjoyed by the recipient, but also an investment from which all society benefits.

In addition to the investment costs, there are operating expenditures. In the past few years, 45 percent of the operating expenditures went to salaries, 26 percent materials, 7 percent scholarships and fellowships, and 22 percent to miscellaneous (half to science and research and half to subsidized student room and board). With respect to the 71 percent (45 percent plus 26 percent) of operating expenditures now going to instruction, basically the "normative budget," the state could agree to continue basic support with an ever-decreasing share in exchange for freeing the universities to earn and control income from such items as tuition, investments on reserves, savings and cash flow, gifts and bequests, sales of supplies and accommodations rentals, overhead charges, fees, bookstores, and so forth. The scholarships (7 percent) should be continued, but focused on vouchers for the most able students pursuing careers of priority national interest. The resources (11 percent) now devoted to subsidizing student room and board could be decreased every year to a point where the most needy students could apply for grants or loans for room and board and others would pay the cost, thus relieving the state of that expenditure. The fellowships and scholarships, 7 percent of the present state operating expenditures, could then be used by the state to fund academic excellence. This fund could pay for vouchers to the most academically talented students. Such vouchers could be used by the students at any national university for any course of study designated by the state as a priority for national needs. As to the 11 percent spent on research and science, it may be wise to evaluate those expenditures to make sure they are serving national development needs such as a modern industrial policy, but otherwise, that is not a large amount of money for a nation to spend on research and science.

If some policy decision such as those cited were agreed upon, it would mean that the state would be relieved of ever-increasing

Issues in Funding Higher Education in Eastern Europe 231

payments to higher education, and those payments remaining could be more focused on national development needs.

Certain curricula ought to get more attention. The social sciences (especially economics), management subjects (especially accounting and marketing), and world languages are the areas requiring the most strengthening. Some areas of physical and engineering sciences are also below world standards and need strengthening. As a general matter, the theoretical disciplines, and the theoretical foundations for hard sciences, are nearly comparable to European levels. Czechoslovakia falls short on practical, hands-on experimental and empirical techniques supported by equipment such as contemporary computers and lab equipment.

The challenge is to find legitimate ways to retire incompetent faculty and to enable those who are or could be productive. This process can be helped by well designed faculty evaluation techniques, faculty development, and the reduction of faculty sizes. This would allow rectors to reorient curriculum and to improve salaries for the most productive colleagues.

Only 16 percent of age-eligible people are enrolled in higher education; as noted earlier, Czechoslovakia provides higher educational opportunity to roughly half the proportion of its citizens as most OECD countries.[33] A change may be needed to open universities to more people and to expand the curricular offerings to make them more relevant, e.g., two-year degree professional preparation programs, business administration, and English and German language instruction. Higher education should work closely with enterprises to gain financial support and training sites and to give modern, well trained technical education to meet the needs of commerce and industry for highly trained personnel.

These suggestions could yield important new resources for institutions and make them more relevant to the need for the nation to enter advanced technological development. Also, the suggestions could help to educate a greater proportion of the able young people, which will yield political, social, and cultural dividends, and at the same time improve the hopes of young persons for a bright future in a land that has suffered so much from the egregious mistakes of the past.

This chapter, we hope, will contribute to a national debate with regard to the issues raised and lead to policies which will work well and equitably for the nation, the universities, and the students, teachers and staff.

Conclusion

Czechoslovakia has a long tradition of higher education, and that tradition can be expected to guide future development. The years of repression of higher education under Communist governments on balance had a negative effect, leaving a legacy of a poorly developed system, isolation from world scholarship, inadequate funding, repression of autonomy, controlled curriculum, access, research, and teaching in higher education.

The overthrow of the Communist government in 1989 raised hopes for a better, more modern and responsive system of higher education, but changes came slowly, especially since the new governments are trying to be democratic, trying to avoid witch hunts and the rigidly controlled behavior of the regime they replaced. Thus, while the institutions have become democratic and enjoy a great deal of freedom in internal governance, they are to a large extent dependent upon the same faculty, staff, and students, the same facilities, equipment, and organization as before, and with the government as almost the sole source of revenue.

The new higher education law created a radical and fundamental change in the relationships between the universities and the state, but funding from the state for higher education is increasingly tight, and far too few students are served by higher education.

Clearly, new financing methods must supplement the state's budget for higher education. The core financing for higher education institutions has been automatic increases for operational budgets. One of the problems with these budgets has been the lack of connection with the number of students attending a university. The new financing system will help to make that connection. At the same time, institutions are being given more autonomy and encouraged to look elsewhere for additional funds.

New regional universities are starting to make the system a bit more rational, but the need to close weak institutions and those that are no longer needed, or that duplicate others, is still present. A few new programs are starting which have more market emphasis and pay more attention to social demand.

The separation of research and teaching imported by the Communists, using the academies as vehicles, caused a certain sterility and unresponsiveness in the former system. That system is slowly being changed. Universities will need to develop new research agendas, and recombine research and teaching. One mechanism is to create a well-funded competition for those working in universities which will enable them to compete for research funds through the preparation and submission of grant proposals.

Universities may be overstaffed and many faculty members may have become obsolete as a result of their isolation from world class information exchange. Faculty development programs are needed to teach modern techniques. New disciplines are going to demand that some faculty change their specialties.

Despite decades of repression and control, universities have remained an important part of Czechoslovak society. They have retained a certain respected status despite outside invasions, the near destruction of the system in World War II, and the Communist state's use of them as instruments for controlling and reeducating the "new Communist man."[34]

Some individual creativity and initiative managed to survive more than forty years of repressive party and state control. This resiliency is testimony to the courage of the citizens and to the persistence of the ideal of common human rights and values even in the worst of times. It is this persistence, courage, and rededication to national history that is now driving the restructuring of higher education, and indeed society, and that provides hope for the future.

NOTES

1. Charles Homer Haskins. *The Rise of Universities.* (Ithaca: Cornell University Press, 1957).

2. D.P. Daniel. "National Higher Education and Research Systems of Central Europe." Unpublished manuscript of the Slovak Academic Information Agency. (Bratislava, Czechoslovakia, 1992).

3. Eric Ashby. *Technology and the Academics.* (London: Macmillan, 1958).

4. M. Hrabinska, ed. *Higher Education in the Czech and Slovak Republic.* (Bratislava, Czechoslovakia: The Institute of Information and Prognosis of Education, Youth, and Sports, 1991).

5. D. Kallen. *The Open Door: Pan European Academic Cooperation.* (Bucharest: UNESCO European Centre for Higher Education, 1991).

6. J. Koucky. "Czechoslovak Higher Education at the Crossroads." *European Journal of Education* 25, no. 4 (1990): 361–377.

7. D. Kallen. *Op. cit.*

8. D. P. Daniel. *Op. cit.*

9. L. Cyerch. "Renewal of Central European Higher Education: Issues and Challenges." *European Journal of Education,* 25, no. 4 (1990): 351–359.

10. Lubomir Harach, Jiri Kotasek, Jan Koucky, and Jana Hendrichova. *Higher Education in the Czech and Slovak Republic.* (Prague-Bratislava: OECD, 1992).

11. J. Koucky. *Op. cit.*

12. D. Kallen. *Op. cit.*

13. L. Harach, et al. *Op. cit.*

14. *Ibid.*

15. *Ibid.*

16. Centre for Higher Education Studies. *Soucasny Vztah Statu a Vysokeho Skolstvi v CR.* (Prague: Author, 1992).

17. L. Harach, et al. *Op. cit.*

18. *Ibid.*

19. J. Koucky. *Op. cit.*

20. R.W. Harbison. *Education and Training in Czechoslvvakia.* (Durham, England: Birks Sinclair and Associates, Inc. Unpublished report to the Czechoslovak government, 1991).

21. Centre for Higher Education Studies. *Op. cit.*

22. L. Harach, et al. *Op. cit.*

23. *Ibid.*

24. R.W. Harbison. *Op. cit.*

25. *Ibid.*

26. L. Harach, et al. *Op cit.*

27. *Ibid.*

28. *Ibid.*
29. *Ibid.*
30. *Ibid.*
31. D.S. Fogel, ed. *Management Education in Central and Eastern Europe and the Soviet Union.* (Pittsburgh: University of Pittsburgh, 1992).
32. L. Harach, et al. *Op. cit.*
33. *Ibid.*
34. J. Koucky. *Op. cit.*

PROBLEMS OF FUNDING THE TRANSFORMATION OF HIGHER EDUCATION IN EAST GERMANY

Helmut de Rudder

Introduction

The reunification of Germany on October 3, 1989, was not just a political act. It is a social, political, economic and cultural process of radical change which started in the fall of 1989 and which might very well take a generation to be completed. Changing the structures, the objectives, the contents, and the methods of public education—of which higher education is a part—is a major element of this process. Given the importance of higher education in highly industrialized or postindustrial societies, there is no doubt that what happens to and in East German universities and colleges will affect the long-range process of uniting the two German societies, which, in spite of their common past and some enduring common characteristics, have developed away from and against each other since the division of Germany and the beginning of the Cold War in the aftermath of World War II.

This chapter focuses on problems of funding the transformation of higher education in East Germany and its integration into the higher education system of what was West Germany. Our perspective on funding is not a technical one. It concentrates, instead, on the political and societal contexts of funding. The ways, levels, procedures, and problems of funding public institutions—like, in this case, higher education in East Germany—reflect political priorities, societal values, the ways and means of regulating public affairs and of solving problems in the public domain; they reflect the social and economic problems of a society, its structures, its political system, and its culture. For a sociologist, the budget is always a telling document for the analysis of a society, its political agenda and social problems, as Daniel Bell has pointed out.[1] Since public funding always is a decisive policy instrument, a societal perspective on funding must consider the real effects of funding policy.

Applying this perspective to the funding problems of higher education in East Germany, the following will be analyzed:

- in the general context of funding the process of German unification;
- as a key factor in the policy of renewing higher education in East Germany, especially in regard to staffing;
- in a comparative perspective of funding higher education in modern societies.

Contexts of Funding Higher Education

Financing the renewal of East Germany after the breakdown of the Communist regime in 1989 and German reunification in 1990 has become the most demanding public responsibility the federal republic has ever had to shoulder. Because of the breakdown of large parts of the productive capacity in East Germany—in 1992, industrial production was down to about one-third of what it was at the time of unification—most of the money needed has to come from West Germany, mainly from the federal government. In 1991, 140 billion marks of public money were transferred into East Germany, in 1992, 180, and in 1993, it will be 186 billion marks. The estimate for 1994 is 185 billion. By the year 2000 it is expected to go down to 143 billion marks per annum.[2] (For comparison, in 1989, the complete budget of the federal government was 290 billion marks.)

The problems of funding the renewal of higher education in East Germany must be seen in this context. Funding the renewal of East Germany by a mix of reducing spending in other public sectors (which so far has not been done), raising taxes, and increasing the public debt is one of the main problems of domestic policy in Germany. Higher education clearly does not have a very high priority in comparison to the need to invest in the material infrastructure (roads, railways, telecommunication, energy, etc.), to support the buildup of the economy, and to finance welfare measures in East Germany, mainly as a consequence of mass unemployment, which in the old industrial areas and in agriculture is more than 30 percent. Notwithstanding the fact that higher education and research are major factors of economic development and prosperity, the main obstacles to economic growth in East Germany today are certainly not due to existing inadequacies of higher education.

The special problems of funding higher education in East Germany also reflect a general predicament of funding public mass higher education in highly industrialized societies: The more expensive and expansive higher education gets (possibly with a diminishing rate of return) and the more it depends on public funds, the more it has to compete with other public responsibilities (like welfare, defense, or environmental protection). In all of these societies, however, strong as their belief in the market economy may be, governments are increasingly overburdened with growing demands for public funds by organized interests or simply by the problems societies have to solve. Since revenues do not increase accordingly, governments tend to be in a steady state of financial crisis[3] or at least underfunding. This is now more of a structural and principal than a cyclical problem of modern societies, and thus also determines the financial environment for higher education.

Basic Changes in Funding Higher Education in East Germany

Because the German Democratic Republic (GDR) dissolved itself and joined the federal republic, the basic structures and mechanisms of financing higher education were not a matter of choice and discussion for East Germany. With the integration of East German higher education into the West German system, West German ways and means of funding higher education are being introduced automatically in the five new East German states. That means that:

- Higher education—including the financial responsibility for it—becomes a matter of the new states.
- Institutions of higher education get line-item budgets from the state government through the state ministry of higher education.
- The federal government pays for 50 percent of all building investments in higher education.

- Professors become civil servants.
- Academics are eligible for research grants from the German Research Society (which is funded jointly by the federal government and the states) and other funding bodies (like the Volkswagen Foundation).

The West German system of higher education budgeting, financing, and financial control is being introduced without any changes in East Germany at a time when it is being questioned by many university-based critics and by people in government and in business. The catchwords are deregulation, decentralization, flexibility, and institutional autonomy. Under self-imposed pressure to renew the East German system of higher education and integrate it into the West German system as fast as possible, there was no time to sit back and think whether and how things might or should be done differently.

In contrast to American universities, most European universities and colleges generate little or no income of their own. There are, however, some notable new developments in this direction such as in the Netherlands and Sweden. Though the necessity of doing something about this almost complete dependence on government funding is recognized in Germany, and some attempts are being made to change it, the prospects of doing it in East Germany are not encouraging given the condition of higher education and the economy in the new East German states. There are neither very many producers of saleable services in higher education nor potential buyers who have the money to buy such services. Thus, for the present and the near future, higher education in the East German states will continue to depend on public money as the main source of its funding. Whereas in West Germany the development of income and property in the middle classes since the 1950s would allow a considerable number of families to pay for the higher education of their children, there are no comparable financial resources in East Germany.

Institutions of higher education in East Germany have also lost the only financial flexibility they had before the breakup of the GDR: Universities and colleges used to have contracts with industrial combines to undertake research and development projects for them and in cooperation with them for pay. This gave them some financial leeway outside of direct government control. In the 1980s this cooperation accounted for about 50 percent of all research and development activities of higher education institutions.

Academic Staff: Renewal and Reduction

Since higher education is a very personnel-intensive business and depends on what its staff actually does, changes in the structure, the size, the selection, and the funding of academic staff is a key issue in the renewing of higher education in East Germany. In the following section, we therefore focus our discussion of funding and budgetary problems on the professoriate.

For the majority of academic staff in East Germany, the main problem with the renewal of higher education is that they will not survive this process: they will be or have already been dismissed because their positions have been eliminated. It is now apparent that less than 50 percent—possibly only around 30 percent—of the academic staff of 1989 is going to be retained. Budgetary and not political or academic factors are responsible. It was clear from the beginning that there would have to be dismissals in the process of renewing higher education in East Germany. Affected were:

- those academics who were leading functionaries of the old regime;
- those who owed their positions to the party without proper qualification;
- those who had worked for the state security forces;
- those who had harmed others for political reasons.

Furthermore, the new state governments closed down ideologically oriented departments like law, history, economics, political science, and education. In these cases, the complete staff of those departments was automatically without a job because their units no longer existed. The compulsory studies in Marxism-Leninism were discontinued right after the breakdown of the Communist regime, and the teachers of these courses were fired. Some of those who were deeply involved with the regime resigned voluntarily, and quite a few took early retirement. There are no exact figures yet for the redundancies caused by this policy of "political cleansing." It is estimated that they are on the order of 10–20 percent of the academic staff of 1989.

The staff of all units, departments, institutes, etc., which continued to exist had to undergo a two-step screening process instituted by the "higher education renewal laws" which were passed in all five new East German states and for East Berlin in 1991. Though there are procedural variations, the first step in all of the states provides for "personnel commissions" consisting exclusively of "Easterners" ("Ossis"), that review the past political record of every staff member and, if the involvement with the past regime is found to be too serious, may recommend dismissal to the state ministry, which then usually acts accordingly.[4] Those academics who are cleared in this way are then subjected to an academic evaluation usually carried out by a mixed East/West commission of academics of their discipline, which passes judgement on their disciplinary qualification.

One would assume that those who are cleared politically and academically then remain in their positions, but that is not the case: they are just a pool for new appointments. It is at this point that fiscal and budgetary considerations enter into the process. In budgetary terms, "renewal" of staff in higher education means that a completely new staffing plan is developed for every institution of higher education specifying the number and kind of positions. This plan then is included in detail in the line-item budget the universities get from the state government. The new East German states only came into existence in the short period between the breakdown of the old East German regime in November of 1989 and the act of unification in October of 1990. The GDR was a centralized state with one central ministry of higher education in East Berlin, while in the political system of the federal republic, higher education was and is a matter of the states. This applied immediately to the new East German states. They had to start from scratch.

The mode and the procedure of creating a state budget for higher education largely predetermines the staffing policy as the most critical field of dealing with the GDR past in higher education. The method could be called "zero budgeting": the new states would not honor any of the appointments the GDR government had made in the past in higher education. All remaining personnel got only temporary contracts for one to three years without any obligation of the state government for further appointment. Thus, the state governments had created *tabula rasa* for a new higher education system and policy without having to close the shop for renovation. With the exception of closed down departments mentioned earlier and politically driven dismissals, the old institutions and programs and their staffs were still there, and the students who had enrolled before unification were guaranteed that they could continue their studies and graduate (except for those in highly ideological programs which had become irrelevant with the end of the old regime). However, it was all "until further notice." This created a situation of extreme uncertainty for both the staffs, whose jobs and livelihood were at stake, and for the students.

Planning and Budgeting

The problems of creating line-item budgets for the first time that included every academic and staff position were great and required political decisions coordinated between the states on structures, size and kinds of institutions, programs, courses, and numbers of students to be accommodated state by state. All of this had to be done under extreme time pressure in close cooperation between East and West. First, the German Science Council, the main higher education advisory body for the federal government since the 1960s, was assigned the task of evaluating East German higher education and research institutions and making proposals for the future landscape of higher education in East Germany in general and in particular by the treaty of unification.[5] Only ten months were allowed for this tremendous effort. Not until the science council had completed its assignment were the first members from East Germany appointed to the council. All of the new states also appointed higher education reform commissions consisting of members from East and West Germany to draw up plans for state higher education systems.[6] Finally, the new state ministries of higher education had to prepare detailed plans for their states which had to be passed by state governments and legislatures.

On the institutional level, the state government (in cooperation with the institution) would appoint "founding commissions" for new departments and academic programs to prepare a curriculum and draw up a budget proposal, including a staffing plan. These commissions consisted mainly of academics from West Germany, especially in cases of departments and programs focusing on subjects and disciplines which were not represented in the GDR or were closely related to the former regime, such as law. Founding commissions were of particular importance where new institutions were to be founded or developed out of old ones or—like in the case of teachers colleges—where formerly specialized institutions were to be integrated into universities. In all of these cases there is a complex interdependence between political decision making, curriculum development, staffing, and funding. On one hand, the limitations of funding determine the other elements of this process; on the other hand, what is finally funded depends equally on the political intentions and the concept and the importance of a program. Under normal circumstances there would have been consecutive steps from the recommendations of the science council to the budget of an institution, but given the pressure to act very fast, and given the fact that, while being changed, the existing system of higher education was in full operation and required daily decisions, all of these planning exercises went on more or less at the same time, and in many instances, decisions on budgets and staffing plans had to be made before planning processes had been completed. This made the position of the ministries in the process of renewal even stronger than they were anyway.

Based on statewide higher education development plans ("master plans"), higher education budgets for the new East German states are largely determined by:

- the rules, regulations and index figures governing the budget process in the old West German states. They were invariably applied in the new states;
- the financial situation of the new states, which in the third year of unification still is much worse that of the old states;
- the (rather low) position of higher education on the list of priorities in the process of renewal and reconstruction in East Germany; and
- special federal programs for the support of the renewal of higher education in East Germany.

Once decisions are made on the kind and location of institutions, the structure and curricula of academic programs, and the projected number of students in each of them, determining the number and categories of personnel to include in the budget is mainly a matter of computation based on the index figures for academic and other staff in use in West Germany since the 1970s. Because of the general financial misery, the actual staffing plans in the yearly budgets usually will include fewer positions than the master plan projected.

Developing new staffing plans for a thoroughly renewed system of higher education in East Germany means that none of the old staff is taken over automatically. Anybody from the old staff has to reapply for a position in the new staffing pattern, even if the work he or she has to do will be basically the same as before. Though many of the old positions reappear in the same or a similar situation in the new staffing plans, legally and formally they are new positions in a different system of grades, pay scales and types of positions. Furthermore, all new professorships are civil service positions now, which did not exist in the GDR. In accordance with the old West German pay scales, salaries for the new academic positions in East Germany are considerably higher than they were in the GDR, which makes the system more expensive even though there are fewer than half as many positions. This is possibly the most critical point in the process of integrating East German higher education into the hitherto West German system: on the whole, it will have to do with about 40 percent of the academic staff it had before. And in those academic disciplines and programs which are closely related to the political, economic, and social system—fields like law, economics, business administration, political science, and to a large extent also sociology, education, and philosophy—which have to be built up anew, almost all of the new professors and most of the academic staff come from West Germany. Furthermore, many academic programs had to be changed considerably to fit the needs of the labor market for graduates, to adopt to the state of the art in the respective academic disciplines and thus to become or to stay attractive and competitive in the new environment of a united Germany and an open European market. As a consequence, the qualifications and specializations of quite a few East German academics would not fit the specifications and denominations of positions in the new staffing plans and thus they lost out when competing with West German academics who also applied. These developments are probably going to bring down the proportion of East German academics who get new appointments in the East German states to about 30 percent.

Overstaffing in the East Versus Understaffing in the West

The far-reaching reductions of staff in East German higher education are related to the astronomical costs of rebuilding East

Germany and the subsequent necessity to keep down the costs of the public sector as a whole. But they also have to do with the fact that in relation to Western countries, higher education in the GDR, as in other East European countries, seemed to have been overstaffed. This situation contrasts sharply with the overcrowding, underfunding, and understaffing of higher education in West Germany as it has developed since the beginning of the 1980s. The resulting funding problems in West Germany make it more difficult to solve the funding problems of higher education in the new eastern states of the federal republic. Consequently, there is a policy of reducing academic staff to the staff-student ratio of West Germany. Whereas the staff-student ratio in the GDR in 1989 was 1:43,[7] it has fallen to 1:26 at universities and 1:37 at vocational colleges (Fachhochschulen) in 1990 in West Germany.[8] The difference shrinks if we take into account that in the GDR almost all students completed their prescribed course of studies exactly on time, whereas in West Germany it takes students at universities on the average more than seven years to finish a program that is designed for four to five years, with many of the students *de facto* studying only part time, but counted as full-time students. East German institutions of higher education were heavily engaged in further and continuing education as part of their normal teaching loads, although that is not shown in the number of students.[9] But even if we consider these factors, the fact remains that the staff-student ratio in East Germany was much better than that of West Germany, and the West German ratio is also considerably worse than in any other comparable Western country. The federal republic decided in 1977 to keep higher education institutions open for the very large age cohorts of the 1960s, expecting the number of students to go down after that in line with demographic development. The policy was to allow more students in during the years of the expected "student mountain," increase the staff only temporarily, and limit the permanent capacity to the demographically expected smaller number of students after that "mountain." Thus, the finance ministers capped—with the exception of medicine and the new vocational colleges (Fachhochschulen)—the funding of universities at the level of the late 1970s, while the number of students kept growing and the "student mountain" turned out to be a high plateau due to a steady increase in the percentage of young people graduating from "gymnasium" (academic secondary school) and thereby earning the right to enter higher education. And the percentage of those who

The Transformation of Higher Education in East Germany

actually entered also kept going up. Since state governments steadfastly refused to increase university budgets, the staff-student ratio increased from 1:11 in 1977 to the earlier mentioned 1:26 in 1990.[10]

To regain the staff-student ratio of 1976 in West Germany, 30,000 more positions for academic staff would be needed, as the German Rectors Conference has stated recently.[11] Investments in buildings and equipment also did not keep pace with increasing numbers of students: today, there are double as many students as there are places in West German higher education. These are alarming figures, and it is no exaggeration to speak of a funding crisis in higher education in West Germany. This was the situation when Germany was reunited. Almost necessarily the basic policy for higher education (as for all other public spending) had to be "building up East before expanding West" ("Aufbau Ost vor Ausbau West"). In this situation of high funding deficits in higher education in West as well as in East Germany, neither the extremely good staff-student ratio in the east can be maintained, nor can the extremely bad one in the west be left as it is. In the light of the highest national debt ever in the Federal Republic of Germany—conditioned by the costs of rebuilding East Germany—this does not seem to be the best time for higher education in Germany to regain the share of the gross national product (GNP) of 1.32 percent it held in 1975, which had dropped to 1.12 percent (down 15.2 percent) in 1990.[12] The German Rectors Conference requested in 1992 that the annual budget of higher education (states and federal government together) be raised by 9.0 billion (with a share of 2.2 for East Germany),[13] which would be an increase of 30 percent against what higher education got in 1990. As it is not very likely that this is going to happen, "renewal East" and "improvement West" are competing for funding.

Mainly for fiscal reasons, but also because ministries and many university leaders and administrators want to accomplish the renewal as fast as possible, the process of reducing staff after the dismissals for political reasons have been effected is not left to normal attrition. Instead, there are mass dismissals of academics until staff size is reduced to the numbers projected in the new staffing plans. This is possible under the legal arrangements and the budgetary procedure for creating new staffing patterns and plans mentioned earlier. As could be expected, there is a lot of criticism of this policy since it results in the ousting of probably the majority of East German academics who have been positively evaluated. Though it is not the primary objective of this policy to fire these people, it is an unavoidable consequence of fixing—for, it seems, compelling financial reasons—the number of academic staff positions in the new budgets at a level this low without interim arrangements for a period of transition. At first sight this seems to be a case where lack of funds plus the application of West German index figures dictate policy. But it is an intention of this kind of policy of higher education renewal to give priority to fast renewal over a policy containing a stronger social component keeping positively evaluated old academic staff in office as part of an overarching social policy of integrating the two German societies. These, then, were clearly political decisions and not just inherent necessities produced by lack of funds.

It is likely that the present reduction of academic staff may lead to staff shortages by 1995, according to carefully researched forecasts of the number of first-year students expected in East Germany.[14] As part of its overall economic planning, the GDR produced only as many graduates as the employment system was projected to need. Therefore, less than half of the age cohort graduated in the GDR in comparison to the federal republic. It can be assumed that, with the integration of East Germany into the system of the federal republic, the percentage of an age cohort attending institutions of higher education in East Germany is going to increase to about the level in West Germany, resulting in a considerable increase of first-year students from about 1995 on.

Contributions of the Federal Government to Higher Education in the New East German States

Even though higher education is a prime responsibility of the states of the federal republic, the federal government contributes in various ways to the funding of higher education. This also goes for the new states in East Germany. As a matter of course, the federal government pays for 50 percent of investments in buildings and "big equipment." It finances—together with the states—the "German Research Society" (Deutsche Forschungsgemeinschaft), which funds more than 40 percent of all research grants given to academics and higher education research institutions.[15] Public research institutions are also largely funded by the federal government. Furthermore, it is responsible for student aid. The new states automatically participate in these federal programs. But their main problem in funding the renewal of higher education is that they are unable to meet their obligations to provide the operating budgets—including salaries—of higher education institutions because their revenues from state taxes still are insufficient due to the breakdown and low productivity of most sectors of the East German economy. Therefore, the new states receive complementary grants from the federal government to supplement their regular budgets. More important for higher education in East Germany is the "Higher Education Renewal Program" of 1.76 billion marks, jointly sponsored by the federal government (75 percent) and the new states (25 percent). The old states declined to participate—probably mainly because of their own funding problems with higher education. The main features of the program are:[16]

- establishment of "founding professorships" to start new departments and programs in law, economics, business administration, history, philosophy, sociology, and Western languages;
- establishment of key chairs for teacher education in education, psychology, philosophy, and sociology;
- support for the founding of new vocational colleges (Fachhochschulen) by providing funding for 100 professorships, mainly in business administration, social work, and some new disciplines in engineering;
- a special program to integrate scientists from institutes of the former GDR Academy of Sciences and other central academies into universities (for about 2,000 scientists) and into newly established research centers outside of universities (for another 1,500 scientists). (In the Academy of Sciences of the GDR alone there were 24,000 researchers; about 8,500 of them found new jobs). This special program was designed to support a base line of higher education policy in the new states, namely to reintegrate basic research into universities again after the GDR had concentrated it following the Soviet model— in the Academy of Sciences. So far, this policy has not been successful because universities are very reluctant to take over researchers or whole research groups from the academy, since in the end they might have to fire their own scientists for lack of staff positions in the new budget.[17]

These federal programs initiate renewal and provide funding for the first phase of getting the new departments and programs started. After that, the new states will have to pay from their operating budgets. Considering the rather slow pace of economic recovery so far (much slower than expected), it seems to be likely that even after the Higher Education Renewal Program has run out, the federal government will have to continue with complemental grants to the East German states to build up their higher education system.

Conclusion

Even though it is obvious that insufficient funding is a serious drawback in the difficult process of higher education renewal in East Germany, the financial situation is not the first factor that determines higher education policy. With almost the same amount of money, different solutions could have been found—like more equitable treatment for positively evaluated academic staff. In public, the course of action most of the new state ministries of higher education decided to take was legitimized by pointing to the extreme scarcity of funds, but it was still based on a political decision between alternative priorities and strategies. The social effects of mass dismissals of academic staff and the negative impact this policy has on the process of integrating East and West German society were not intended, but forseeable. It was a political decision to put up with these effects in order to achieve fast "renewal."

Our analysis also shows the political importance of public attention, or the lack thereof. In the unification and rebuilding of East Germany there are so many other big problems which catch public attention that this one—mass dismissal of politically "innocent" East German academics—remains below the level of important national news, submerged in the overall mass unemployment and disappearing behind the breakdown of most of the East German economy.

In a comparative perspective of funding policies and mechanisms it is noteworthy that, with the exception of some external research funding, both the former East and West Germany are examples of almost completely state funded higher education systems, with the authority for distribution and allocation of funds resting with the government, with very little open competition for funds, without funding bodies between governments and higher education and with only limited room for the institutions themselves to maneuver within the budget.[18] The urgency of making changes in the system of funding and budgeting in German higher education, which had already been realized by many experts and political decision makers,[19] almost seemed to be forgotten when reunification suddenly came after the demise of the GDR, and the West German system with hair and hide then was taken over in a hurry by the new East German states. A careful study of the problems of funding and budgeting in East German higher education today might provide useful insights into the basic relationships between funding, planning, and policy making in higher education in general, especially if these processes in East Germany are compared with developments in other former Eastern Bloc countries which did not have the opportunity (or the problems) of being reunited with a prosperous Western brother.[20]

NOTES

1. Daniel Bell. *The Cultural Contradictions of Capitalism.* (New York: Basic Books Inc., 1976), Chapter 6.
2. *Wirtschaftswoche*, no. 37 (1990): 14.
3. James O'Connor. *The Fiscal Crisis of the State.* (New York: St. Martin's Press, 1973).
4. Wolff-Dietrich Webler. "Eine Schlacht fur den Rechtsstaat gewonnen? Personalkommissionen an ostdeutschen Hochschulen." *Das Hochschulwesen*, 40, no. 2 (1992): 52–62.
5. *Die Vertrage zur Einheit Deutschlands.* (Munchen: Verlag C.H. Beck, 1990), p. 64.
6. Ulrich Teichler. "Zur Arbeitsweise von Hochschulstrukturkommissionen auf Landesebene." Projektgruppe Hochschulforschung, *Zur Hochschulerneuerung in den neuen Bundes-landern.* (Berlin: Projektgruppe Hochschulforschung, 1992), pp. 8–15
7. Anke Burkhardt, Doris Scherer, and Sabine Erdner (EDV). *Personalbestand an Hochschulen der ehemaligen DDR 1989 und 1990.* (Berlin-Karlshorst: Projektgruppe Hochschulforschung, 3/1991) .

8. Hochschulrektorenkonferenz. "Konzept zur Entwicklung der Hochschulen in Deutschland." *Das Hochschulwesen,* 40, no. 5 (1992): 206.

9. Anke Burkhardt and Doris Scherer. "Personal an Hochschulen in den neuen Bundeslandern." *Beitrage zur Hochschulforschung,* no. 3 (1991): 186.

10. Hochschulrektorenkonferenz. *Op. cit.,* 206.

11. *Ibid.,* 215.

12. Der Bundesminister fur Bildung und Wissenschaft. *Grund- und Strukturdaten 1991/92.* (Bad Honnef: Verlag Karl Heinrich Bock, 1991), p. 275.

13. Hochschulrektorenkonferenz. *Op. cit.,* 215.

14. Henri Adler and Irene Lischka. *Erste Prognose der Studienberechtigten und Studienanfanger aus den neuen Bundeslandern bis 2010.* (Berlin-Karlshorst: Projektgruppe Hochschulforschung, 2/1991); and Klaus Klemm, Wolfgang Bottcher, and Michael Weegen. *Bildungs- planung in den neuen Bundeslandern.* (Weinheim und Munchen: Juventa Verlag, 1992), pp. 165–168.

15. Wissenschaftsrat. *Empfehlungen des Wissenschaftsrates zu den Perspektiven der Hochschulen in den 90er Jahren.* (Koln: Wissenschaftsrat, 1988), p. 39.

16. Hans Rainer Friedrich and Ludger Viehoff. "Erneuerungsprogramm. Drei Ziele: Sichern, Eingliedern, Erneuern." *Deutsche Universitatszeitung,* 15–16 (1991): 24–25.

17. Wolf-Hagen Krauth and Doris Scherer, "Das Wissenschaftlerintegrationsprogramm." *Das Hochschulwesen,* 40, no. 5 (1992): 202–204.

18. Edgar Frackmann. *Selbststeuerung im Hochschulbereich. Ein Beitrag zur okonomischen Theorie der Hochschule.* (Munchen: Verlag V. Florentz, 1987): 53–170.

19. Loccumer Protokolle. *Mehr Freiheit fur die Hochschulen.* (Rehburg-Loccum: Evangelische Akademie Loccum, 1992): 12.

20. Burton Bollag. "Osteuropa: Kredite der Weltbank gegen Reformen." *Deutsche Universitatszeitung,* no. 23 (1991): 24–25.

HIGHER EDUCATION FUNDING IN AUSTRALIA

Brian G. Wilson

Governments play an important role in Australian education, although this role varies significantly between the various education sectors. Postschool education is provided in institutions which are almost entirely publicly established, coordinated, and financed. In contrast, a significant proportion of primary and secondary school pupils are enrolled in private schools—approximately 20 percent in Roman Catholic schools, and 8 percent in non-government, non-Catholic schools.

Constitutionally, in the six states and two territories, education is a matter for the individual state or territory government rather than for the federal authorities. However, by virtue of popular pressure and its control over the major sources of revenue, in particular retaining the sole right to levy income tax, the federal (or commonwealth) government has become increasingly involved in education. Initially, this occurred at the university level, but the federal government is now heavily involved in the support of education at all levels, in both the public and private sectors.

Australian universities have a shorter history than their North American and European counterparts. However, throughout this relatively short history, there have been major changes in the means by which higher education has been funded. Financial support for students in higher education has had a similar history of variation.

During the past thirty-five years, three major shifts in regulation and administration of higher education funding—initiated by changes in government attitudes and policies—have had significant impacts on the development of universities, on the attitudes of students, on university-community relationships, and on the ways in which university resources are procured and managed. Before discussing these issues, however, some background on higher education in Australia may be necessary.[1]

The first university in Australia, the University of Sydney, was inaugurated in New South Wales in 1850, sixty-two years after the arrival of the first British colonists. A powerful force for its establishment was to protect students from the perceived "baleful influence of the universities of Oxford and Cambridge"! Over the following seventy years, each of the other five states established a university in its capital city—a situation that was to remain unchanged until after World War II. Each of these institutions was set up under a state act of parliament and higher education was almost exclusively a state responsibility.

In the 1940s, however, to help cope with wartime demands and subsequently the postwar increase in student numbers, the commonwealth government began to provide significant financial assistance. This was continued until the late 1950s, but was largely an *ad hoc* arrangement; there was no formal acceptance by the commonwealth of a long-term commitment to universities, with the one exception of the Australian National University, established directly by the federal government in 1946.

The first major change in the balance of formal responsibilities between federal and state governments with regard to universities was initiated by Prime Minister Sir Robert Menzies, who, in 1956, invited the chairman of the British University Grants Committee, Sir Keith Murray, to preside over a committee of inquiry into the future of Australian universities. This committee recommended new relationships between state and commonwealth governments with regard to university support, including the appointment of an Australian University Grants Committee to advise the commonwealth government, after consultation with the states, in order to ensure balanced development.

The Murray Report

The Murray Report of 1957[2] was largely accepted by the commonwealth government. The commonwealth agreed to share

Higher Education Funding in Australia

financial responsibility for universities with state governments on a matching grant system (dollar for dollar for capital expenditure, and a dollar of federal support for each A$1.85 of state support for recurrent expenditure). However, a decision was made to establish an Australian Universities Commission as a statutory agency rather than a grants committee.

From the establishment of the commission until the mid-1970s, this matching system of financial support for universities operated, and over this period the Universities Commission worked on a system of triennial planning and reporting. Every third year, after considering detailed submissions from each university and after visits to campuses and consultations with various parties, including state governments, the commission recommended the level of financial support to be given to each institution for both capital and recurrent expenditure for a predicted number of students, and what new major academic developments should be approved. In effect, the commission acted as a broker between the universities and the state and federal governments; this mechanism encouraged increased involvement by the states in order to gain the benefits of additional matching funds from the commonwealth.

The six original universities (Sydney, founded 1850; Melbourne, 1853; Adelaide, 1874; Tasmania, 1890; Queensland, 1910; and Western Australia, 1911) had been augmented by only three others, apart from the ANU, through the 1940s and 1950s. However, significant expansion of the system developed through the 1960s and 1970s, with nine more universities being established by 1975. The first private university was not founded until 1987; there are now two, both small.

State governments had been considerably slower than the commonwealth in establishing special statutory coordinating agencies for higher education. Until the mid-1960s, there was little incentive for them to change their traditional administrative patterns: in most cases, they had to relate directly to only one or two universities, while teachers' colleges, technological institutes, agricultural colleges, and technical colleges within the state were under the direct control of relevant government departments.

But non-university higher education also grew rapidly after World War II. Existing institutions expanded quickly and many new teacher colleges and other specialist institutions were established.

Following the recommendations of the Martin report,[3] from the mid-1960s, the commonwealth government provided financial help to many of these non-university institutions and guided their development to form a separate "advanced education sector," parallel to the university sector. These institutions were not funded to do research. Called colleges of advanced education (CAEs), they were, however, funded by a similar mechanism to universities, and by 1972, there also existed a parallel commission for CAEs, the Australian Commission on Advanced Education. The higher education structure thus formed in Australia became known as the "binary system." The Australian higher education system in 1970, therefore, was similar to those of many other countries, with funding provided by a combination of government grants and fees paid by students.

The second major change in funding mechanisms occurred from January 1974, when the matching system of university financial support was discontinued. The commonwealth government, in agreement with the states, assumed full responsibility for providing all capital and recurrent funds to universities and colleges of advanced education. This led to the unusual situation, still current, in that almost all higher education institutions remain under state influence, with state governments appointing about a third of the membership of governing boards, senates, or councils, even though their total financial support comes from the commonwealth. The advisory mechanisms—the two commissions—continued, however, as did the triennial funding arrangements.

Concurrently, the federal government abolished tuition fees in universities and CAEs to provide a broader spectrum of socio-economic access. It is important to recognise that, in 1973, only about 25 percent of people actually paid full fees for their university education—a situation made possible through the provision of full commonwealth scholarships awarded on academic merit and state systems of teacher scholarships which entailed working for the state governments for some years after graduation.

The triennial system of planning was interrupted for the 1976 calendar year as a result of a government decision to treat that year outside the triennial progression because of the country's major financial difficulties. However, following a change of government in late 1975, the system of triennial planning was reinstated in 1976—this time on a rolling basis. Under this revised system, plans were made for

Higher Education Funding in Australia

a three-year period; then, as each year of the triennium was completed, plans for the remaining two years were reviewed and updated and proposals to the federal government made for a new third year. Since then, with a couple of brief breaks, this rolling triennial system has continued to operate.

As might be expected, growing federal involvement in the planning and funding of higher education has been associated with an enlarged governmental bureaucracy and increased centralised control. In June 1977, the Tertiary Education Commission (later renamed the Commonwealth Tertiary Education Commission, or CTEC) was established by bringing together the previous Universities Commission, the Commission on Advanced Education and also the trades-oriented Technical and Further Education (TAFE) Commission, as councils within a single commission, reporting as before to the commonwealth minister for education.

Nevertheless, as far as the universities were concerned, these structural changes had limited impact on their financial support; of more significance was a decade of virtually static enrollment. Although operating budgets were adjusted to meet agreed salary increases, "incremental creep" of salaries reduced the effective budgets progressively throughout the decade.

The Dawkins Reforms

In July 1987, a new combined department of employment, education, and training was established at the federal level, and Mr. John Dawkins was appointed as minister. Much to the surprise of the tertiary education community, the federal government announced that the Commonwealth Tertiary Education Commission would be abolished, and institutions would henceforward negotiate directly with the department.

This was the beginning of the third series of major changes to affect Australian higher education. A variety of issues was raised for discussion purposes in a green paper in 1987;[4] and subsequently government policy was officially announced in a white paper released by the new minister in July 1988.[5] These changes included the following major elements.

First, the binary system, with its separate sectors for universities and CAEs, was to be abolished and replaced with a so-called "unified national system" comprised of institutions whose "educational profiles" were required to be negotiated annually with federal authorities. Increased funding would be based on the agreed increases in student numbers, taking into account the relative cost of the relevant degree programs.

A second element was the federal government's commitment to having fewer and larger institutions, in the declared belief that this would increase student choice and credit transfer, provide better academic services and facilities, offer better career opportunities for staff, and achieve greater efficiencies. This policy has been achieved through amalgamations, with the sixty-seven members of the binary system in 1987 being reduced to just thirty-six current members of the unified national system. The exercise has been facilitated through a combination of implied threats and promises—smaller institutions being potentially limited in breadth and depth of research development, and access to additional financial support to facilitate the amalgamation process. The use of the word "implied" recognises the inability of the federal government to legislate formal changes in the status and structure of state institutions.

Third, the government committed itself to significant expansion of student numbers in order to achieve increased numbers of graduates, and to renewed efforts to achieve greater equity of access to higher education. Special emphasis was also given to promotion of increased enrollments in areas considered by the government to be of high priority for economic growth.

Fourth, special efforts were to be directed to the increase of research activity and output, with a newly established Australian Research Council to undertake a major role in allocation of research funds. At the same time, however, operating grants to higher education institutions were reduced by 1 percent to provide funding for projects of national priority, while operating grants to the pre-1987 university sector were progressively reduced by 5 percent over a four-year period to provide additional research monies for allocation over the enlarged system by the Australian Research Council (and, to a lesser extent, the

National Health and Medical Research Council), with distribution being determined in each case through national competition for grants.

A fifth element was the planned rationalisation of external studies programs, reducing the numbers of providers of distance education from forty-one to eight, named as distance education centres.

The most far-reaching of the Dawkins initiatives have been the elimination of the formal binary system of research oriented universities and the colleges of advanced education, unfunded to undertake research, coupled with the pressure on smaller institutions to amalgamate with others in order to be part of the new unified national system of higher education.

Other Initiatives

The green paper laid out a proposal that institutions with less than 2,000 FTE [full-time equivalent] students would be required to negotiate annually with government for funding for teaching purposes alone; institutions with more than 2,000 but less than 5,000 FTE students would gain triennial funding but would not be funded for research; institutions with enrollments in the range of 5,000—8,000 FTE students would have a broader teaching profile with some specialised research activities, while institutions with greater than 8,000 FTE enrollment would be largely autonomous in research directions.

The white paper representing government policy, released only seven months later, reaffirmed these enrollment benchmarks; however, the higher education system had already moved rapidly to respond to the perceived threat of tighter government control with many suitors seeking optimal marriage agreements with other small or, more usually, larger institutions. Some institutions chose to over-enroll significantly in 1988, to achieve the magic enrollment benchmark by themselves, even though the excess load was unfunded.

Despite the large amount of activity that commenced well before the formal delivery of government policy, only a limited number of amalgamations had been finalised by the end of 1988. Consequently, in February 1989, the commonwealth minister announced the establishment of a special task force to report on progress to date on proposed institutional mergers, to identify areas where the commonwealth might assist through the allocation of capital resources for 1990 and 1991, and to consider applications for assistance from the National Priority [reserve fund].

The task force reported in April 1989,[6] outlining the potential benefits of consolidation of institutions, such as educational effectiveness and administrative cost efficiencies, and recommending appropriate resource allocations to facilitate desirable outcomes. However, the final outcomes of amalgamation in Australia were achieved only in 1992, in which year the first report of a likely breakup of an amalgamated set of institutions was released.

The process has reduced the number of independent institutions from sixty-seven to thirty-six. No institution has been closed in the process. In each amalgamation process, formal agreements were negotiated between representatives of the relevant universities/colleges of advanced education and endorsed by their governing bodies. These agreements often have involved definition of a transition period during which administrative policies and procedures, developed separately, would be phased into a single set. Of particular importance were issues related to tenure and promotion, where university expectations were usually quite different from those in the college sector. Entrance of the consolidated body into the unified national system required satisfaction of five basic conditions: one governing body; one chief executive; one educational profile; one funding allocation; and one set of academic awards (e.g., degrees and diplomas).

Inevitably, satisfying these conditions has required reassignments of responsibilities of senior administrative staff, but there have been few, if any, redundancies in the system. Since all the merging institutions have been state instrumentalities, each amalgamation has required an act of parliament to make it legally effective. In general, this process has taken place without significant problems or delays, since it has involved open discussion and, finally, agreement by the parties. The influence of state governments has been variable; however, as all funding derives from the federal government, state interests have been more oriented to ensuring a fair share of commonwealth funding coming to the particular state.

Not all these institutional mergers seem, on the face of them, other than marriages of convenience. Some new universities have constituent campuses lying scores, even hundreds, of kilometres apart, with little previous commonality of interest. Most face the difficulty of incorporating two sets of academic staffs, hired using different criteria, with different career expectations, with different cultures and, industrially, represented by different unions. In some cases, entrance standards for students are quite disparate between the partner campuses, yet all study for a single university degree qualification.

As noted, the professed government intent was to improve diversity of learning experiences for students and to obtain economies in operation by increasing the size of the amalgamated institutions. As yet, no detailed studies as to the success in these expectations have been published. Anecdotally, however, the impression grows that the former college sector elements are moving to achieve the perceived status of the "university" with increasing orientation to research activity and seeking additional research funding. The diversity of learning experience issue is more open, dependent on whether the distances between campuses permit commuter access. One might surmise, however, that the general interest in the "university" as providing the norm of behaviour will gradually reduce interest of academics in teaching at certificate and associate diploma level rather than at the "real" degree level, reducing current options which relate more directly to practical training. Consequently, instead of increasing diversity, the amalgamation process may reduce it.

With respect to economic gains, there is great scepticism about potential success. Where campuses are contiguous, there are clear economies possible in administration, provision of library and computing resources, and use of building facilities. But these are likely to be significant only where one of the combining institutions is small. After all, institutions are funded for teaching purposes on a per-student basis, taking into account faculty mix and the undergraduate/graduate proportions. This suggests, *a priori*, that there are no significant advantages of scale in a developed system. Where constituent campuses are widely separated, a condition more common than not, communication costs, particularly in person-hours, are likely to outweigh any marginal economies of scale.

It is perhaps ironical that the most potentially detrimental (perhaps the only detrimental) result of the 1988 initiatives, at least in the short to medium term, has been one where the commonwealth had no legislative power to compel changes (except in Canberra, where it was singularly unsuccessful!), but influenced both institutions and state governments to act where few could see any advantage.

In this new "unified national system," recurrent funding has continued on the rolling triennial basis, with allocations being made as a single block sum to replace previous fragmented funding arrangements. New growth in student load is being financed at close to average operating costs—unusual in these straitened financial times. The massive expansion of student numbers—almost 50 percent since 1987—has also been associated with a significant increase in the amount made available for capital development in the university sector. While this has largely been centrally allocated for the provision of approved facilities for undergraduate students, there has been some spin-off for research and postgraduate training. It follows, moreover, a relatively stagnant fifteen–year period when provisions for maintenance of buildings—upgrading, renovation, and replacement—have been totally inadequate.

Current Funding Patterns

The commonwealth has, in late 1992, moved to allocate future—post 1994—funds for capital development on an institutional rather than on an individual building approval basis, calculated on weighted student enrolments. Where has this additional operating and capital funding come from in a time of economic recession? When the changes were initiated in 1988, the commonwealth indicated very clearly that it was not prepared to support higher education financially at a level significantly greater than its current commitment; therefore, it began to advocate more strongly a philosophy of "user pays," even though this was contrary to established Labour Party policy.

Since the mid-1980s, however, there has been considerable public debate about the desirability of the reintroduction of tuition fees for at least some higher education students, and in the 1986 budget, the federal government imposed a Higher Education Administration Charge (HEAC) of A$250 per annum, payable by both Australian and international students. The introduction of this relatively small charge produced an outraged response from students, including occupation of government offices. The subsequent political reaction was the appointment of a committee to review the initiative.

Following recommendations from this committee, the administration charge was superseded in 1989 by a new arrangement, the Higher Education Contribution Scheme (HECS), which has become known as the "graduate tax." Under this scheme, students are required to contribute to the costs of their courses, either through a discounted "up-front" payment or through a special taxation levy imposed when their income levels reach the average Australian weekly wage. Progressively, 2, 3, or 4 percent (initially 1, 2, or 3 percent) additional taxation is applied, until the outstanding obligations, inflated only by the CPI (consumer price index), are paid off.

The HECS scheme has been remarkably successful. The discounted pay-up-front charge or payment on the "never-never" must be seen as the most successful innovation of the Dawkins revolution. Remarkably, other than in New Zealand, it seems not to have been introduced overseas, although there has been a lot of interest expressed in it. Indeed, the June 20, 1992, issue of *The Economist* devoted one of its feature columns to the fact that the Australian model of higher education funding, specifically as it relates to HECS, was causing much comment in the northern hemisphere.

It is important to recognise that the HECS administration is handled by the universities for the government; there is no direct income to the institution. HECS has the advantage that, if one recognises the value of higher education towards a future career and can afford it, the 1992 discounted contribution at A$1,912.50 (out of $2,250 for a full year standard program) is not large compared to fees world wide. A married woman whose children are now in school, or an Aboriginal person, for example, with doubts about future employment after graduation, can utilise the HECS scheme which requires no repayment until after success in gaining a reasonably high-paying position. The acceptability of HECS is attested to by the lack of concerted opposition to its imposition in 1989, even though it is much greater than the HEAC. Its effectiveness may be studied in Figure 1, which shows how contributions have largely paid for the recent major expansion of the system. It is hoped that it will match these costs within three years, and to this end the commonwealth has increased the discount for HECS charges paid up front from 15 percent to 25 percent for 1993.

Figure 1. Cost of New Places Compared to HECS Receipts, 1990–1995 (a) (b) (July 1991 prices)

[Bar chart showing cost of new places and HECS receipts from 1990 to 1995, with values ranging from approximately A$150 to A$650.]

Cost of new places   HECS receipts

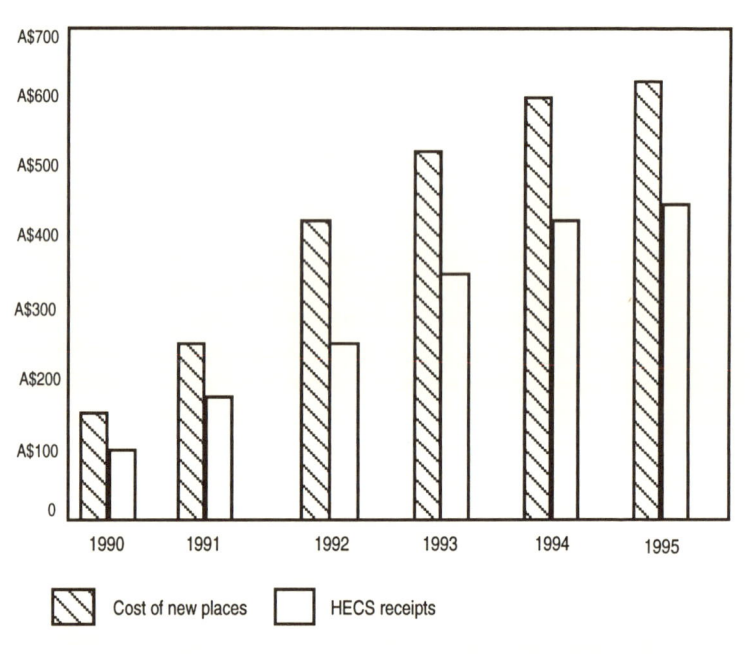

(a) Includes cost of continuing students from previous increases in the student intake.
(b) Cost of new places estimated at A$9,344 per equivalent full-time student unit.
Source: *Commonwealth Government*, 1991–92 budget statement.

As observed earlier, in 1973, before direct tuition fees were abolished, only about a quarter of the students actually paid their own fees. In 1974, with the abolition of fees, the merit-based Commonwealth Scholarships Scheme was replaced by a non-competitive, means-tested grants scheme for student income support—the Tertiary Education Assistance Scheme (TEAS). This was described by the then minister for education as being expected "to produce a revolution of access to education" to "ensure that hardship or poverty would not prevent a student taking advantage of the opportunity for further study."

TEAS (from 1987 called AUSTUDY) has remained the basic mechanism for student income support, subject to minor adjustments from time to time regarding eligibility. Since 1982, the eligibility of students to gain a grant has been about 40 percent. Recently, a review

Higher Education Funding in Australia

of AUSTUDY was contracted by the commonwealth government.[7] Its draft recommendations included introducing a mixture of grants and interest-free loans to replace the means-tested grants system. The level of student opposition to this broadening of approach has convinced the government not to accept the full recommendations in an election year. A most interesting element of the review, however, was the suggestion that the HECS arrangement (for repayment of tuition costs) also be used to handle loan repayments.

The opposition parties, the Liberal-National Coalition, however, have taken an even stronger user-pays approach in their pre-election material. A factor in their policy is the proposal to introduce a voucher system whereby students would carry the government operating grant fraction, with their fees, to the institution of their choice, so that universities would receive *no* direct government support. Full details of the policy have not been released. The HECS, however, has proven so successful and acceptable that the coalition has been forced to accept the continuation of the mechanism. The introduction of pure market forces into the economics of university budgeting is not one that can be viewed with general equanimity.

The implementation of the HECS does not imply that the universities' financial worries are a thing of the past. As a result of the federal government's unpreparedness or inability to fund other than basic operating requirements, it has become imperative for universities to find other ways of raising money in order to maintain institutional traditions of excellence and specialisation.

Although many foreign students have been educated in Australian universities, particularly since World War II, through Aid-supported and other scholarships, it is only since 1987 that the offering of tuition to *full fee-paying* overseas students has been permitted. This opened a new window of opportunity to universities and other educational institutions. Students in overseas countries, particularly in Southeast Asia, are now aggressively recruited through a variety of strategies: indigenous local agents; "education fairs"; relying on reputation relayed through previous students; and, more recently, through the International Development Program (IDP), representing the Australian education system; and government trade organisations. These activities are, of course, in competition with organisations from many countries operating in the same market.

More interesting and promising, perhaps, has been the recent initiation of university fund-raising activities in several institutions, soon to become the norm in most or all. Alumni and/or development offices have been set up by virtually all universities. The number of development officers in Australian universities is reported to have tripled in 1991–1992 from ten to about thirty. It is expected that highly organised graduate networks will emerge within a few years; and it is hoped these could be raising well over $100 million a year for universities by the end of the decade, according to a study by the Australian University Graduate Council. It is recognised that these totals are "small beer" by North American standards, but they represent a total reversal of past Australian university attitudes, despite the fact that there have been some notable bequests in the past.

Private sector sources of funding are being sought in other areas also. Clearly, a university with strong emphases in medicine, dentistry, engineering, and agriculture will have relationships with industry, the professions, and relevant government departments. As one example, the Julius Kruttschnitt Mineral Research Centre at the University of Queensland has been a prime example of research and development interaction with the mining industry for twenty years. However, there has been little organised interaction between universities and the external business and industrial communities before the last decade.

The development of university consulting and/or applied research companies has also mushroomed over the same period, with reasonable success. As yet, however, Australia has not found the way to move effectively from bright ideas to commercialisation, which might lead to greater returns to universities from intellectual property development.

As an example of these developments, the University of Queensland set up a foundation to support research in 1982 and an applied research/consultancy company in 1983; commenced recruiting for full fee-paying overseas students in 1988; and set up a development office in a central downtown location in 1989. In 1974, when fees were abolished for Australian students, the university's income from sources other than the commonwealth grant amounted to 13.3 percent. In 1991, 35.7 percent came from other sources.

Developments in New Zealand have followed a similar approach, but with significant differences in detail. There are no private universities in New Zealand. From 1961 through to 1989, universities were funded by government through a buffer body called the University Grants Committee (UGC), which was modeled on the UK body of the same name. It negotiated operating funds for universities within a system of quinquennial block grants. The process required universities to submit plans for development on a five-year basis: these were then submitted to scrutiny and a final amount negotiated with government. The funds were augmented during the quinquennium by additional amounts for any general increases in salaries and wages negotiated or determined by salary-fixing bodies that had been agreed to by government. In this model, tuition fees were small and there were quite generous living allowances available to all students who succeeded academically. The UGC also operated a capital works fund that provided for the construction and equipping of major new university buildings. It also allocated scholarship monies and a small research fund designed to assist with purchase of research equipment.

In 1989-90, the New Zealand government disestablished the grants committee, and universities now negotiate directly with the ministry of education. Operating grants are based on a formula related to the cost of education (in particular degree programs), multiplied by the number of students per category. The main scope for negotiation is the number of students that an institution estimates it can enroll in each cost category. In practice, the ministry is unable to fund bids fully, and in 1992, most universities had more students than were funded. The quinquennial approach has given way to a rolling triennial model. In recession, however, the result is more like annual funding. Capital works funding is distributed on a flat per capita basis across the sector.

Student fees have risen substantially and are set by each university council. Government operating grants are allocated on the basis that they are a "subsidy" on tuition costs. This year, the subsidy is 85 percent of costs for most students, declining to 75 percent by 1994. Student allowances have been subject to stringent means testing since 1992, and about 65 percent of students now receive no allowances. To assist students with fees and living costs, a loans scheme recoverable through the tax system has been introduced in 1992. This operates like the Australian HECS, but repayments cut in at a much lower salary level.

As in Australia, to assist with diversifying sources of income and as part of the overall drive to export services, universities are developing capacity to attract full fee-paying overseas students.

Previously (before 1989), educating overseas students was thought of mainly in an Aid context. There is also a much more vigorous effort by universities to commercialise parts of their research expertise and to develop funding support from private business, alumni, and the like.

Conclusion

In summary, although Australia has a federal system and New Zealand a national one, the starting points and ending points in funding processes for universities are similar in many ways, even if their developments have followed different paths. Initially small and largely autonomous, both systems developed greatly in size through the 1960s and early 1970s under the guidance of (and buffered by) a grants commission responsible for funding both operating and capital expenditures from government sources, with relatively modest fee structures supported by scholarship schemes. While this process continued for New Zealand until 1989–90, Australia moved away in 1974, with the commonwealth abolishing tuition fees, taking over states' funding responsibilities, and moving to non-competitive, needs-based student support to broaden entry to higher education.

At the end of the 1980s, however, both systems had moved to a user-pays environment, incorporating fees or charges of the order of 20 percent of costs, responsible directly to government, and funded by government on an agreed student profile. While increasing student numbers in Australia are funded at close to real costs, much of the student increase in New Zealand is unfunded as the grant (now "subsidy") per student is decreasing each year. In Australia, funds have thus far been augmented to meet increases in salaries and wages negotiated or determined by salary-fixing bodies that have been agreed to by government. While this was true in New Zealand until June 1990, salaries are now negotiated for all university staff by the employers—legally the vice-chancellors (presidents)—either collectively or individually.

A common feature now is the arrangement for students to pay fees up front or to pay them through the taxation system when the graduate's salary reaches some proportion of the national average weekly wage. Since this mechanism has produced revenues to government in Australia to fund a large proportion of the substantial increase in student numbers, it seems likely to remain a key element in the funding mechanism for universities.

Finally, the diminished real level of funding to the university systems has led to: a greater internationalisation of university student bodies as Australia has opened its doors to overseas fee-paying students; the development of more comprehensive profitable relationships with business and industry through applied research contracts and consultancies; universities rediscovering their graduates, graduates' needs for professional upgrading and extension courses, and, ultimately, to their emotional, political, and financial support of their *alma maters*. All of these latter developments must be seen as long overdue.

NOTES

1. More detailed accounts of the development of higher education are available in, for example, G.S. Harman. *The Universities of Australia*. (London, Association of Commonwealth Universities, 1992).
2. K. Murray. *Report of the Committee on Australian Universities*. (Canberra, Government Printer, 1957).
3. L. Martin. *Tertiary Education in Australia: The Report of the Committee on the Future of Tertiary Education in Australia*. (Canberra, Government Printer, 1964).
4. J. S. Dawkins. *Higher Education: A Policy Discussion Paper*. (Canberra, Australian Government Publishing Service, 1987).
5. J.S. Dawkins. *Higher Education: A Policy Statement*. (Canberra, Australian Government Publishing Service, 1988).
6. G. A. Ramsey. *Report of the Task Force on Amalgamations in Higher Education*. (Canberra, Australian Government Publishing Service, 1989).
7. B. Chapman. *Austudy: A Review* [draft options paper]. (Canberra, Australian National University, 1992).

CANADIAN UNIVERSITIES AND THE POLITICS OF FUNDING

Howard Buchbinder and P. Rajagopal

Introduction

The thrust of social and economic policy over the past half century has been dominated by welfare liberalism, informed by the theories of John Maynard Keynes. The emergence of the welfare state provided the vehicle for the implementation of social and economic policy. Governments began to manage the economy through fiscal and economic policies geared toward the manipulation of aggregate demand. The moral basis for this policy agenda was couched in terms of social justice. The results of the policy (aided and abetted by World War II) ameliorated the ravages of the depression and put North American capitalism back together and encouraged a long period of economic growth which extended through the 1960s (with occasional "slumps"). The Canadian university system is by and large a product of that growth. The subsequent emergence of economic crisis in the mid 1970s accompanied by contraction and restraint, contrasted sharply with the period of growth and expansion of the 1960s. The emergence of harder times was accompanied by a shift in the ideology which informed social and economic policy. The 1980s continued the directions which began to develop during the 1970s.

The result is that the financial context of the Canadian university has, for the past decade and more, been bleak. Universities have been chronically underfunded in a period where enrollments have steadily climbed. From 1980 to 1990, there was an enrollment increase of more than 30 percent across Canada while operating grants during the same period rose only 3 percent in real dollars. In 1990 the federal government froze the level of transfer payments to the provinces for higher education and health until 1995.[1] In November of 1991, the Council of Ontario Universities indicated that member universities would be forced to cut faculty and staff and limit student enrollment unless they got an increase of 7% from the provincial government.[2] In fact, the provincial government announced an increase of 1 percent. One can cite examples from across Canada. All add up to the same grim picture; rising enrollments, reduced funding, growing deficits, and drastic exercises in budget cutting.

The period of contraction and restraint which emerged in the early 1970s was accompanied by a major ideological shift; "the bloom was off the Keynesian rose."[3] The shift was to the ideology of neo-conservatism. Monetarism, supply side economics, social Darwinism, and laissez-faire all reigned as the new roots of policy. The politics of austerity reigned. Instead of expansion and growth, "tighten the belt," "bite the bullet" became the watchwords.[4] The new policy direction reversed many of the earlier social policy directions. Free trade, privatization, the Goods and Services Tax (GST), clawbacks of Old Age Security payments, reductions in the Established Programmes Financing (EPF) and the Canada Assistance Plan (CAP), changes in tax legislation, were all on the agenda. Higher education was affected directly by these policy initiatives—especially by changes in the EPF, which reduced funding for postsecondary education in a significant way.

> The freeze on per capita transfer payments which began in 1990–91, and which Bill C-29 is designed to continue has led to a major drop in cash transfers, amounting to 7.7% in 1990–91 and approximately 21% in 1994–95. The amounts lost to post-secondary education (or "savings" to use the language of the budget) were $321 million in 1990–91 and will be $971 million in 1994–95.[5]

These policy initiatives occurred in a context of economic globalization and restructuring of capital. In this context, universities were identified as a potential aid to the national economy. The method for accomplishing this begins to emerge in the early 1980s with initiatives to encourage corporate-university linkages. These linkages took many forms: technology transfer, research and development, and providing access to corporate clients. Centres of excellence, university offices for technology transfer, and innovation offices began to spring up, but *outside* of university collegial decision-making structures such as senates and faculty associations. Instead, they directly engaged central managerial structures in the university. This led to further expansion of managerial structures and greater differentiation from the collegial constituency. These developments did not take place in as obvious a way as did the campus struggles of the 1960s. Nevertheless, they did take place. What begins to emerge is a new agenda for the universities which is best characterized as the creation of the "service university," a term which emerged from the Science Council of Canada's involvement in the creation of this new agenda. The reference is to the corporations—the linkage between universities and industry.[6]

This linkage oriented universities more and more towards the market. The effects of this amounted to an institutional transformation. Administration of universities was significantly altered as it centralized and proliferated while taking on the trappings of managerial practice: not serving the academy in an administrative sense, but rather, dictating a managerial agenda from above. It is the consolidation of this agenda that characterized the 1980s. The shift from administration to management was completed with a corresponding decline in the power of collegial bodies. The role of the professoriate shifted with the development of entrepreneurial professors, the creation of spin-off companies, the diminution of any force at the departmental level and the marginalization of academics and academic work. These developments diminished academic autonomy and altered even further the role of democratic process in the universities as they chased after the establishment of a corporate model. This brief review of the past three decades can be further amplified by considering them from the perspective of the actual funding policies and process.

We look initially at the ways in which universities were funded (and the way in which the provincial government was funded) during these periods. Initially, there was a recipe for growth which was expressed via an enrollment-driven funding formula. This formula supported a policy of accessibility; more students meant more money. Universities grew and the opportunity for access to postsecondary education grew as well.

As the political economy changed, so did the recipe. During the transition from growth to contraction, the funding formula was altered to ensure that more students meant less money per student. This did not seem to faze the universities, which continued to accept burgeoning enrollments. Finally, with economic crisis intensifying, a policy which initiated a system of corridors developed, providing greater penalties for those who exceeded their assigned corridor.[7] The universities continued to enroll students. The move to raise tuition fees significantly was a way of lessening the governmental burden by placing more of the load on the shoulders of the students.

In this chapter, we track the policies and the processes of funding formulae, enrollment policies, and tuition fees. We wish to show how they work and what change they bring about in the way universities are governed. The battle is fought over decisions regarding funding formulae, enrollment projections, provincial resources and federal policy—all of which are managerial issues. The policies described in this chapter move away from accessibility, move toward privatization of a public institution and later the form of university governance. Yet, while universities seem to pay lip service to elitist prescriptions, they take in more and more students on a fees-only basis, which could be construed as a desire on the part of universities to resist the move away from accessibility. After all, students are the life blood of universities. What is a government to do under the circumstances? It can encourage restricted accessibility while it encourages an aggressive business sector to penetrate the universities, or it can reward universities by increasing funding to cover the costs of increased enrollment, or it can even earmark funding for specific expenditures in assigned "envelopes."

Funding Policies and Processes

In the 1960s in Ontario, the funding formula for universities was tied to what were known as basic income units (BIUs). These units were based on assigned weights for each student, associated with the level of a course and its subject category. These were then calculated for all students in all courses and subject categories across a university to arrive at the total number of BIUs for the entire university. The provincial government then announced a dollar value for each BIU. The government also determined what tuition fees might be charged and subtracted that total amount from the grant income for the university. Each institution was then able to calculate its actual grant income by multiplying the number of BIUs by the dollar value of the BIU, and subtracting from that amount the standard (i.e., permitted) fees they collected from the students. Thus, the income for a university was composed of the grant income and the fee income; together, the total was referred to as the "operating grant income." There were additions to this such as endowment income, research grants, funds raised from occasional fund-raising drives, and the additional fees (over and above the standard fees) they charged for incidental expenditures. Only a small number of universities in Ontario were well endowed or had alumni of several decades' standing. Most of the other universities were relatively new (established after the 1960s), and they received very little income from such sources. Such a comment would apply to university systems in other provinces of Canada as well, so that in the Canadian system, the government grants plus tuition fees represented the major source of funding. This sort of funding formula arrangement was enrollment driven. The greater the enrollment, the greater the grant income and the fee income; thus, there was a greater possibility for new appointments, expansion, and increased infrastructure. It was a wide-open arrangement: more students equalled more dollars.

In the mid-1970s in Ontario, there was a change in the BIU allocation mechanism described earlier. Instead of announcing the dollar value of a BIU, the government announced the total amount of dollars granted to the university system as a whole. This represented the size of the total funding "pie." The distribution of this "pie" was undertaken by the Ontario Council on University Affairs (OCUA) acting as a buffer body between the government and the universities. OCUA distributed the money to the universities by calculating the total number of BIUs, then dividing the system grant by the number of BIUs, and thereby arriving at a BIU value. The rest of the exercise followed the 1960s scenario with the "pie" being divided up in terms of the number of BIUs. In effect, the value of the BIU fluctuated; if there was an increase in enrollment, the value of the BIU went down. There were other features built into the new allocation mechanism such as slip year financing, and later on, a three-year moving average; these were intended to cushion the effects of too rapid a change in the enrollment. This arrangement was a competitive one. There was a fixed number of dollars and each institution "fought" for its share.

This arrangement represented a significant change from that of the 1960s. Now, more students did not necessarily mean more money. In fact, more students in the system meant a lowered BIU value. However, *within* the system, larger enrollments were favoured over decreased enrollments. The government attempted to address this seeming inequity by setting a cap on the permitted *rate* of increase. Increases of more than 3 percent above the cap meant that no grant income would be given to any university for those students over and above the cap, although tuition income continued to be forthcoming. In the next few years, some universities had a large number of "above 3 percent" students, and they started complaining that they were being penalised for being faithful to the policy of accessibility. Some universities were talking about getting only 85 cents on the dollar.[8]

This process was very complicated. It required maintaining records for each university, taking into account the different cohorts of students (for slip year, for three-year averaging, for over 3 percent cap, for different years and different special envelopes of funding), and needed outlays of revenue—which were affected by teaching the increasing number of students.[9] There was a striking lack of resolve against this new technological offensive on the part of the university system. "Technological offensive" it was in that the administering produced in its wake an increasing number of administrators both at the government level (these were working for the OCUA), and at the level of the individual university.

In 1990, in Ontario, the government came up with a new plan by which all the students were included in the enrollment entitlement. All the students who were above the 3 percent cap were brought into the accounting system and a new BIU corridor was set for each university. The university received a block grant for the number of BIUs it was entitled to. Within permitted limits, it was to translate the number of BIUs into a number of students. Under this arrangement there is no prospect of enhancing a university's income by increasing enrollment and thereby increasing pressure on the government for a change in the allocation mechanism, since all universities in the system have a corridor midpoint. This recipe represents an imposed, bureaucratic arrangement which is management oriented. Not only are the number of BIUs allocated for each university, but in certain areas of "social need," universities are asked to increase enrollment at the expense of other areas already in operation. Surprisingly enough, universities have not come up with any critique of these changes; they seem to be confounded by the barrage of policies and white papers and proposals (some of which may well have been designed to rekindle confidence in progress).

During the first year of operation (1991–92), universities have enrolled students way above the corridor (by about 5 percent to 9 percent). For such enrollments the universities receive no operating grants, only the fees they collect. It is too early to tell whether this enrollment above the ceiling will continue for 1992–93.[10] What is fascinating is that this corridor exercise is imposed from the top. It is a bureaucratic exercise which is quite different from the previous funding formulae. As we have indicated, funding policy has proceeded from a wide-open arrangement in which more students meant more money to one in which more students meant lowered value per BIU, and finally to one in which a corridor has been imposed which regulates university admissions by imposing penalties if corridor limits are exceeded. This centrally imposed policy correlates with the development of a centralized managerial process within the universities. This is the status of the system. What are the options?

Possible Responses to the Funding (or Underfunding) Policies

Option 1: Increase Fees

Until 1976, the Established Programmes Financing (EPF) agreement between the Canadian federal and provincial governments required that funds transferred under this programme from the federal government to the provincial government for health and higher education be spent on health and higher education, respectively. In 1976, the provincial governments wrung a concession from the federal government allowing them to spend the EPF money as they saw fit. Funds not spent on intended programmes became part of provincial general revenue, and as a result, each province spent the EPF funds in different ways. The province of Quebec continued to spend more than 85 percent of higher education EPF funds for that purpose. As a result, tuition fees in Quebec remained low (but about five years ago Quebec started raising fees and since then they have increased sharply).

Ontario, on the other hand, diverted EPF funds to other purposes so that by 1988 less than 65 percent of higher education EPF funds were being spent for that purpose. As government spending on higher education diminished, tuition fees increased, often at the same rate as the provincial operating grants. But in 1991–92, provincial operating grants increased by 1 percent and tuition fees by 7 percent. Overall federal contributions to this programme were cut as a result of federal deficit reduction policies. The federal government, in 1988, capped the EPF transfers to the provinces. This action was severely criticized by the provincial governments as a unilateral withdrawal by the federal government from an established joint agreement.

In the face of this deteriorating situation, the Association of Universities and Colleges of Canada (AUCC) attempted to address the need for an effective policy by establishing a special commission.[11] Since student fees represent the largest source of income outside of government funding, it is not surprising that tuition policy played a prominent part in the recommendations and discussion of this commission. What is surprising is that the commission expressed so optimistic a view of the universities after more than a decade of serious underfunding. The commission found "that Canadian universities today are fundamentally healthy and are serving the country well."[12] Again, another optimistic note: "the universities protect their students from the full consequences of underfunding."[13] It is strange to perceive what has happened as protecting the students, since students have indeed suffered—but not only students. The university infrastructure, insofar as teaching and associated service is concerned, has absorbed an increase of more than 30 percent in students over the past decade without a corresponding increase in full-time academic staff and ancillary personnel, but with an increase in part-time teachers. Thus, the burden of this increase in an atmosphere of chronic underfunding has been carried by an overloaded faculty, including a large number of underpaid (and underprivileged) part-time faculty, and students subjected to very large classes, large tutorials (if any), poor library facilities, and an increasing amount of computerised processing (so-called "voice registration" and "press-button administration").

This commission's rather benign view, which sees the universities as "weathering the storm" as they negotiate the turbulent currents of underfunding, is at odds with many views: "Universities face massive layoffs and enrollment reductions unless government funding increases, says the Council of Ontario Universities . . . in a report released on November 21, 1991. The COU predicts that if universities do not receive 7 percent government grants next year, enrollment will be reduced by as much as 17,737, faculty will be cut by 1,045, and staff by 1,312. The report also says that universities would have to increase tuition fees by up to 33 percent to cover the loss."[14]

The report of this special commission suggested increasing tuition fees to the level of about 25 percent of the total operating cost of the universities (at that time it was about 18 percent in Ontario). In September 1992, a government memo from the deputy minister of revenue was reported as proposing for consideration a series of initiatives designed to increase provincial revenues; one of them was to raise tuition fees by 500 percent.[15] Among the proposals were plans to levy a 3 percent income tax on recipients of Ontario Student Aid Program (OSAP) funds, sell the administration of student loans to the banks, and increase tuition to "full cost recovery," thereby making students pay the full cost of their education.[16]

Option 2: Reduce Enrollments

Another option in dealing with the funding crisis is that of reducing enrollments. This represents a departure from the commitment to accessibility. In addition to reducing overall enrollments, the provincial government appears to be "steering" enrollments. It makes statements about the increased need for people in specialized areas of science, technology, and business. The application of such policies leads to an overall reduction in enrollments accompanied by increased enrollments in certain high cost areas. This would have the effect of shifting resources from sectors such as the humanities and science, technology, and business.

Option 3: Redefine the Mission of the Universities

If the earlier scenario is implemented and the marketability of various educational programs dictates the academic emphasis in the universities, what will be the results for students and for the educational process? It is necessary to keep in mind that when one moves into the area of marketability, the emphasis is on "efficiency" rather than on "equity."

A possible shift to admit more graduate students by the concurrent reduction of undergraduate students has been proposed. Graduate programmes and research centres are the prized parts of the new universities; they bring prestige and visibility; they are home to the "stars," and they attract money. The combination of low cost undergraduate education with high-powered research represents the new definition of service in market-oriented universities. This shift in mission is in keeping with the push to encourage more corporate–university linkages. Research in this area describes the development of knowledge as a marketable commodity rather than as a social good.[17]

Option 4: Seek Other Sources of Revenue

Canadian universities are public institutions supported by government funds and by tuition fees. University presidents in Canada were never heavily involved in direct fund raising as were presidents of universities in the United States. This is changing; Canadian university administrations are seeking to include active fund raising in their structures.

Final Observations

We have examined in this paper the changing political economy over the past three decades and the resulting policy options which have influenced the directions for higher education in Canada. The institutions of higher education have been reacting in a defensive, ad hoc manner to the continuing crisis in university funding. Although funding policies encourage and even dictate enrollment reductions, universities continue to increase enrollments. At the same time, there is an internal redistribution of enrollments—from undergraduate to graduate, from social sciences and humanities to hard sciences and technology.

Canadian Universities and the Politics of Funding 281

Within the universities, the professoriate and the university management join in a common denunciation of government funding policies, yet the professoriate does not appear to play a critical role as management redistributes internal resources in an ever-tightening belt of austerity. This managerial response to austerity has a severe impact on the integrity of academic work as conditions deteriorate within the academies: large class sizes, reductions in the range of courses, examinations instead of essays, inadequate library and reading room facilities, and insufficient student advising.

The increasing use of part-time faculty has been one of the ways in which universities have coped with the enrollment increases that have accompanied the underfunding. The large number of Ph.D.s educated in graduate programs begun in the late 1960s and early 1970s have provided the pool from which part-time faculty are recruited. Many of them are women. They have no hope of being absorbed in the regular faculty ranks; they are a "lost generation" of academics. It has been estimated that in the Ontario system, the part-time salary total in 1987–88 was about $53 million, contrasted with full-time salaries of about $651 million. Part-time salaries come to about 7.6 percent of the total, even though part-timers represented 32.4 percent of total faculty members and did about a fifth of the total teaching. Also in that year, women as full-time faculty was 17 percent, the percentage of women as part-time teachers was 38 percent; for the year 1989–90, these percentages were 20.2 percent and 44.3 percent respectively.[18]

The increasingly restrictive funding policies outlined in this paper are part of the deficit-reduction strategies which dominate public policy formulations. Declining tax revenues, increasing deficits, economic stagnation, and rising unemployment develop side by side with greater demands on the social assistance system and the health care system. In this context, funding of universities will continue to fall. In addition, the shift in ideology discussed earlier leads to tuition fee policies which are privatizing as the cost of studying is shifted more and more onto the shoulders of the students. Spokespeople for our provincial government continue to extol the virtues and the importance of higher education. However, the context changes to a focus on "restructuring" the institutions of higher education with greater emphasis on "training" opportunities.

The crisis of funding is exacerbated by a climate of deficit reduction which generates restrictive social policies in which universities slip in governmental priorities. Business orientation is encouraged as a response, and public knowledge education becomes more market oriented. This undermines the real purpose of the universities, namely, teaching and research in an open environment. Academic autonomy and openness in the production and exchange of knowledge are threatened. What has been public knowledge now becomes private knowledge, and knowledge is treated as private property.[19] These changes signal an overall transformation in the universities in which intellectual excellence, free inquiry, and scientific imagination may be at risk.

The issue of the universities as respondents to external events or rather as primary agents for change runs through our remarks. This paper deals with the linkage between the state of the political economy, the resulting funding policy options, and their impact on universities. The range of institutional change is wide, deep, and penetrating. The options for action are influenced by the forms of institutional change. However, the shifts in the state of the political economy have been accompanied by an ideological shift which influences the outcome. Right now, the initiatives have been grasped by the higher levels of management and the university workplace is less and less the terrain of academic workers. Students are preoccupied with negotiating the obstacles imposed by escalating tuition fees and deteriorating conditions for learning. As a result, they seem to have opted for a role of "let us get on with our careers," and so are not joined in the debate in a major way.

We are not able to account for why universities have acted the way they have with regard to enrollment growth or with regard to governmental funding policies. Contractions in funding ought to suggest a corresponding decline in enrollment, not the opposite. It is remarkable that the last three governments in the province of Ontario (Conservative, Liberal, and social democratic New Democratic Party), when faced with economic contraction have been unified in their response: all have pronounced on prosperity but have acted in response to their concern for the cumulative deficit. The cumulative deficit has continued to escalate and funding has continued to decline.

We are left with a major question on which to reflect. Why has the process described in this paper proceeded apace without any significant resistance from the professoriate; in fact, without so much as a whimper. University professors serve as advisors to governments, consultants to corporations, experts for the media, and public policy advocates. Yet, when it comes to directing our insights to our own organizations, the professoriate seem to lose interest. As a result, the initiative has been grasped by the higher levels of management and the university workplace is less and less the terrain of academic workers. Might we consider the impact of such factors as academic and staff careerism, entrepreneurialism as a frame for academic work, and growing allegiance to corporate benefactors? The politics of funding reveal a university system in the throes of major readjustments. No sector is exempt from scrutiny, certainly not the professoriate.

NOTES

1. Scott Feschuck. "Ontario Universities Fear Payment Freeze." *The Globe and Mail*, Jan. 20, 1992. These transfer payments are part of the Established Programs Financing program. Cash and tax credits are transferred to the provincial governments, although, it should be noted, they are compelled to spend it for those items.

2. Jennifer Lewington. "Universities warn of staff cuts without 7 percent funding increase." *The Globe and Mail*, Nov. 22, 1991.

3. P. Armstrong and H. Armstrong. *The Global Ghetto* (1984) Revised Edition. (Toronto: McClelland and Stewart, 1984).

4. Paul Gingrich. "Unemployment: A Radical Analysis of Myth and Fact." *Our Generation,* 12, no. 3, (1977): 16–31.

5. Robert Leger. "University Financing Policies Consistently Cut into PSE Core Funding." *CAUT Bulletin* (December, 1991).

6. Philip Enros and Michael Farley. *University Offices for Techology Transfer: Towards the Service University* (discussion paper). (Ottawa: Science Council of Canada, 1986).

7. A corridor refers to identifying and assigning an enrollment floor and an enrollment ceiling for each university.

8. This is not a reference to the exchange rate to the U.S. dollar, but to the fact that the income they received was 85 percent of what they would receive if all of their enrollment was included in the count.

9. The students were being increasingly taught by part-time instructors; these were the products of the graduate schools that were started in the 1960s. They had no prospect of obtaining a normal tenure track teaching position.

10. During the Autumn of 1992, statements and pronouncements from governmental sources include: how the provincial tax revenue will be staying constant in real dollars till the end of the century; how the share of health costs will increase; how enrollments in universities may go up by as much as 34 percent by the end of the century, and so on. Task forces have been set up to look the postsecondary sector. There is also a task force on accountability. In our own university, it is being let out that there is no guarantee that every retirement will necessarily be replaced. It is not clear whether there is an assumption that technology—microelectronic technology that is, not accountancy technology—will come to the rescue.

11. Stuart Smith. *Report the Commission of Inquiry on Canadian University Education.* (Ottawa: Association of Universities and Colleges of Canada, 1991).

12. *Ibid,* p.14.

13. *Ibid,* pp.16–17.

14. Naomi Klein. "Leaked Document Has Students up in Arms." *The Varsity* (Sept. 21, 1992).

15. *Ibid.*

16. In the last thirty years, the province of Ontario has had conservative governments, liberal governments, and new democratic governments. There has been a persistence of a mind-set through all of them: conservative democratic governments, liberal democratic governments, and social democratic governments have all continued with the same policy sequence—a remarkable consensus, indeed!

17. David Dickson. *The New Politics of Science.* (Chicago: University of Chicago Press, 1988); Martin Kenney. *Bio-technology, The University-Industrial Complex.* (New Haven: Yale University Press, 1986); Janice Newson and Howard Buchbinder. *The University Means Business* (Toronto: Garamond Press, 1988).

18. Indhu Rajagopal and William D. Farr. "The Part-Time Faculty in Canada." (Private communication, and a pre-publication copy of a paper to be published in *Higher Education*, Winter 1993).

19. Howard Buchbinder. "The Market Oriented University and the Changing Role of Knowledge." Paper presented at the Conference at the Ontario Institute for Studies in Education, October, 1992.

CONSTRUCTING THE "POST-INDUSTRIAL UNIVERSITY": INSTITUTIONAL BUDGETING AND UNIVERSITY-CORPORATE LINKAGES

Janice A. Newson

> It is only recently that policy makers have begun to understand the critical links between expenditure patterns, cost and efficiency in higher education and the mechanisms by which institutions receive funds, . . . Many governments now see financial incentives as a more effective way *of influencing the pattern of activities in higher education institutions* than administrative intervention.[1]

In most advanced societies of the West, the post-World War II period has engaged universities in new kinds of relationships within the state, insofar as governments have invested increasing amounts of public moneys in higher education. Their increasing reliance on public funds has released them from the parochial and privatized controls of, for example, religious organizations that funded and administered many of them in earlier periods. In fact, it can be argued that state support and regulation has provided institutions of higher education with a form of social, economic, and political embeddedness that is more compatible with their project of expanding the rational-scientific knowledge base.

Yet, the higher level of public investment has meant a deeper involvement on the part of governments in what takes place in universities to ensure they are serving social purposes that justify this investment. Consequently, higher education policies implemented through the state are increasingly significant to how universities carry out their tasks. How and in what ways they are significant, however, is not a matter of simple cause and effect. Two points are particularly important. First, state policies do not enter the minds of politicians and their aides "out of nowhere": they arise from, and reflect, a variety of social pressures and influences. I therefore do not consider the organs of government that formulate and adopt official public policy, or the associated legislative enactments themselves, to be the originators, causes, or prime movers of state policy. Nor do I consider the changes that appear to flow from policies simply to be "effects." Rather, the idea needs to be preserved of a more interactive, dynamic, and mutually reinforcing relationship between "policy" on the one hand, and changes that appear to be associated with it on the other.

A sociological analysis of "policy" should not be limited to a study of the legislative enactments of governments. For one thing, legislative actions are often narrowly focused; they may simply provide for the allocation of funds to the programs and projects of particular ministries. In order for a wider pattern of changes and institutional realignments to flow from these enactments, a very complex social process must unfold, involving the participation of an often wide array of social agents. For another thing, a policy does not magically become manifest simply because legislation is enacted. The implementation of policy is a practical matter: that is, the policy comes into being in the real world through changes in practice that have real consequences. Universities in particular are complex institutions with conflicting and often contradictory patterns of internal decision making. Government legislation, constitutionally speaking, is several steps removed from the "ground level" of the academy. It is, therefore, not a simple matter to account for major transformations "inside" universities which appear to correspond with narrowly focused legislative enactments from "outside." At the very least, an adequate analysis of changes in universities must take into account the broader political, economic, and social contingencies in which they function during particular historical periods, as well as the processes of decision making and reorganization that characterize universities as social institutions.

Since the end of World War II, two relatively distinct policy approaches have contextualized university development in advanced western societies: the expansionist period of the 1950s and 1960s and the period of contraction that began around the early 1970s until the present. Some scholars have collapsed these two phases into a single story—the story of the university entering what is designated as the era of "post-industrialism." Theorists such as Daniel Bell and Alain Touraine have very different perspectives on post-industrialism, but they nevertheless agree that "knowledge" has become the central valuable commodity of this period. For this reason, the university or some other form of knowledge institute is seen by these theorists as the central institution of post-industrial society, replacing the business firm and the factory of the mechanical-industrial age. [2]

Taken in this light, the postwar expansion of higher education signals the movement of the university to a centre stage position in social development, supported by the huge influx of public funding and the increased emphasis given to academic credentials as the *sine qua non* of social and economic mobility. From this position, the expansionist university became, among other things, both a site and an agent of social mobility. The organizational practices which were aimed toward providing broad accessibility and the internal attempts to "democratize" traditional academic structures were as much a part of dismantling the economically and socially restrictive character of society at large as they were of dismantling the elitist character of the academy.

But what has the subsequent period of contraction signaled, and what has the university become an agent of during this period? To many advocates and defenders of the university, contraction has signaled a litany of ills that are serious enough to threaten the very existence of the university. Donald Savage, the executive director of the Canadian Association of University Teachers, has described the resulting "deep malaise" on university campuses this way:

> No one seems to care that universities are sliding into a period of decline. Classes grow in size. Libraries are able to buy less. Research funds vanish. Equipment becomes obsolete. Building maintenance disappears. One has to wage a major war to get photocopying done. Secretarial services gradually vanish. Wages are frozen . . .[3]

This description of the material conditions of the "contracting" university in Canada is echoed in recent descriptions of the university in Britain, Australia, the United States, and Western Europe. But more significant and longer term than the material conditions themselves or even the demoralizing climate, are the organizational and ideological changes that have accompanied them. For example, most students and many faculty members no longer think about the pedagogical significance of class sizes, given that larger classes in most disciplines and at most levels have become standardized according to "cost efficient" formulae. Professors rely less and less on the support infrastructure of the university. Instead, they furbish their homes with computers, modems, and fax machines, keyboard their own papers and memos, and look after their own photocopying. Moreover, in spite of inadequate research funding, "time for research" assumes an increasing priority when divided among the three activities of teaching, service, and research. Departmental meetings, faculty councils, senates and their committees—the structures that give substance to collegialism—are either held less frequently or with fewer in attendance. Decisions about curricula, course allocations, new positions, etc., are often made, whether because of necessity or choice, without debate and discussion.

The university in the 1990s appears to be no longer simply reacting to—even resisting—a fiscal "crisis" imposed on it from the outside, as it might have been characterized in the 1970s.[4] Instead, it appears as an institution which is actively generating a culture of restraint, one which emphasizes norms of cost efficiency and budgetary accountability; which cultivates privatized, individualized, and where possible, "profitable" intellectual activity; and which substitutes technological and bureaucratic mechanisms for the pedagogical, educational, and collegial activities that are now constricted by a reorganized "research-teaching-service" hierarchy.

One way of accounting for these shifts in "thinking" in the academy is to consider the relationship between the funding policies that have produced contraction, and the associated changes in the ways universities accomplish their objectives. Contraction has actually consisted of two interrelated approaches to funding: fiscal restraint itself, and the reallocation of significant portions of higher education dollars to develop closer collaboration between universities and corporations. A recent OECD publication, *The Changing University*, demonstrates that this double-pronged approach has been taken in most of the economically advanced societies of North America, Great Britain, and Western Europe as well as in areas of the developed Pacific Rim region. The purpose of this paper is to show how this double-pronged policy of funding has interacted with the "pattern of activities" in universities, to the degree that fundamental changes in the institutional character of universities have begun to emerge along with new ways of thinking about the way the university should respond to the exigencies of its times.

The Exigency of Fiscal Restraint

The funding shortfalls that began in the early to mid-1970s were often viewed within the academic community as short-term, requiring strategies that would bridge between the difficulties of the present moment and a not too distant future when funding would return to the more affluent (or realistic, depending on point of view) levels of the late 1950s and 1960s. However, as annual budget shortfalls transmuted into a chronic state of fiscal restraint which universities were expected to live with into the foreseeable future, different kinds of responses and justifications emerged. The earlier idea of "fat" in the budget extended to a more general diagnosis of universities as being insufficiently managed institutions which did not deliver their services as efficiently and as cost effectively as they could. "Restructuring" became a recurrent theme in policy discussions—"restructuring" in forms that would secure increased efficiency in the delivery of educational and research programs, and greater value for the public tax dollar. Moreover, the idea that a one-time experience of fiscal restraint had been a "good thing" in forcing institutions to think through priorities, provided a justification for inserting an agenda of financial discipline and budgetary centrality into university decision making.[5]

Fiscal restraint in the form of government funding cutbacks thus established the basis for *budget-based rationalization*, a process that has involved significant changes in the way universities are internally organized and routinely carry out their objectives. For example, fiscal restraint provided the opportunity for university administrations to take up the practical task of "managing the budget." Through a complex sequence of moves, the activity of administration—centered around the management of increasingly constrained fiscal resources—moved to the centre of institutional decision making. The more "democratized" governing structure, which was largely achieved under the conditions of expansion, came now to be seen as cumbersome, indecisive, and above all, ill equipped to deal with budgetary matters. In fact, in the 1970s and on into the 1980s, a number of books written about the university tended to emphasize these aspects of organizational inefficiency, and to implicitly, if not explicitly, characterize both "collegialism" and "democratization" as "part of the problem"[6] The face-to-face talk and lengthy debates of academic senates and faculty councils were assessed, not in terms of their democratic representativeness or collective decision making, but rather in terms of their effectiveness in making "the tough decisions." The argument for "a more managerial approach" was premised on a need for the local interests of departments and faculties to be transcended by a purportedly neutral body which would give primacy to meeting budgetary constraints rather than to preserving and defending academic territory.

As "management" has moved to the centre of decision making, academic decision making has moved to the margins. This does not mean, of course, that academics are no longer involved in decision-making practices. On the contrary, as they have remained involved, they have acquiesced to, or actively participated in, a process of change in which clearly academic considerations have taken a secondary, even tertiary, place in a reorganization of academic work. For example, the division of the academic work force into separate "bargaining units" (e.g., full-time/part-time; tenure track/limited contract), each organized according to its own terms and conditions of employment and pay scales, has made it possible to implement cost-saving policies even though these policies may undermine *academic* objectives. For example, enrollment levels can be manipulated according to the current funding policy of government. Decisions to increase enrollment when it is profitable can be accommodated by the cheaper labor of part-time instructors, who are contracted only to teach and paid by the course. Cutting back on enrollment when expansion is not profitable is also readily achieved because a significant portion of the teaching staff work on "one course at a time" temporary contracts. The academic criteria for increasing or decreasing enrollment, such as grade levels, new intellectual developments, pedagogical considerations, etc., become secondary to this manipulation, if they are even considered at all.

In a similar fashion, the separation of teaching from research provides a more "budgetarily accountable" way of allocating the scarce "human resource" of faculty time according to its income generating capabilities. Members of the more costly full-time tenured faculty who are successful at generating income for their research endeavors can have their teaching obligations "bought out" at the cheaper rate of part-time instructors. In the process, the long-standing academic debate about the intrinsic interdependence of scholarly production and scholarly transmission is thus bypassed by budgetary considerations which are favorable to a division between those who "do research" and those who "teach." This fragmentation of academic workers and their activities in the interest of being able to pursue cost-efficient financial strategies is in turn reflected in the divided political objectives of the academic workforce. Different categories of workers develop different "workerist" interests, both with regard to the way their work should be organized and remunerated, and with regard to their role in shaping institutional policy. As academic workers, they do not speak with a single voice to these issues, but with many often contradictory and conflicting voices.[7]

In a mutually reinforcing way, "management" assumes an even greater importance for coordinating these "fragments" and divisions, and thus the activities of management in the academy have become more comprehensive and pervasive, as is reflected in the expanding managerial structure. Systems of management have been applied to aspects of decision making and judgment that once belonged within the realm of "the collegium." In fact, the face-to-face debating of policies and practices within academic decision-making bodies like departments, faculty councils, and senates have been displaced in large part by a documentary form of decision making. The process of constructing documents like five-year plans, mission statements, and green and white papers establishes the guiding parameters from which are derived the specific decisions for each academic unit about enrollment levels, class sizes, the creation of new positions, program initiatives, and the like. Although academics and various collegial bodies may have input into this documentary process, it is highly centralized and less open to scrutiny and intervention. It is more difficult politically to challenge the content of these documents or to subsequently question the parameters which constrain all decisions. At the same time, local academic units and even individual professors can be thought of, and can think of themselves, as self-directing decentralized mini-cost-and-revenue centres, even while their freedom to choose their own priorities is contained within a previously established set of parameters.

Finally and more importantly, the budgetary criteria of "efficiency," "productivity," and "accountability" have become ends in themselves: that is, they are substituted for academic/professional judgments and adopted as the *valued* criteria for assessing and deciding how to carry out a wider and wider range of academic activity— initiating new curricula and phasing out others, putting forward new research projects and deciding which ones to support, and even carrying out activities such as the registration and advising of students. It is, therefore, of little consequence whether academics themselves are or are not active in the decision-making process, because the very criteria that have relevance for decision making subordinate academic and professional judgments to the limitations of the budget.

The Exigency of Collaboration Between Universities and Corporations

The second prong of government funding policy in the era of contraction began with the idea that universities should develop closer relationships with the private corporate sector as a means of alleviating some of their funding difficulties. Among other things, "closer collaboration" means that university research and teaching programs should be more clearly focused on the needs of the corporate sector for workforce training which is suited to the demands of high-tech production, and for new knowledge to facilitate technological innovation and economic development. Through this collaboration, it has been argued, universities will acquire new sources of funding to counteract the effects of government underfunding, and corporations will gain much needed expertise—a window on science—to provide them with a competitive edge in the international marketplace. In the face of dwindling resources, members of the academic community who believed it to be the only game in town for maintaining and improving the quality of academic activity, have become actively engaged in implementing this proposal.

However, the idea of a mutually beneficial tradeoff to assist universities through their funding crisis has extended into the argument that the partnership between universities and business is a good in itself that should be actively promoted and that universities in particular should be willing to accommodate. In fact, the first report published by Canada's Corporate-Higher Education Forum (parallel to the Business-Higher Education Forum in the USA and similar organizations in other countries involving university presidents and corporate executives)—*Partnership for Growth*—argued that governments *should maintain*

Constructing the "Post-Industrial University" 293

their underfunding of universities as a means of pressuring them into partnerships with corporate clients. As well, it argued that universities need to abandon some of their treasured "cultural" ideals, such as the maintenance of autonomy and academic freedom, in order to establish the needed compatibility with industrial culture.

More importantly, the idea of a tradeoff between "access to knowledge" and financial support has encouraged a new way of thinking about knowledge itself and the role of the university in society as a producer and distributor of knowledge. In fact, even more than a way of thinking, it has offered a formulaic solution to the university's underfunding dilemmas as well as to the need of governments to devise a new way of funding universities in the face of economic and political changes.

For example, the idea that universities can enter into partnerships in which knowledge is traded for money implies that "knowledge" can be bundled up into neat packages and a precise money value attached to them. To accomplish this end, knowledge needs to be quantified and measured in terms of its economic "exchange" value. Practical questions must be resolved. How much money for how much knowledge? How is it possible to ensure that the "search for knowledge" will produce a result that will be of marketable value to the client? Who will then "own" the knowledge that is produced?

Answers to these practical questions are found in the various types of contracts, and a wide range of university-industrial linking mechanisms that are worked out by university researchers and administrations with the funding bodies—government agencies, research councils, and corporate clients. Patent agreements, licensing arrangements and the expanding jurisprudence around "intellectual property rights" concretely embody the idea that knowledge can be commodified and thus can be offered for sale or be appropriated as the protected (even private) property of an owner. Within this conceptualization of "knowledge," university professors are encouraged to think of themselves as intellectual entrepreneurs, and university administrators orient their activities toward seeking out (mainly paying) clients and markets for the university's "products."

Moreover, around the edges of the traditional university emerged new structures that have begun to have a central place in defining and achieving the (shifting) objectives of the university. For example, spin-off companies, centers of excellence, discovery parks, offices of technology transfer, and various other units which embody a corporate-university partnership draw on the university's resources, such as faculty, operating funds, and share of research moneys to achieve their objectives. Typically, these structures are not governed by the academic policies of the university, for example, the academic policies guiding research, hiring practices, and collective agreements covering terms and conditions of employment. In a sense, they represent a shadow institution which gains legitimacy from its connection to the academy, but at the same time is not subject to the kind of academic controls that have been associated to date as accepted university practice. It remains to be seen whether the "shadow" will supersede the "real," or what kind institution will emerge from their intermingling.

Government funding policies over the past decade have been crucial in encouraging and supporting these institutional changes. For example, governments have provided the funds for programs that are specifically designed to bring together industrial and academic researchers in order to facilitate the development of knowledge for commercial and practical application. They have also provided funds to develop on-campus innovation centres to facilitate collaborations between university researchers and corporate clients, on-campus technology transfer centres, and "matching funds" approaches to research grant programs whereby government money matches research funds that are obtained from corporate clients.

Linking universities and corporations and achieving budgetary rationalization are mutually reinforcing (although at times conflicting and contradictory) processes which constitute significant changes in the university as a social institution. Moreover, these changes have not resulted from the mechanical imposition of various government funding policies. Rather, they represent strategic choices, the resultants of the complex internal maneuverings and active participation of various constituencies within the university community in response to fiscal restraint. On the one hand, budgetary rationalization represents a methodology through which the university can exist in the world as an efficient, cost-effective business. On the other hand, linking universities to corporations has produced and legitimized a practical conception of knowledge as a commodity, and of the university as a producer and conveyor of knowledge for privatized and predetermined uses. The university thus becomes on the one hand, a site and an agent for promoting this methodology and its associated culture and, on the other, for transforming knowledge from a social resource to a commodity that can be prepackaged and targeted to specified markets and clienteles.

Exit "Ivory Tower"— Enter "Service University"

These changes in the institutional character of universities are not entirely new, of course. Some of them can be traced back through a long period of historical development in which universities have become increasingly reliant on larger and larger amounts of external (in Canada, almost exclusively public) funding at the same time as they have become key instruments of the social, political, and economic policies of the state. However, in the political, and economic context of the 1970s and 1980s, the convergence of these two policy directions has signaled a potentially *qualitative* transformation of universities and their role in, and relationship to, society as a whole.

One way of expressing this qualitative transformation is to refer to the shift from collegial self-governance to managerialism as the dominant mode of institutional decision making, one which links the *programmatic* activities of the university more directly to the control and influence of external constituencies like governments, the business community, funding agencies, and the like. Another points to a shift in the primary objectives of the university from the creation, preservation, and dissemination of social knowledge to the production and distribution of market knowledge. Still another expresses the change in the essence of the university as a social institution and in the way it produces and reproduces itself in the world: that is, the shift from an institution whose practices emerge from its distinctively academic and educational character, to one whose practices emerge from its character as a business organization which delivers largely prepackaged or predefined academic and educational services to paying customers and targeted markets. To be sure, all of these descriptions of transformation are simplistic and over-generalized; rather than describing an altered state, they are more useful from an analytical perspective if they are seen as pointing toward a potential direction of development.

A 1986 Science Council of Canada study report by Philip Enros and Michael Farley has articulated this potential direction in their conceptualization of a "new species" of university—*the service university*—which, they argue, has been emerging over the last two decades under the conditions of underfunding. They describe the service university in the following terms:

> Just as the research university emerged in Canada at the start of the twentieth century, perhaps a new species, the service university, is evolving in the last decades. In such an institution teaching and research would not be displaced so much as they would be re-oriented. The essence of such a university would be a dynamic, integral relationship with society. Just as the research university underwent structural and functional change, so too will the service university.[8]

Enros's and Farley's study is one of ten Science Council studies carried out in the 1980s which advocated the development of new structures, programs, and approaches to decision making that will integrate "into the fabric of universities" various forms of collaboration between business/industry and the academy. Moreover, a recently edited collection of articles presented at a NATO advanced workshop on "The Changing University and the Education and Employment of Scientists and Engineers" displays that a similar conception of the "dynamically integrated university" is being realized in other industrialized and industrializing countries. Robert Rosenzweig's review summarizes the overall thrust of the collection of essays this way:

> ... the news is not good for those who hold to the classical view of the university both as an institution committed to the search for truth and to the dissemination of this knowledge without hindrance, and as a body opposed to all forms of parochialism. It is clear that in the United States and Europe at least, the perceived economic value of research and training in science and technology has produced a market for what universities have to offer, and even those institutions most faithful to their traditions are finding it hard to resist the market's claims on their resources and policies.[9]

Rosenzweig's observation underscores the extent to which the dynamically-integrated, market-oriented university is to be distinguished from the idea of the university as "ivory tower." In the climate of the 1980s and 1990s, the ivory tower university based on collegialism and "traditional" academic values is often represented as a thing of the past. In fact, some advocates of the dynamically integrated academy argue that corporate funding has the advantage of diversifying the university's funding source, allowing it to be less directed by state policy and therefore more autonomous. Others challenge the desirability of institutional autonomy entirely. For example, John Fairclough, the science adviser to the British prime minister in 1987, argued that universities can "no longer set their own research agendas; . . . industry should set them because it better understands the nation's needs."[10]

The Service University as a Tool of Post-Industrialism

One fruitful way of understanding the idea of the dynamically integrated, market-oriented service university is in the context of "post-industrialism." Daniel Bell based his predictions of an emerging post-industrial society on a configuration of specific changes in the social structure comprised of the "economy, technology, and occupational structure."[11] These changes arise, according to Bell, because of the increasing "centrality of theoretical knowledge as the source of innovation and of policy formation for society."[12] Universities and research institutes are assigned an increasingly central role in the post-industrial order as "axial structures" engaged in the important task of codifying and enriching theoretical knowledge. Because, as Bell argues, "every society now lives by innovation and growth and it is theoretical knowledge that has become the matrix of innovation,"[13] it follows that universities in post-industrialism will become key centers of innovation and growth.

It is precisely here that the vision of post-industrialism and the "service university" policy initiative converge. Both assume that knowledge and its technological manifestations are the motor drive of social development. The "service university" policy views universities as key instruments of economic recovery and growth, insofar as scientific discoveries and the training of a highly skilled, technologically literate, motivated, and productive workforce are the instruments of technological innovation and new product development. Richard Teitelman illustrates the point well in his study of the partnerships formed in the 1970s and 1980s in the U.S. between academic science and Wall Street. He argues that biotechnology and microelectronics were assumed to constitute technological innovations that would set off a new "Schumpterian" style industrial revolution. Whole new industries would be created, thus leading to a renewed era of economic growth and prosperity.[14]

There is a price to be paid for the university moving to the center stage of social and economic development. For one thing, those who advocate the dynamically integrated, market-driven "service university" model admit, and even advocate, that traditional ideas of institutional autonomy, academic freedom, unlimited access to knowledge discoveries, and a sharing and cooperative research climate will have to be modified or sacrificed in order to establish an institutional climate that is more compatible with the needs of corporate development and technological innovation. For example, the changes previously described which have accompanied budget-based rationalization and university-corporate collaboration have introduced new forms of decision making into the university. These new forms of decision making are closely akin to Bell's idea of "technological forecasting," through which the post-industrial society is uniquely able to control and plan for social change. Five-year plans, undergraduate and graduate program audits, workload studies, and other measurement tools are the means through which the goals and objectives of departmental and faculty units are linked to centrally coordinated *strategic plans* for the institution as a whole; and these in turn, to regionally and nationally coordinated social, political, and economic strategies.

Thus, in contrast to the self-governing collegialism of recent decades, the post-industrial "service university" functions through centrally controlled and coordinated initiatives in response to, and in relationship with, external agencies and constituencies. These new forms of decision making fundamentally undermine a conception of the university as an autonomous, self-directing, peer-review and professional-authority based institution, and thus changes the politics of how academic work is accomplished. Dorothy Zinberg observes that, "if basic research in the university is expected to lead directly to

Constructing the "Post-Industrial University" 299

discernible health benefits, information science to national economic competitiveness, or condensed matter physics to military security, the real purpose of the university—namely teaching and research in an open environment—can be severely undermined."[15] But herein lies a major contradiction of Bell's post-industrial vision which is built into the model of the dynamically-integrated, market-driven university. On the one hand, Bell argues that societies will have unprecedented opportunities to shape their own futures because of the innovative and virtually limitless applicability of theoretical knowledge. On the other hand, he also predicts and advocates the development of intellectual technologies for *planning and controlling* technological change. But if the knowledge to be produced—new knowledge—is governed by these intellectual technologies based on algorithmic formulas and the elimination of intuitive judgments, where will be the basis for innovation? The knowledge to be produced will be restricted by knowledge already acquired, as well as by the interests that shape and determine the knowledge production and distribution process.

Some scholars who have been witnessing the "service university" policy in action have begun to express concerns about these effects on the knowledge-seeking process. For example, Maureen Woodhall argues that changes in funding patterns which create greater reliance on conditional grants and market mechanisms may actually impede, rather than promote, scientific progress.

> There has been a shift (over the 1980s) in the balance of research away from pure research, funded through general research grants and concerned primarily with the advancement of knowledge, toward more applied research, funded through contracts and concerned with the use of *existing knowledge* to solve specific problems. There has been some concern that excessive growth of applied research may cause a decline in the rate at which new knowledge is created.[16]

Moreover, the planning and controlling of knowledge creation and distribution which are achieved through the "service university" policy threaten to undermine the traditional role of the university in evaluating and criticizing established ways of doing things. If the university's economic well-being is invested in predetermined solutions to problems, as is the case when the university or its researchers own shares in a private company which will economically benefit from patent rights and licensing agreements for particular kinds of marketable products, how likely is it that the same university will support research that is critical of the science that leads to these products? Even more so, if the economic fate of the university is integrated into an economic strategy that is tied to the economic successes of industrial and governmental partners, how much freedom can it have to maneuver independently of this strategy or of the other policies of its partners? In fact, Teitelman's analysis of the "partnerships" between academia and Wall Street that were designed to achieve profitable results for both through an explosion of marketable biotechnology discoveries, reveals that universities can become even more economically vulnerable if the optimistic predictions of profitability are not achieved.

Conclusion

In the latter section of this paper, I have been arguing that current policies that are being implemented in universities in most industrially advanced societies share many of the assumptions of Daniel Bell's post-industrial vision. Post-industrialism, however, is not simply or even primarily a description of the political and economic realignments that flow from the application of theoretical knowledge. Post-industrialism is also a discourse which attempts to implement the vision that it describes. Similarly, the prevailing model of the dynamically integrated, market-driven "service university" is not merely a codification of inevitable institutional changes: it is a discourse which attempts to implement a vision of a "newly emerging" institution of higher education.

Moreover, there are critiques of post-industrialism even as there are of the service university policy—critiques of the predictions, critiques of the discourse, and critiques of the social order and social institutions that they advance. Among other things, these critiques point to contradictions in the overall vision of social life and social organization that is represented by post-industrialism.[17] As well, the very existence of these critiques reveals that there are other contrary and competing visions able to mobilize social resources which may be self-destructing in this latter decade of the twentieth century. These contrary and competing visions are finding a place in the university, even while it is being transformed by the policies that are designed to implement the dynamically integrated, market-driven "service university."

For example, even assuming that society is becoming increasingly subject to the application of theoretical knowledge, new social movements have arisen in the last decade or two which challenge some of these applications and advocate different visions of social progress and social development. Environmentalism and aboriginal peoples' revival are only two examples. Insofar as the "service university" policy links universities to the implementation of specific government policies, and to serving specific economic interests, it is predictable that these challenges to particular knowledge applications will be directed toward universities as well as toward governments and industrial organizations. One by now infamous example is the case of a land-grant university in California which was taken to court by its local community, largely made up of small farmers. The farmers successfully argued that the university had violated its mandate to serve its local community because research on tomato production carried out by university researchers for the benefit of agri-business clients had driven local farmers out of business. Other examples include the challenges of environmentalists, animal rights activists, and the peace movement to the university's role in carrying out research that is believed to be dangerous to the planet and to its species, or that supports military objectives.

Tensions and conflicts that have surfaced in universities over the past decade or so over such issues as creating a just gender and racial balance within the faculty and student body will not be made to disappear through the innovations advanced by the service university policy. In fact, it is arguable that the service university will accentuate these divisions, as it feeds into the development of a workforce divided into an elite cadre of "educated" technological experts to control and coordinate the use of technology and the large mass of "trained" workers to carry out relatively low level tasks. [18]

Perhaps most challenging of all are the post-modernist attacks on the perceived universalism of the rational-scientific knowledge base itself. The expression of gender, race, and class divides have spawned a growing discontent with the existing and accepted knowledge base, and this discontent is increasingly shared not only by various community groups which represent the interests of, for example, women and racial and ethnic minorities, but also by academics who critique the established "canon" of their own disciplines. In many respects, new epistemologies and theoretical approaches are emerging from these critiques that are fundamentally contradictory to the theories and epistemologies on which post-industrialism is based (and by implication, the model of the dynamically-integrated, market-driven "service university").

These few examples suggest that at the very time that the university appears to have been appropriated by privatized economic interests, and to have begun to transform itself into a business organization that offers educational services to predetermined clienteles, there are signs that the broader public constituency of the university is being aroused. Moreover, these newly aroused publics may be inspired by, even as they inspire, *new* theoretical knowledges that challenge the premises of the theoretical knowledge underlying the post-industrial vision—ironically, a source of innovation that Daniel Bell did not foresee. Even as the expanded university of the 1960s became the site of struggle over who controls the university as an institution, the contracted university of the 1990s may increasingly become a site of struggle over who controls knowledge itself.

NOTES

1. Dorothy Zinberg. *The Changing University: How Increased Demand for Scientists and Technology Is Transforming Academic Institutions Internationally.* (Boston, Mass.: Kluwer Academic Publishers, 1992), p. 45. Italics mine.
2. James Rhinehart. *The Tyranny of Work.* (Toronto: Harcourt, Brace, Jovanovich, 1987 edition), p. 74.
3. Donald Savage. "CAUT Response to Dr. Stuart Smith's *Issues Paper.*" Ottawa: circulated by the Canadian Association of University Teachers, (July 12, 1991).
4. Howard Buchbinder and Janice Newson. "The Academic Work Process, the Professoriate and Unionization." *The Professoriate—Occupation in Crisis.* Edited by Cecily Watson. (Toronto: OISE-Higher Education Group, 1985), pp. 221–247.

5. For an example, see H. Buchbinder and J. Newson. "Managerial Consequences of Recent Changes in University Funding Policies: a Preliminary View of the British Case." *European Journal of Education*, 23, (1988): 151–165.

6. George Keller. *Academic Strategy: The Management Revolution in American Higher Education.* (Baltimore: Johns Hopkins University Press, 1983.)

7. H. Buchbinder and J. Newson. *Op. cit.*

8. Philip Enros and Michael Farley. *University Offices for Technology Transfer: Toward the Service University.* (Ottawa: Science Council of Canada, 1986), p. 16.

9. Robert Rosenzweig. "Market Research: A Review of the Changing University: How Increased Demand for Scientists and Technology Is Transforming Academic Institutions Internationally." *Nature*, 355 (January 1992): 121.

10. Zinberg. *Op. cit.*, 65.

11. Daniel Bell. *The Coming of the Post-industrial Society: A Venture in Social Forecasting.* (New York: Basic Books, 1973), p. 12.

12. *Ibid.*, p. 12.

13. *Ibid.*, p. 344.

14. Richard Teitelman. *Gene Dreams: Wall Street, Academics and the Rise of Biotech.* (New York: Basic Books, 1990).

15. Zinberg. *Op. cit.*, 3.

16. Maureen Woodhall. "Changing Patterns of Finance for Higher Education: Implications for the Education of Scientists and Engineers." *The Changing University: How Increased Demand for Scientists and Technology is Transforming Academic Institutions Internationally.* Edited by Dorothy Zinberg. (Boston: Kluwer Academic Publishers, 1992), 49. Italics mine.

17. Rhinehart. *Op. cit.*, Chapter 4.

18. Heather Menzies. *Fast Forward and Out of Control.* (Toronto: Macmillan of Canada, 1989).

CONTRIBUTORS

Philip G. Altbach is director and professor of the Comparative Education Center, State University of New York at Buffalo. He is also a senior associate of the Carnegie Foundation for the Advancement of Teaching. He is editor of *International Higher Education: An Encyclopedia.*

Ignaz Bender, a lawyer, is chancellor (administrative head) of the University of Trier, Germany. He is a general secretary of the International Conference on Higher Education.

Ernest L. Boyer is president of the Carnegie Foundation for the Advancement of Teaching, Princeton, New Jersey. He has been commissioner of education in the United States government and chancellor of the State University of New York. He has written widely on higher education. His most recent book is *Scholarship Reconsidered.*

Michael A. Brown is executive pro-vice chancellor at De Montfort University, Leicester, England. He has taught physics at Grenoble and Loughborough Universities.

Howard Buchbinder is professor and the chair of the department of social science, Atkinson College, York University, Toronto, Canada. His research and publications focus on the politics of higher education.

Helmut de Rudder is professor of higher education, director of the Institute of Higher Education, and former president of the University of Lüneburg, Germany.

Ihsan Dogramaci established Hacettepe University in Ankara, Turkey, and was instrumental in the creation of the Council of Higher Education, serving as its president from 1981 to 1992. In 1984, he established Bilkent University, the only private university in Turkey, where he is president and chairman of the board of trustees. He is also one of the founders of the International Conference on Higher Education.

Daniel S. Fogel is professor of business administration and director of European programs, school of management, University of Pittsburgh.

John Fürstenbach has been deputy head of administration at Stockholm University, Sweden. He is currently serving as advisor to the ministry of education.

Richard A. Hartnett is director of the Center for the Study of Chinese Higher Education and professor and chair of the department of educational administration at West Virginia University. He is currently writing a history of Chinese higher education with Professor Min Weifang of Beijing University.

Cornelius A. Hazeu is senior policy officer, national and international coordination, directorate of research and science policy in the ministry of education and science, government of the Netherlands.

Michael C. Hulfactor received his Ph.D. from the higher education program at Stanford University in 1992. He is affiliated with the Stanford Institute for Higher Education Research.

D. Bruce Johnstone is chancellor of the State University of New York. He has been president of the State University College at Buffalo and has written widely on higher education. He is author of *Sharing the Costs of Higher Education* and other works on international comparative higher education finance.

Peter A. Lourens is coordinator of budgeting in the ministry of education and science, government of the Netherlands.

William F. Massy is professor of education and business administration and director of the Stanford Institute for Higher Education Research. He has served as Stanford's vice provost for research and vice president for business and finance. He has published widely in higher education and business administration.

James E. Mauch is professor of educational policy and administration, School of Education, University of Pittsburgh.

Janice A. Newson has held a faculty appointment at York University in Toronto, Canada, since 1971. She is currently working on a collection of essays on the Canadian university in the 1990s.

Linda Parker is program analyst at the National Science Foundation, Washington, D.C. Her areas of interest include developing scientific capacity and the role of science and technology in economic development.

George Psacharopoulos is on the staff of the World Bank, Washington, D.C. He has published widely in the area of economics of education.

P. Rajagopal is professor of mathematics and computer science at Atkinson College, York University, Toronto, Canada. His research and publications have been in the areas relating to mathematics and computer science (numerical) analysis.

Karel Tavernier is general director (head of administration) at the Catholic University of Leuven, Belgium. He is one of the founders of the International Conference on Higher Education.

Teshome G. Wagaw is professor of higher education at the University of Michigan. He was professor and dean at Haile Selassie I University in Ethiopia and has wide experience in Africa.

Brian G. Wilson is vice chancellor of the University of Queensland, Australia. He is also professor of astrophysics.

David M. Wolf is planning support manager at De Montfort University, Leicester, England. He also teaches in the field of business management.

INDEX

Academic freedom, 50, 92, 96, 98, 102, 120, 167, 175, 214, 229, 293
Academic goals, 27, 61, 185, 290, 292; and resource allocation, 36
Academic values, 102
Access, 7, 215, 227, 231, 258, 273, 274, 279, 287
Accountability, 28, 29, 52, 67, 89, 91, 174, 194, 214, 227, 288, 290, 291
Administration, 55, 105, 106, 114, 167, 175, 260, 273, 278; administrative support, 27; centralization 29; control of budgeting, 30, 47, 50
Admissions, 155, 223
Africa, 14, 18, 20, 64, 151–169
Al-Azhar University, 153
Allocation models, 194–198
Argentina, 19, 20
Ashby, Eric, 208
Asia, 111, 112, 134, 156, 267
Australia, 7, 18, 19, 253–269, 289
Australian National University, 254
Australian University Grants Committee, 254
Austria, 208, 213

Autonomy, 49, 51, 72, 85, 89, 90, 91–92, 96, 98, 137, 141, 146, 167, 198, 202, 214, 217, 224, 227, 232, 240, 273, 282, 293, 297

Bangladesh, 18
Basic income unit (BIU), 274, 275, 276, 277
Behrman, J.N., 110
Beijing University, 138
Belgium, 18, 46, 83–99
Bell, Daniel, 237, 286, 297, 298, 299, 300, 302
Bennett, William, 25
Bilkent University (Turkey), 81–82
Brain drain, 109, 112, 140, 164, 229
Brazil, 19, 20, 109
BRITE, 88
Budget, 10, 15, 29–31, 139, 173, 175–177, 179, 180, 192, 193, 194, 195, 197, 198, 204, 218, 219, 220, 289; block allocation budgeting, 30, 179–181; center budgeting, 30–31, 223, 242
Business enterprises, 20, 54, 81, 160, 229, 296

309

Canada, 7, 18, 19, 271–284, 292, 295, 296
Cash flow, 71
Centers of excellence, 85, 87, 88, 90, 96, 97, 272
Central and Eastern Europe, 12–13, 14, 19, 111, 207, 210, 215, 227, 246
Centralization, 35, 131, 137, 143, 144, 211, 257, 277
Centre National de la Recherche Scientifique (CNRS), 54
Change and reform, 83, 98, 117, 127, 161, 174, 181, 185, 191, 192, 213, 214, 216, 220, 227, 232, 272, 275, 282, 286, 294
Charles University (Czech Republic) 207
Chevaillier, Thierry, 3
China, 16, 18, 20, 21, 127–149
Colombia, 19, 20
Competition, 87, 89, 108, 110, 111, 227, 228
Competitive funding, 85, 90, 91, 94, 97, 211, 275
Congo, 154
Control, 86, 104, 106, 131, 138, 183, 184, 186, 198, 210, 211, 294, 299. See *also* Cost control
Corporate colleges, 87
Cost, 3–24, 72, 77, 181, 220, 223, 230; allocation methods, 33–35; categories, 4–5; control, 22; cost accounting, 52; cost centers, 174, 175, 179; cost efficiency, 186, 199, 287, 288; cost recovery, 53, 58, 61, 67, 68; cost structure, 194; individualization of, 88; politics of, 9–11; staff and non-staff costs, 173; unit cost, 8, 65, 133, 134, 135, 137, 156, 157, 174, 186, 193, 197. See *also* Effectiveness, cost
Cost-benefit analysis, 158
Curricula, 164, 194, 195, 210, 211, 213, 227, 231, 244, 291
Czechoslovakia (the Czech Republic and Slovakia), 207–35

Dawkins, John, 257
Dawkins Reforms, 257–262
Decentralization, 35, 36, 98, 189, 213, 214, 240
Decision making, 35, 96, 131, 137, 203, 227, 244, 251, 273, 290, 295, 296, 298
Demands for higher education, 64, 65, 67, 84, 89, 152, 159, 166
Democratization, 97, 273, 287, 289
De Montfort University (Britain), 173–174, 179, 185–87
Deng Xiaoping, 127, 128
Developing countries, 61–64, 65, 67, 74, 75, 76, 101, 102, 103, 110, 111, 113, 114, 116, 156

Index   311

de Zagottis, Decio, 109–110
Disadvantage, 113, 119
Distance education, 259
Donors, 6, 21; international, 160

East Germany (GDR), 237–52
Economic development, 119, 127, 239, 271, 297; growth, 12; decline, 105
Economy, 151, 156, 157, 196, 228, 261
Educational policy, 83, 85, 91, 95, 96, 145, 197, 248, 286
Effectiveness, 106, 133, 138, 161, 183, 186, 213, 263; cost, 161, 162, 260
Efficiency, 5, 7–8, 25, 31, 65, 67, 76, 86, 89, 133, 135, 143, 145, 158, 184, 197, 224, 280, 291, 294. *See also* Cost efficiency
Egypt, 153, 154, 159
Eicher, Jean-Claude, 3
England, 162
Enrollments, 62, 63–64, 74, 93, 94, 95, 128–31, 135, 145, 153, 155, 159, 173, 174, 191, 193, 213, 246, 247, 254, 259, 271, 275, 276, 277, 282, 290
Enros, Philip, 296
Entrepreneurialism, 114, 119, 285
Equity, 7, 161, 163, 258, 280
Erasmus, 89
Ethiopia, 153, 159, 160
EURAM, 88
EUREKA, 88

European Economic Community (EEC), 87, 88; funding, 88
European Institute of Business Administraiton (INSEAD), 87
European integration, 87
Exchanges of students, 89
Expansion, 64, 128, 130, 133, 135, 137, 153, 155, 159, 164–165, 168, 255, 258

Faculty, 4, 6, 25, 26, 27, 39, 47, 56, 72, 92, 95, 96, 97, 98, 102, 104, 105, 106, 114, 130, 139, 147, 162, 273, 281, 283, 288, 290, 291; faculty resource, 28, 162, 167, 173, 210, 216, 227, 228, 231, 241–43, 244–45
Fairclough, John, 297
Farley, Michael, 296
Fees, 67, 97, 109, 139, 155, 160, 177, 224, 256, 262–263, 267, 275, 277–79
Financial crisis, 3, 11, 26, 175, 239, 274, 282, 288
Finland, 18
Fischer, W. A., 110
Foregone earnings, 5
Foreign students, 82, 97, 223, 225, 262, 265, 268
Foreign universities, 87
Foundations, 53–54
France, 14, 20, 47, 55, 73, 84, 90, 92, 162
Free education, 155, 213

Geographic region, 11, 142, 163; and national and regional development policies, 50, 277
German Research Society, 248
Germany, 14, 18, 73, 78, 86, 90, 105, 208, 213
Ghana, 20
Governance of universities, 49–50, 138, 211, 217, 220, 263
Government control, 85, 86, 89, 93, 111, 131, 143, 146, 154, 255, 259
Government funding, 190, 191, 192, 193, 194, 202, 238, 240, 248, 249, 253, 256, 275, 281, 294
Graduate education, 106, 108, 113, 114, 120, 140, 280
Grants, 19, 78, 80, 90, 189, 196, 240, 249, 250, 254, 258, 259, 264, 265, 267, 275, 276, 277
Greece, 14
Gross domestic product (GDP), 156
Gross national product (GNP), 157, 247
Guangdong, 142
Guinea, 159

Higher Education Funding Council (U.K.), 173
Hospitals, 38–40
Hungary, 208

Impulse funding, 86

Income, 63, 81, 101, 104, 111, 119, 139, 158, 175, 177, 179, 181, 191, 219, 224, 240, 274, 275, 276; operating grant income, 275
India, 18
Indonesia, 16, 18, 19
Industry, 131, 138, 273, 293; industry-university research collaboration, 101–124, 272, 292, 296
Inefficiency, 66, 219, 289
Inequity, 66, 68,
Inflation, 9, 144, 220
Information, 108, 109, 196, 197, 211, 299
Innovation, 108, 115, 119, 138, 140, 141, 147, 203, 263, 298; technical, 110
Institutes Universitaires de Technologie, 14
Institutional culture, 101, 114
Institutional multiplication, 133, 137
Intellectual property rights, 114, 293
International Center for Chemical Studies, Slovenia, 106–107
International community, 160, 161
International donors. *See* Donors, international
International Institute for Management Development (IMED), 87
Internationalism, 89, 106, 107, 113

Index

International organizations, 160, 161
Inventions, 58
Italy, 14

Jamaica, 20
Japan, 7, 14, 18, 19, 113, 208
Johnstone, D. Bruce, 72–73, 185–186
Joint venture, 138, 139

Kenya, 20
Keynes, John Maynard, 271
Knowledge, 85, 89, 102, 108, 117, 119, 120, 162, 167, 282, 286, 292, 293, 294, 295, 297, 299, 301
Korea, 7, 18, 19, 20, 108–109, 113, 119, 120
Korean Advanced Insitute of Science and Technology (KAIST), 113
Korean Science and Engineering Foundation (KOSEF), 108
Kornhauser, A., 107

Labor market, 94, 143, 159, 164, 245
Latin America, 7, 14, 19, 62, 74–75, 156
Leadership, 112, 161
Legislation, 87, 89, 91, 95, 96, 103, 104, 117, 214
Lesotho, 20
Libraries, 16, 34
Libya, 154
Line-item budgeting, 86, 89, 239, 243

Loans, 19, 73, 77, 78, 88, 139, 160, 189, 229, 265

Malawi, 20
Malaysia, 18, 19, 20
Mali, 159
Management, 16, 54, 86, 146, 176, 179, 185, 186, 273, 281, 289, 291, 295; budget, 175; cash management, 55; of facilities, 141
Market, 107, 110, 111, 113, 119, 120, 127, 143, 239, 265, 273, 280, 282, 295, 297, 299; demands, 57; labor, *see* Labor market
Martin, L., 269
Masaryk, Tomas, 208
Mass education, 65, 174
Massy, William, 186, 187
Menzies, Robert, 254
Mexico, 11, 14, 19, 102
Modernization, 127, 151
Morocco, 154
Multinationals, 87
Murray, Keith, 254
Murray Report, 254–257

National Academy of Sciences (USA), 115
National Autonomous University of Mexico (UNAM), 10–11
National Endowment for the Humanities (USA), 25
Nationalized property, 226
NATO, 296

Netherlands, 14, 18, 19, 47, 78, 86, 90, 91, 93, 189–206, 240
Netherlands Organization for Scientific Research (NWO), 190, 204
New Zealand, 266, 267, 268
Nigeria, 20, 153, 159, 160
Non-degree continuing education, 137
Non-government sources, 160, 224, 232, 280
Non-university sector, 13–14, 90, 255
Nyerere, Julius, 151–152

Obligations, 72
Ontario, 275–277
Ontario Council on University Affairs (OCUA), 275
Open university, 79, 87, 190, 194, 198
Organizational structure, 138, 147, 174
Organization for Economic Cooperation and Development (OECD), 7, 17, 219, 231, 288
Overhead costs, 34–35

Pacific Rim, 12, 111, 134
Pakistan, 76
Parental wealth, 66, 67, 68, 77, 155
Performance evaluation, 98, 176–179, 248
Permanent education, 87, 97
Philanthropic sources, 21, 46
Philippines, 7, 18, 19, 20

Planning, 15, 52, 117, 144, 162, 197, 199, 211, 219, 243–45, 248, 255, 256, 267, 298, 299
Politics, 26, 68, 86, 89, 118, 127, 128, 152, 154, 157, 161, 167, 168, 189, 210, 211, 237, 250, 251, 262, 272, 287
Portugal, 14
Primary education, 76, 132, 161
Princeton University, 73–74
Private funding 6, 67, 146, 168
Private sector, 10, 18–19, 63, 65, 66, 67, 74, 75, 81, 111, 113, 120, 138, 140, 145, 253, 266, 292
Privatization in higher education, 19, 61, 67, 89, 140–141, 274
Production standards, 118
Public expenditures, 6, 17, 46, 51, 67, 75, 76, 132, 134, 144, 189, 218, 219, 220, 225, 230, 255
Public funding, 63, 65, 72, 74, 82, 88, 91, 93, 95, 107, 239, 240
Public sector, 7, 9, 15, 63, 64, 74, 78, 81, 186; and budgeting and control, 10; subsidies, 10
Public trust, 26, 110, 151

Qinghua University (China), 138
Quality, 25, 26, 37, 40, 51–52, 57, 85–86, 89, 95, 97,

Index

108, 176, 177, 183, 184, 185, 197, 200, 292
Quantity of output, 85

Ranis, G., 113, 122
Reform, 131, 137, 227
Religion, 153, 287
Research, 4, 29, 31–35, 50, 81, 85, 86, 88, 90, 102, 103, 107, 110, 138, 162, 190, 200, 201, 203, 210, 230, 239, 259, 266, 288, 290, 299; and teaching, 36–38; department research funding, 32; faculty, 55, 120; financing of, 48; foundations, 51; funding, 93, 173, 174, 201, 202, 204; institutional funding, 33; interdisciplinary, 108; program funding, 32; project funding, 31–32
Resources, 5, 28–31, 64, 132, 159, 186, 227; human, 111; independent of, 59; resource allocation systems and centralization 25–27, 41–43
Responsibility, 89, 138, 152, 174, 189, 214, 239, 254
Restructuring, 26–28, 96, 128, 137, 145, 181, 227, 289; elements, 27; need for, 26; strategies for, 41–43
Revenue, 95, 101, 109, 115, 119, 160, 278; sources of, 21, 71–82; budget, 173
Rosenzweig, Robert, 296

Salaries, 13, 14, 31, 92, 104, 111, 132, 228, 249, 281
Savage, Donald, 287
Science, 110, 118, 201, 230
Science parks, 101, 118, 119
Secondary education, 76, 95, 132
Selection (student candidate), 67; project, 113–114
Services, 27–28, 84
Sierra Leone, 153
Slovenia, 106, 120
Social justice, 77–78, 229, 271
Social relevance, 201–202, 231
Somalia, 159
Southeast Asia, 113–114
Soviet Union (Russia and CIS), 13, 20, 21, 63, 210
Spain, 14, 18, 48
State Education Commission (China), 131
State financing, 78, 95, 113, 154, 174, 211, 214, 219, 224, 230, 232
State University of New York, 14
Student-faculty ratio, 14, 16, 130, 134, 135, 145, 158, 195, 217, 229, 246, 247
Students, 4–5, 15, 16, 18, 66, 81, 94, 97, 108, 128, 139–141, 167, 223, 225, 229, 230, 246, 274, 282
Student unions, 10
Study abroad, 140
Subsidies, 7, 77, 78, 79, 90, 92, 96, 113, 139, 224, 267
Sweden, 48–49, 53, 73, 240
Switzerland, 18

Talent, 115, 127, 163
Tanzania, 151
Taxation, 10, 88, 229, 262
Technology, 12, 16, 88, 103, 108, 110, 111, 117, 298; and computers, 12, 50
Teitelman, Richard, 298, 300
Teleclassing and satellite education, 87
Thailand, 14, 16, 18, 111
"Third stream" of income, 45–59
Touraine, Alain, 286
Training, technical, 118; on-the-job, 137
Tuition fees, 7, 10, 17, 18, 77, 78, 80, 139, 140, 145, 173, 225, 262, 264, 265
Tunisia, 154
Turkey, 20, 77, 78, 79–82, 103, 111, 116, 118, 119, 120

Uganda, 153
Undergraduate education, 32, 137, 280
Unit cost. *See* Cost, unit
United Kingdom, 14, 15, 18, 19, 20, 73, 105, 115, 119, 173–187, 255, 267, 287, 288

United States, 7, 14, 18, 19, 21, 31, 32, 33, 63, 73, 75, 108, 109, 115, 118, 208, 216, 217, 240, 287, 292, 298, 301
University Grants Committee (UGC) (New Zealand), 267
University of Ljubljana, 106–107
University of North Carolina, 73
University of Salford, 120
University output, 86

Value of physical plant, 226
Voucher-like system, 90, 94, 230, 265

Williams, Gareth, 7
Wilson, R.T.J., 177
Wolf, D.M., 177
Women, 163, 281
Woodhall, Maureen, 299
Workforce, 64, 162, 167
World Bank, 158

Zimbabwe, 20
Zinberg, Dorothy, 298